Protecting Your Home From Radon

A Step-By-Step Manual For Radon Reduction

Protecting Your Home From Radon
A Step-By-Step Manual for Radon Reduction
Copyright © 1993 by Colorado Vintage Companies, Inc.

Colorado Vintage Companies, Inc.
525 East Fountain Boulevard, Suite 201
Colorado Springs, Colorado 80903

This book is dedicated to the memory of
Jacob Kladder
the ultimate do-it-yourselfer.

Disclaimers

Colorado Vintage Companies, Inc. strives to provide accurate, complete, and useful information. However, neither Colorado Vintage Companies, Inc. nor any person contributing to the preparation of this document makes any warranty, expressed or implied with respect to the usefulness or effectiveness of any information, method, or process disclosed in this manual. Each person who uses the information or methods disclosed in this manual is thereby assuming any and all risks associated therewith, and shall have no claim against Colorado Vintage Companies, Inc., any author, or contributors to this manual for damages or expenses related thereto.

Mention of firms, trade names, or commercial products in this document do not constitute endorsement or recommendation for use.

****

Neither the State of Wyoming, the Department of Health, nor the Division of Preventive Medicine, nor any person, employee, or agent of the same, contributing to the preparation of this document makes any warranty, expressed or implied with respect to the usefulness or effectiveness of any information, method, or process disclosed in this manual. Each person who uses or utilizes information or methods disclosed in this manual is thereby fully assuming any and all risks associated therewith, and shall have no claim against the State of Wyoming, the Department of Health, nor the Division of Preventive Medicine for damages or expenses related thereto. Further, the mention of firms, trade names, or commercial products in this document do not constitute endorsement or recommendation for use by the State of Wyoming, the Department of Health, or the Division of Preventive Medicine, or any person, employee, or agent of the same.

Warning: If you only read isolated parts of this book, you will not have sufficient details to complete a radon mitigation system. This could result in poor radon reductions and serious injury.

Acknowledgments

This manual was created by Colorado Vintage Companies, Inc., with partial funding from the State of Wyoming. The need for a course and an instructional guide of radon repairs for the do-it-yourselfer has been growing as rapidly as the public's awareness of the health threat posed by radon gas. The authors of this manual have certainly felt this way for several years, based upon both the number of calls from interested homeowners, and the discovery of several self installed systems that fell off the mark. However, it was the support and urging from Ms. Jan Hough, Coordinator of the Radon Project for the State of Wyoming, that provided the catalyst to develop a structured Do-It-Yourself class for Wyoming using this as an instructional manual. In her role of helping the general public address radon concerns, it also became apparent to her that there was a great need to help people reduce their radon exposure without increasing the safety and health concerns associated with radon mitigation efforts. Merely encouraging further testing or the hiring contractors is no longer sufficient response to the concerned homeowner.

We would also like to acknowledge the efforts of the U.S. EPA, who over the last several years have funded research in the area of radon mitigation. This research was done in concert with the private sector. This partnership between the EPA and the private sector has now yielded technology for reliable reduction of radon in homes. This effort has taken the radon mitigation field out of the era of experimentation and into practice. This manual takes many of these tried and proven techniques out of the sole arena of the contractor and into the hands of the accomplished do-it-yourselfer. If it was not for the efforts of the U.S. EPA and their involvement of Colorado Vintage Companies, Inc. in many of these development efforts, this manual would not be possible at this point.

We would also like to acknowledge the indulgence of many homeowners over the years who not only had the foresight to address radon in their homes, but also for having the tolerance to allow us to experiment on their homes. We would like to thank these pioneering clients of ours in the Rocky Mountain Region, and especially those in Colorado Springs, Colorado.

We would also like to acknowledge the following contributors and corroborators:

James F. Burkhart, Ph.D., Chairman of the Physics Dept., University of Colorado, Colorado Springs for his contributions on the over-view and measurement chapters and overall editing of this book.
Mr. James Gustafson, Chief Financial Officer for Colorado Vintage Companies, for his assembling of the material supply data, and non-technical review of this manual.
Ms. Julie Hodges, Impact Images, for translation of the figures and illustrations into a format for presentation.
Ms. Jan Hough, State Radon Project Coordinator for the State of Wyoming for her inspiration, overall editing and contributions to the book.
Ms. Debi Nelson of the State Radon Project for the State of Wyoming, for coordinating our efforts with the State of Wyoming.
Mr. Steven R. Jelinek, Special Projects Manager, Colorado Vintage Companies, Inc. for his illustrations and experiential contributions.

Mr. Douglas L. Kladder,
President, and Primary Author.

PREFACE

Is this book for me, and do I really want to do this?

This manual is designed to provide sufficient information to a homeowner to make many of the basic repairs that can significantly reduce radon levels in the home. The techniques described in this manual are not experimental. They work, if done properly. The same methods that are detailed in this manual are identical to those which are used by professional mitigators. The only difference between the use of methods described in this book by the professional as opposed to the amateur is the time and tools available to do it.

There are, however, certain types of mitigation systems that have been deliberately left out of this manual. These are approaches that involve a higher skill level than those that may be generally held by the typical weekend do-it-yourselfer. There are also some systems that have greater dangers associated with improper installation. The authors recommend that in these specific cases you seek the advice of a contractor who is listed on the U.S. EPA's Radon Contractor's Proficiency Program or is certified in Radon Mitigation with your state.

The techniques in this book describe methods for reducing radon entry from the soil beneath the home. This applies to the vast majority of problem homes in the world. This book will not assist the homeowner who wishes to reduce radon that may enter the home either from a water source or if radon emanates from the home's building materials.

Professional help is strongly recommended for the following situations:

1. If the house is constructed partially or completely over a crawl space that is inaccessible. To use this manual and perform repairs on houses of this type you will have to be able to crawl through the crawl space and have good access to the walls of the crawl space.

2. If the house is constructed partially or completely over a crawls space that has asbestos covered piping or ductwork. To perform the repairs described in this book, personal access into the crawl space is required. Working in these areas without suitable respiratory protection is dangerous and should not be undertaken by a person who is not trained and licensed to remove or work in asbestos environments.

3. If you desire to reduce your radon levels by increasing the ventilation in the home. Increased ventilation is one of the least effective radon reduction techniques and the most costly to install and operate. For this reason it is not commonly employed unless other indoor air quality problems exist in the home that can only be corrected by increased ventilation. Ventilation systems that minimize the operating costs and the loss of comfort are complex. It would be appropriate to consult with a professional if your intention is to employ ventilation as a radon reduction technique.

4. If your home has a basement whose walls are made out of masonry block and whose internal cores have not been filled with concrete during its construction. This book will still have significant value. However, if the hollow block walls still allow significant radon entry into the home after the methods described within the book have been followed, a professional will be needed to finish off the installation. Systems that deal with removing air from within hollow block walls have a high potential of causing dangerous back drafting of combustion appliances and should only be installed by a professional. Generally, the methods described in this book adequately reduce radon levels in the home without having to address hollow block walls, and if not, the same methods described in this book would still be needed with slight modification. Therefore, it is still prudent to use this book, but beware that these methods may not be sufficient by themselves to totally accomplish the desired result.

5.   If the house is built over an old landfill or a low grade coal deposit, or any other formation that may be generating methane gas. The systems detailed in this manual collect radon gas and concentrate it for exhaustion above the home. These systems will also collect other soil gases such as methane. If methane is a problem in your area, consult a professional to insure that flammable levels of methane are not created.

6.   If your forced air heating or air-conditioning system have ductwork located beneath the slab, the active soil depressurization systems described in this manual may not be as effective as desired. Consult a professional.

The repairs described in this manual apply to more than 90% of the homes in the United States that have elevated radon concentrations. So unless the above exceptions apply to you, this manual is appropriate for use, provided that you have some basic remodeling skills. Tenacity and the willingness to get good and dirty are the other qualifications that you will need to embark upon this project. To do the work in this manual you may find yourself:

Slithering through dark crawl spaces,

Cutting holes through concrete floors,

Cutting holes through your roof,

Cutting holes through your ceiling,

Applying several tubes of solvent based caulking,

Digging deep holes along side of your house,

Cutting, gluing and fitting PVC pipe together.

The methods described within this book are not that difficult. The authors have tried to share every detail from their experience to make the installation go as easily as possible. Each mitigation approach included in this book is broken into three segments:

1.   How it works.

2.   How to plan the installation.

3.   How to install the system.

There are chapters in the manual that support the system installations such as general safety precautions, how to install piping systems, how to interpret your radon measurements both before and after the installation, and where to find some of the specialized equipment and materials needed for this work are discussed.

So, if you take your time reading about and planning for the system you should have little difficulty in installing these systems. If you can do all this, you stand to save several hundred dollars and improve the safety of your home.

Good Luck!

Radon
Reduction
Flow Chart

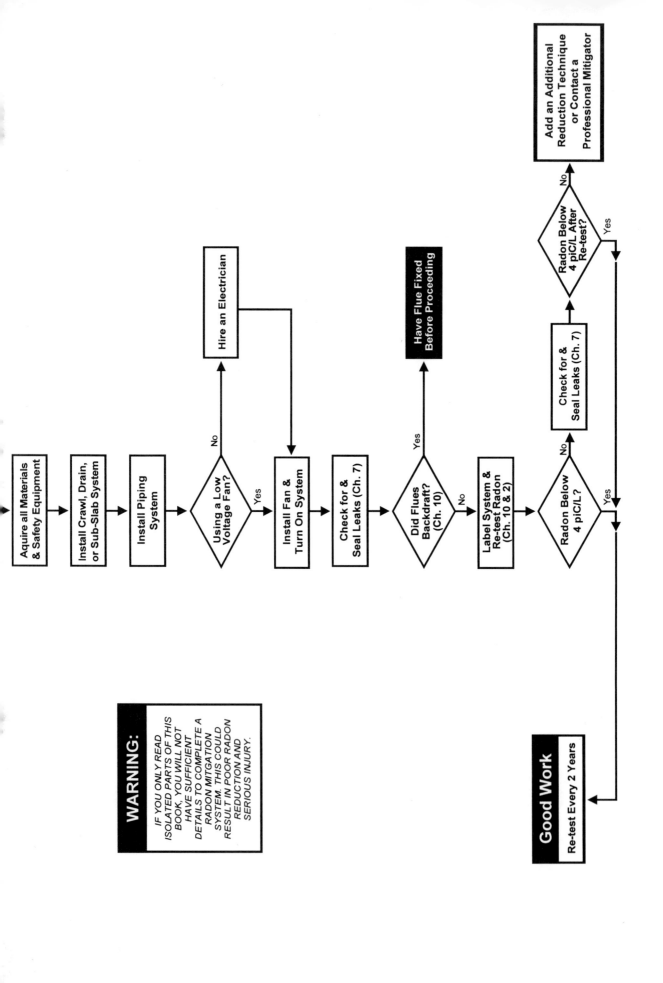

WARNING:

IF YOU ONLY READ ISOLATED PARTS OF THIS BOOK, YOU WILL NOT HAVE SUFFICIENT DETAILS TO COMPLETE A RADON MITIGATION SYSTEM. THIS COULD RESULT IN POOR RADON REDUCTION AND SERIOUS INJURY.

Aquire all Materials & Safety Equipment

Install Crawl, Drain, or Sub-Slab System

Install Piping System

Using a Low Voltage Fan?

No → Hire an Electrician

Yes

Install Fan & Turn On System

Check for & Seal Leaks (Ch. 7)

Did Flues Backdraft? (Ch. 10)

Yes → Have Flue Fixed Before Proceeding

No

Label System & Re-test Radon (Ch. 10 & 2)

Radon Below 4 piCi/L?

No → Check for & Seal Leaks (Ch. 7) → Radon Below 4 piCi/L After Re-test?

No → Add an Additional Reduction Technique or Contact a Professional Mitigator

Yes

Yes

Good Work

Re-test Every 2 Years

Radon
Reduction
Flow Chart

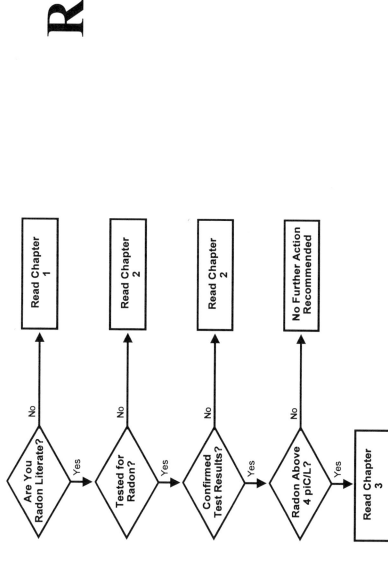
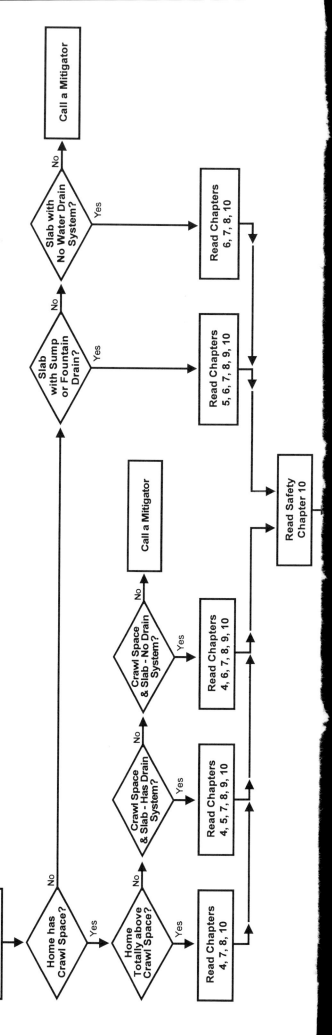

Are You Radon Literate? — No → Read Chapter 1

Tested for Radon? — No → Read Chapter 2

Confirmed Test Results? — No → Read Chapter 2

Radon Above 4 piC/L? — No → No Further Action Recommended

Yes → Read Chapter 3

Home has Crawl Space? — No → (to Slab with Sump or Fountain Drain?)

Yes → **Home Totally above Crawl Space?**

Yes → Read Chapters 4, 7, 8, 10

No → **Crawl Space & Slab - Has Drain System?**

Yes → Read Chapters 4, 5, 7, 8, 9, 10

No → **Crawl Space & Slab - No Drain System?**

Yes → Read Chapters 4, 6, 7, 8, 9, 10

No → Call a Mitigator

Slab with Sump or Fountain Drain? — Yes → Read Chapters 5, 6, 7, 8, 9, 10

No → **Slab with No Water Drain System?**

Yes → Read Chapters 6, 7, 8, 10

No → Call a Mitigator

Read Safety Chapter 10

Protecting Your Home From Radon

A Step-By-Step Manual For Radon Reduction

Protecting Your Home From Radon
A Step-By-Step Manual for Radon Reduction

Radon Reduction Flow Chart

Chapter 1   **An Overview of the Health Effects of Radon**
What is radon?
Why should you reduce radon in your home?

Chapter 2   **Confirming That You Have Tested for Radon Properly**
What are some of the proper testing devices?
Was my house tested according to EPA protocols?
Do the test results say I should now fix my house?

Chapter 3   **Radon Entry and An Overview of Reduction Techniques**
How does radon enter a home?
What types of radon problems will this book address?
How is radon reduction typically achieved?

Chapter 4   **How to Reduce Radon in Homes that are Completely or Partially Built Over Crawl Spaces**
What mitigation system will give you the best radon reduction?
What are the best materials?
How is it installed?

Chapter 5   **How to Make Use of Existing Water Drainage Systems to Reduce Radon**
How to make use of a sump system.
How to make use of an exterior foundation drain.
How to use these systems without affecting their water drainage capability.

Chapter 6   **Sub-Slab Depressurization**
How to reduce radon in slab-on-grade or in basement homes that do not have crawl spaces or existing drainage systems.

Chapter 7   **Depressurization System - Fan and Piping**
How to install the piping and fan for sub-membrane, drainage and sub-slab depressurization systems.

Chapter 8   **Sealing**
How to improve the performance of active soil depressurization systems by caulking and sealing air leakage points.

Chapter 9   **Combining Radon Mitigation Systems Together Where More Than One Foundation Type Exists**
Discussion of Other Mitigation Techniques.

Chapter 10   **General Safety Precautions**
Backdrafting Concerns.

Appendix   Safety Equipment, Tools, and Material Checklist
Listing of Radon Material Suppliers
U.S. EPA's Citizen's Guide to Radon
U.S. EPA's Consumer's Guide to Radon
U.S. EPA's Radon Contractor Proficiency Program Interim Radon Mitigation Standards

Chapter 1

An Overview of The Health Effects of Radon

What is radon?

Why should you reduce the radon in your home?

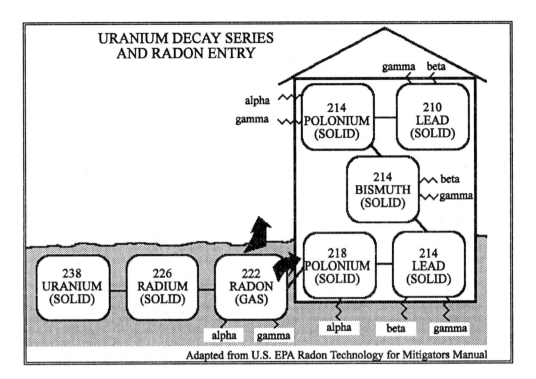

Adapted from U.S. EPA Radon Technology for Mitigators Manual

Since you are reading this manual, you probably are interested in fixing your house to reduce the radon in it. That's great! But before you invest your hard earned money (and time) into this project, you may want to have a few questions answered first. In this section, you will learn the answers to the following questions:

1. What is radon?

2. Why should you reduce radon in your home?

So, please set aside your hammer, drill, and caulking gun for a few minutes and read this section. Let's make sure you really are ready to begin the mitigation process.

1. What is radon?

For billions of years a very common type of uranium has been gradually changing into radon gas. The uranium, which is found in small amounts everywhere in the soil beneath our houses , does not move out of the soil and the rock (see picture above). Uranium changes into radon gas which, however, is free to move up out of the soil and into the air above.

When the radon makes its way into the outdoor air, it mixes with the vast amount of fresh air in the atmosphere and is usually diluted to relatively low levels. However, when the radon enters your house through the basement floor, crawl space, or slab flooring, it can build up inside your house to levels far in excess of that found outdoors.

The occupants of a home with elevated levels of radon can breathe the radon gas. But, believe it or not, that is not the main worry with radon. The real culprits of the "Radon Story" are the small particles created as radon continues to radioactively change - remember, it started as uranium. These radon decay products are continuously produced by the radon in the air inside the home. It is these radon decay products that cause the damaging health effects when breathed in.

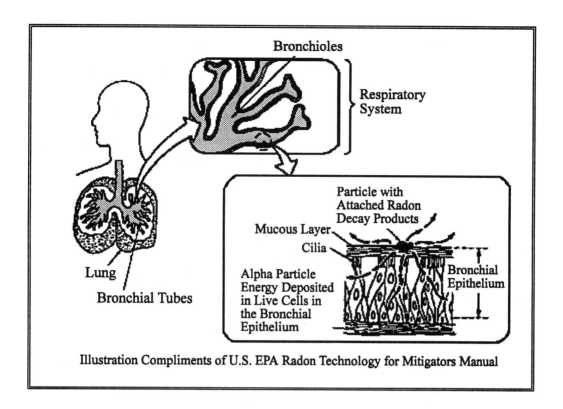

Illustration Compliments of U.S. EPA Radon Technology for Mitigators Manual

The radon decay products are very small particles. Since they are made in the air inside the home they tend to float in the air and can be breathed into the lungs. Many of the radon decay products then stick on the walls of the air passages leading to the lungs and in the lung tissue itself.

Two of these radon decay products are especially troublesome; polonium 218 and polonium 214. It happens that these two particles release a high speed particle called an alpha particle. When this alpha particle, which is like a small atomic "bullet", strikes lung cells, the cells can be damaged. The damaged cells, in turn, may become changed in a way that can eventually turn them into cancerous cells.

At present, the only known hazard from breathing radon (or actually the decay products of radon) is an increased potential of developing lung cancer. No other health effect has been directly traced to radon, although lung cancer is bad enough. There is no current evidence that breathing radon causes asthma, allergies, colds, flu, or other respiratory illnesses.

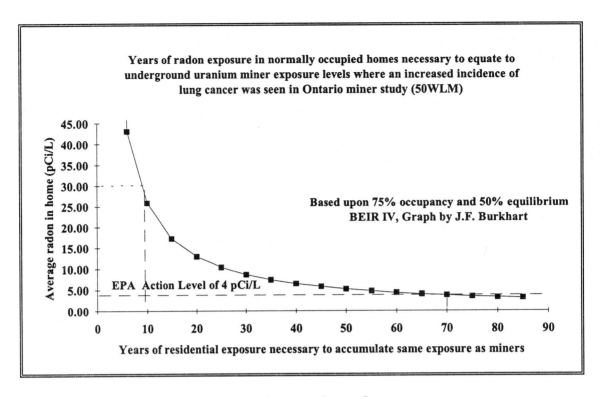

Years of radon exposure in normally occupied homes necessary to equate to underground uranium miner exposure levels where an increased incidence of lung cancer was seen in Ontario miner study (50WLM)

Based upon 75% occupancy and 50% equilibrium
BEIR IV, Graph by J.F. Burkhart

EPA Action Level of 4 pCi/L

Average radon in home (pCi/L)

Years of residential exposure necessary to accumulate same exposure as miners

2. Why should you reduce the radon in your home?

Radon is called a Class "A" carcinogen by the United States Environmental Protection Agency (U.S. EPA). This means that it is known to cause cancer in humans. At the present time, the only known health hazard coming from breathing radon decay products is lung cancer.

As you would suspect, the higher the concentration of radon and radon decay products in your home the greater is your risk of developing lung cancer by breathing the air inside your home.

The graph above represents one of the many underground miner studies that were used to determine the health risks for radon. Using the graph at the top, and looking at the vertical axis on the far left, follow the horizontal dashed line representing 4.0 pCi/L (pCi/L is an abbreviation for PicoCurie per liter that is the unit of measurement for radon gas concentrations) to the right until it intersects the curve. After intersecting the curve drop down to the horizontal axis to find the number "70 years". This says that you would have to be exposed to 4.0 pCi/L for 70 years to approximate the Ontario miner's exposure, the lowest exposure at which lung cancers were observed in this particular study.

By comparison, locate the number 30.0 pCi/l on the vertical axis on the graph above. Following the dashed line to the right until it intersects the curve, and dropping straight down leads us to 10 years. Thus, it only takes 10 years to receive the same radioactive dose at 30 pCi/L as was received for 70 years at 4 pCi/L. So, by reducing the radon in your home, you can increase the amount of time you can live in the home before accumulating an exposure equivalent to the affected uranium miners. It is possible, by performing the repairs described in this book, to lower radon levels to below 1 or 2 pCi/L, thus significantly reducing radon as a concern in your home.

The following table illustrates some examples of radon risk assessments, modified for people who live in homes (not in mines). This chart has been taken from the U.S. EPA's 1992 publication "A Citizen's Guide to Radon" (Second Edition). A copy of this publication is included in the appendix of this manual.

RADON RISK IF YOU SMOKE

Radon Level	If 1,000 people who smoked were exposed to this level over a lifetime...	The risk of radon exposure compares to...	WHAT TO DO: Stop smoking and...
20 pCi/L	About 135 people could get lung cancer	100 times the risk of drowning	Fix your home
10 pCi/L	About 71 people could get lung cancer	100 times the risk of dying in a home fire	Fix your home
8 pCi/L	About 57 people could get lung cancer		Fix your home
4 pCi/L	About 29 people could get lung cancer	100 times the risk of dying in an airplane crash	Fix your home
2 pCi/L	About 15 people could get lung cancer	2 times the risk of dying in a car crash	Consider fixing your home between 2 and 4 pCi/L
1.3 pCi/L	About 9 people could get lung cancer	(Average indoor radon level)	(Reducing radon levels below 2 pCi/L is difficult)
0.4 pCi/L	About 3 people could get lung cancer	(Average outdoor radon level)	(Reducing radon levels below 2 pCi/L is difficult)

RADON RISK IF YOU NEVER SMOKED

Radon Level	If 1,000 people who never smoked were exposed to this level over a lifetime...	The risk of radon exposure compares to...	WHAT TO DO:
20 pCi/L	About 8 people could get lung cancer	Risk of being killed in a violent crime	Fix your home
10 pCi/L	About 4 people could get lung cancer		Fix your home
8 pCi/L	About 3 people could get lung cancer	10 times the risk of dying in an airplane crash	Fix your home
4 pCi/L	About 2 people could get lung cancer	The risk of drowning	Fix your home
2 pCi/L	About 1 person could get lung cancer	The risk of dying in a home fire	Consider fixing your home between 2 and 4 pCi/L
1.3 pCi/L	Less than 1 person could get lung cancer	(Average indoor radon level)	(Reducing radon levels below 2 pCi/L is difficult)
0.4 pCi/L	Less than 1 person could get lung cancer	(Average outdoor radon level)	(Reducing radon levels below 2 pCi/L is difficult)

Chapter 2

Confirming That You Have Tested For Radon Properly

What are some of the proper testing devices?

Was my house tested according to EPA protocols?

Do the test results say I should now fix my house?

Testing for Radon

Since you probably have already tested your house the questions we will try to answer in this chapter are:

1. What are the proper testing devices and techniques? That is, did you do the test right?

2. How do you interpret the measurement results to determine if you should mitigate or fix your home?

When you have finished reading this chapter you should be able to make an intelligent decision on whether or not to mitigate your home.

1. What are the proper testing techniques?

First, we need to provide some definitions. We will be talking about short-term and long-term tests. Short-term tests are all tests less than 90 days long with a minimum of 2 days. Most short-term tests are, in fact, only a few days long (for example: a 48 hour test). Long-term tests, on the other hand, are 90 days or longer in duration. Most long-term tests tend to be a full year long.

The U.S. EPA recommends a two-step testing strategy. This strategy has been worked out after years of testing experience. It is designed to make sure, or as sure as possible, that:

♦ You find out very quickly if you have a potential radon problem.

♦ You **do not** fix a house that does not have elevated levels of radon.

♦ You **do** fix a house that does have elevated levels of radon.

The two step strategy goes like this. First, test your house with a short-term test - usually 2 to 7 days). If the initial test reveals a radon reading below 4.0 pCi/L, you are finished. If the reading is 4.0 pCi/L or greater go to the second step.

The second step is to re-test your house with either another short-term test device or a long-term test device. If the second test confirms that the house is at, or above, 4.0 pCi/L, you should then do something to reduce the radon to below 4.0 pCi/L.

There are many radon testing devices available. Some of the common short-term test devices are:

♦ Charcoal Canisters
♦ Electret-Ion-Chambers
♦ Continuous Radon Monitors
♦ Charcoal Liquid Scintillation Bottles

The most often used long term test device is the alpha track detector. Both the electret-ion-chamber and the continuous radon monitor can be adapted for long term testing use.

CLOSED HOUSE TESTING CONDITIONS

Attic Fans Off

Kitchen & Bathroom Fans Off

Door & Windows Closed

Short-Term Tests

Short term tests are usually 2 to 7 days long and are done under "closed-house" conditions. Closed house conditions means that the house was closed up for at least 12 hours before the test and for the duration of the test. Exterior windows and doors are kept shut except for normal walking in and out of the doors (don't leave doors open). Also, fans and blowers which move air from the outside of the house to the inside or exhaust inside air to the outside are turned off. Whole house fans should be off and air conditioners should be put on "recycle" or "max.-cool", but not on the "fresh air" setting.

Of course, you *can* live in the house during the testing. Since it is sometimes difficult to keep all the windows closed during warm weather, try to schedule the testing period when it will not be inconvenient or uncomfortable to keep the house closed up. If you must test during warm weather, keep the air-conditioning on but simply put it on total recycle rather than the "fresh air setting". On the other hand, "swamp coolers" or evaporative coolers that blow air into the home should be turned off during the test.

The test device should be placed about table height (2 to 5 feet) and left undisturbed for the duration of the test. The test device should not be placed in direct sunlight or on hot or cold surfaces. The test device should not be placed in a moist environment such as bathroom, the kitchen, or the laundry room. Finally, the test device should not be placed directly in moving air, such as in front of a fan or an air duct.

Note: **Closing up the room in which the test device is placed and opening doors and windows in the rest of the house is not following proper test procedures and can give erroneous readings. This can falsely report the radon too high, or even worse, too low.**

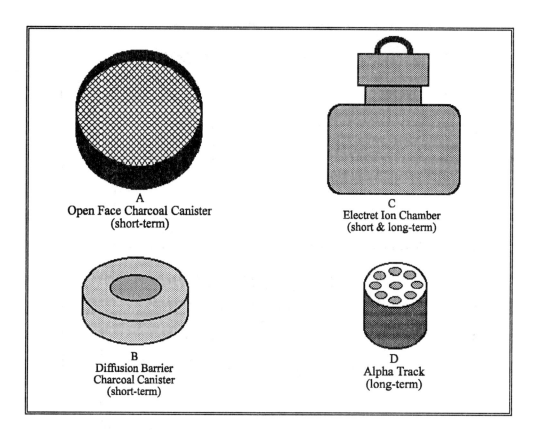

A
Open Face Charcoal Canister
(short-term)

C
Electret Ion Chamber
(short & long-term)

B
Diffusion Barrier
Charcoal Canister
(short-term)

D
Alpha Track
(long-term)

Test Devices

The illustrations above show four very common testing devices. The **Open Face Activated Charcoal Canister** (Fig. A) is probably the most frequently used short-term testing device. It works by absorbing the radon from the room air into the charcoal beneath the screen. It should be deployed in the home for 48 hours.

The **Diffusion Barrier Charcoal Canister** (Fig. B) works the same way as the open face canister, but can be in the home for up to a week. Some people prefer the longer testing time allowed by this device because they can get an average of the radon for a week rather than for just two days. These devices can also be charcoal filled paper pouches.

The **Electret Ion Chamber** (Fig. C) is usually placed by a radon testing firm rather than by a homeowner. An electric charge on the interior surface of the device changes as a result of radon exposure. By varying the size of the chamber and the type of charged surface inside, a testing firm can use the device for either short or long term testing.

The **Alpha Track Device** (Fig. D) is for long-term testing only with a 90 day minimum. It is an inexpensive and reliable device that can be placed by the homeowner. A special piece of plastic inside of the device is struck by alpha particles from the decay products of radon. The resulting craters, or tracks, are counted in a lab with a microscope.

All of these devices, and others not described here, should come with instructions for their proper use. The important thing is to follow the instructions and make sure that the devices are provided and measured by a laboratory that is listed with the U.S. EPA's Radon Measurement Proficiency Program and your state's Health Department.

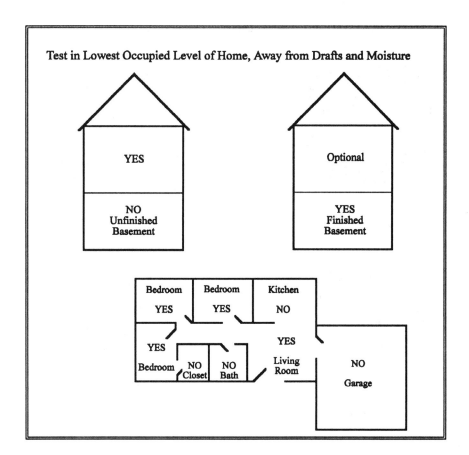

Test in Lowest Occupied Level of Home, Away from Drafts and Moisture

Where is a Good Location for a Radon Test?

Since the purpose of the first, short-term test is to be able to identify homes that are clearly below 4.0 pCi/L, it is necessary to place the test device in a part of the home that would be expected to have the highest radon level. Then if the reading comes back below 4.0 pCi/L there is good reason to believe that the rest of the home also has a low radon level. Furthermore, if the closed house test protocols were followed, there is a good reason to believe that a low short-term test result means that the average radon throughout the year will probably not be above 4.0 pCi/L during normal use of the house (non-closed house conditions).

However, if you live in a climate that results in air conditioning for much of the year, the short-term results will be closer to the year long average than if you lived in a cold climate.

Therefore, in order to have confidence in the radon reading, the device should be placed in the lowest **occupied** space of the home. A finished basement is normally chosen in parts of the country that typically have basements. After the lowest occupied area of the home is selected, the device should be placed in a room that is frequently occupied but where high humidity in the air would not be expected. Examples of good locations would be bedrooms, dining rooms, and family rooms. Never place the device in a closet, crawl-space, storage areas, kitchens, garages or bathrooms.

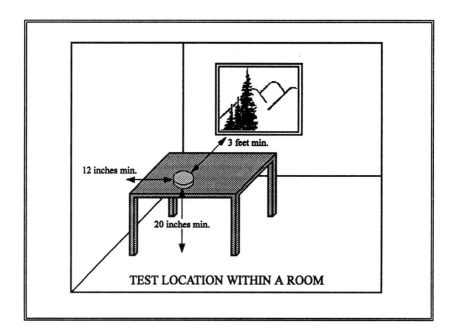

TEST LOCATION WITHIN A ROOM

A proper location should be selected to obtain a good measurement of the radon in the home. A measurement should represent the breathing space of the home. The minimum distance for a test device is at least 20 inches from the floor, 4 inches from another object, 12 inches from a wall, and 3 feet from an outside window.

Was the Short-Term Test Performed Correctly?

Before you begin to even think about fixing your house, you will need to perform a short-term test. Therefore, use the check list below to make sure you did the test right.

SHORT-TEST CHECK LIST		
QUESTIONS	YES	NO
Have you done a short-term test?		
Was the result at or greater than 4.0 pCi/L?		
If you did the test yourself - did you follow all the instructions?		
If the test was done by someone else - are they listed with U.S. EPA's Radon Measurement Proficiency Program?		
Was the house closed for 12 hours before the test began (not necessary if the test itself was longer than 3 days)?		
Was the test device placed at least 20 inches above the floor?		
Was the test device kept out of drafts and temperature extremes?		
Was the device placed in the lowest lived-in area of the house?		
Were the closed-house conditions maintained for the duration of the test?		
Was the test device promptly read by the laboratory (within a few days of the end of the test)?		

If you can check "yes" to all of the above questions, then you have indeed completed the first step toward fixing your home. Why? Because you now know that you do have a potential radon problem. If you do not feel confident that you can check "yes" to all of the above questions then you should repeat the short-term test yourself or hire a professional tester to do it for you. The professional should be listed on the U.S. EPA's Radon Measurements Proficiency Program and have a U.S. EPA identification card as proof.

Confirming the Short-Term Test Result

You have now completed the first step of the two step testing process. To proceed you should have done a short-term initial radon test under closed-house conditions and obtained a result of 4.0 pCi/L or greater.

The second step is now to confirm the initial reading so that you do not unnecessarily fix your home. At this point, you have an option of either doing another short-term test as the confirmatory measurement **or** doing a long-term test instead. Ideally the confirmatory test would be a long-term test (90 days or longer) because this would give you the best data about long term radon exposures to you and your family. However, if the initial test was in excess of 10 pCi/L or the house is being sold, the EPA, along with the need for quick results, would recommend that the confirmatory test be a second short-term test.

In any case, the confirmatory test should be placed in the *same location as the first* short-term test.

If the second test is a short-term test then closed-house conditions have to be used again. All of the testing procedures outlined on the previous pages must also be followed.

However, if the second test is, a long-term test (from 90 days to a year) all of the placement procedures outlined on the previous pages should be followed with the exception that it is not necessary to close up the house prior to or during the test. Merely place the test device in the same location as the first test and occupy your house as you normally would. An alpha track detector would be an appropriate test device for this measurement.

Use this check list below to make sure that your confirmatory test was done correctly.

CONFIRMATORY TEST CHECK LIST		
QUESTIONS	YES	NO
Have you done a confirmatory test?		
If it was long-term - was the result at or greater than 4.0 pCi/L?		
If it was a short-term test - is the average of the first short-term test and the confirmatory short-term test at or greater than 4.0 pCi/L?		
If you did the test yourself - did you follow the directions?		
Was the test device placed in the lowest lived-in area of the house?		
If the test was done by someone else - are they listed with US EPA's Radon Measurement Proficiency Program?		
If the second test was a short-term test - was the house closed for 12 hours before the test began (not necessary if the test itself was longer than 3 days)?		
If the second test was short-term - was the home under closed-house conditions?		
Was the test device placed at least 20 inches above the floor?		
Was the test device kept out of drafts and temperature extremes?		
Was the test device promptly read by the laboratory (within a few days of the end of the test)?		

If you can check yes to all the relevant questions then you have completed the second step toward fixing your home. Why? Because you have now confirmed that you have unacceptable levels of radon in your home.

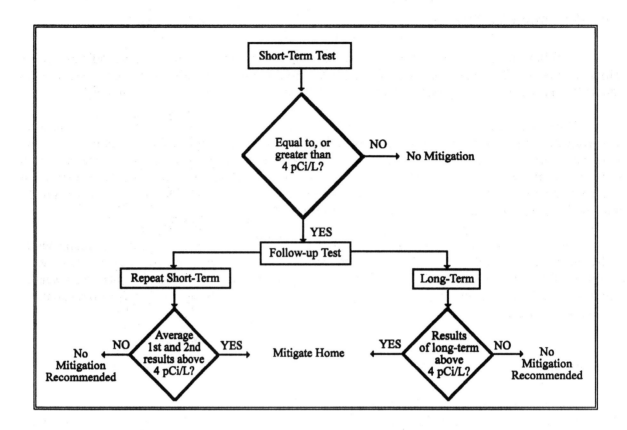

How do you interpret the measurement results to determine if you should mitigate (fix) your home?

The U.S. EPA is very clear on this point: if your confirmatory test was short-term then you should average the initial short-term test and the confirmatory short-term test. If the average is at or above 4.0 pCi/L then you should mitigate your home.

If, on the other hand, your confirmatory test was long-term, you should fix your home if the long-term test is at, or above, 4.0 pCi/L. **Don't** average this result with any other measurement.

The urgency of getting your home fixed is related to the amount of radon in your home. Homes with radon around 4.0 pCi/L do not present as serious of a situation as homes around 20 pCi/L or greater (there are many homes above 20 pCi/L). Common sense tells you that the higher the radon in your house, the more quickly you should start repairs.

Note: It is now getting to be very common place for houses at, or above, 4.0 pCi/L to be mitigated before they are sold. The moneys used to fix the home can be part of the negotiations at the time the contract is being written on the house.

Post Mitigation Testing

A follow up short-term test should be done after you have completed the installation of the mitigation system. This should be done within 30 days of the systems installation, but no sooner than 24 hours after the system is operational. The test should be done under "closed house conditions."

If the post mitigation test is at or above 4.0 pCi/L, review the installation of the system for leaks then evaluate the need for further mitigation work. If the post mitigation test is under 4.0 pCi/L, a long-term test for one year should be done to confirm the short term results. A test should be performed at least once every two years thereafter to confirm that the radon level is staying low and that the system is still performing well. Also, if you remodel your home, retest in the lowest lived-in area to make sure the construction did not reduce the effectiveness of the system.

The simplest procedure for testing your home after mitigation is to always place the testing device in the same location as the very first short-term test. By using the same location, you will have some confidence that the post-mitigation readings can be compared to the earlier measurements. You want to insure that the differences in readings were actually due to your mitigation efforts and not from variations seen between different test locations.

Caution and Advice

There are different types of testing devices used for diagnosing where radon entry is occurring. These are referred to as grab sampling devices. Although they can be quite accurate, they only sample the air for a few minutes. Radon levels vary from hour to hour. This is why the minimum sampling time established by the EPA, to provide a reasonable measurement, is 48 hours. *Do not use these types of devices for short or long-term testing.*

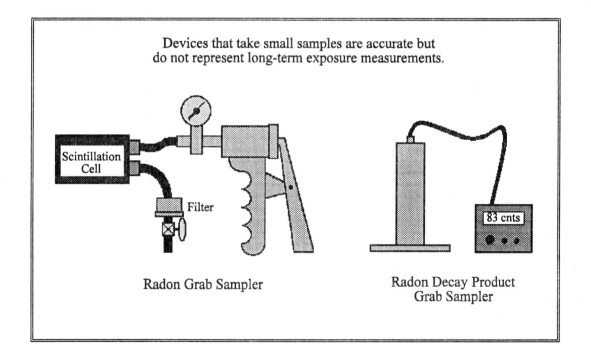

Devices that take small samples are accurate but do not represent long-term exposure measurements.

Radon Grab Sampler

Radon Decay Product Grab Sampler

Chapter 3

Radon Entry And An

Overview Of Radon Reduction Techniques

How does radon enter a home?

What types of radon problems will this book address?

How is radon reduction typically achieved?

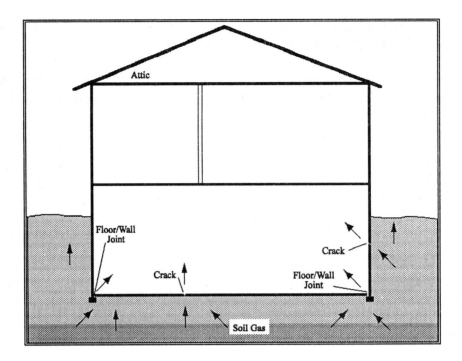

How Radon Enters A Home

To understand how radon reduction techniques are able to reduce radon we should start by understanding how radon enters a home in the first place. There are three factors that affect the amount of radon that enters a home.

1. Source.

Radon is a gas that is constantly being created from the decay of naturally occurring uranium and radium in the soil. Radon that is created in the soil either breaks down to form particulates that are trapped in the soil or finds its way to the surface and enters the atmosphere or house, where it also breaks down and is diluted to very small concentrations.

2. Pathways.

As a gas, radon acts just as air does. It freely moves through the open spaces in the soil. These open spaces can be as small as the space between individual particles of dirt in the soil. The larger the particle size of the soil the larger the open spaces will be (e.g., gravel versus sand) and therefore it will be easier for radon to move up through the soil. These open spaces provide the pathway for radon to move from its source in the ground (the natural deposits of radium) and into your home. Pathways for radon migration into your home may be through the soil below or through cracks and crevices in the soil. Piping trenches and drainage systems that were installed during your home's construction can also be entry pathways.

3. House Vacuum.

To make matters worse, your home creates a vacuum on the soil beneath it and virtually sucks the radon out from the soil along with other soil gases. This happens for two main reasons:

A.   During colder seasons we close our windows and heat our homes. This causes a difference in temperature between the air inside the home as compared to the air outside. This temperature difference causes a thermal stack effect. This thermal stack effect causes warm air to rise in a home (the same phenomena that gliders and hawks use to gain altitude). This thermal stack effect causes air in the lower part of the home to rise. As the warm air rises, a vacuum is created in the lower portions of the home. This suction on the lower level, such as a basement, draws air from below in the soil into the home. This air can contain radon as well as other undesirable soil gases (e.g., methane).

B.   The second reason why radon is drawn into the home is because of the home's mechanical depressurizing devices. We intentionally build and install devices that will remove air from a home. The exhaust fans found in kitchens and bathrooms are one example of this type of device. Another are the flues on our hot water heaters, furnaces and chimneys for stoves and fireplaces. These exhaust fans and flues remove objectionable odors and poisonous combustion by-products. They work by drawing air out of the house thus creating an additional vacuum effect.

Both stack effect and mechanical depressurization devices contribute to the suction force that your home exerts on the soil. The greater the suction force the more make-up air needed and the greater the entry of soil gases. The severity of the radon problem depends upon the source, pathway and house vacuum.

**THE LEVEL OF A RADON CONCENTRATION DEPENDS UPON:
SOURCE, PATHWAY, & HOUSE VACUUM**

♦   **The amount of radon being created beneath your home is called the: SOURCE**

♦   **The ease at which radon can move through the soil is called the: PATHWAY**

♦   **The amount of suction force exerted on the soil is called the: HOUSE VACUUM**

There are two other ways for radon to enter your home. These are usually minor contributors compared to the soil gas entry described above.

1.   **Well Water.** Radon can enter the home with the water supply. If your home is supplied directly from an underground water well you should have the water tested for radon. Maximum contaminant levels for radon in water have not been firmly established as of this printing. However, a rough estimate is that for every 10,000 pCi/L of radon that is found in the water an additional 1 pCi/L of radon is added to the home's overall airborne radon concentration. Using this guideline you can predict how much of the indoor radon may be from the well water and how much is from the normal soil gas entry routes.

Example: Indoor radon concentration of the home was determined to be 20 pCi/L and the well water was determined to be 20,000 pCi/L. Using the guidance that 10,000 pCi/L in water yields 1 pCi/L in the air, one can see that 2 pCi/L (20,000 divided by 10,000) of the overall 20 pCi/L found in the home comes from the water. The majority of radon found in this home comes mainly from the entering soil gas. Therefore, the greatest health benefit would come from reducing the soil gas entry. This book will concentrate on reducing the radon from soil gas entry. Contact your local health department if you find that you have elevated levels of radon in your water or if the techniques described in this book do not sufficiently reduce radon levels. The health department can supply a list of radon professionals who have knowledge of reducing radon from water supplies.

2. Radon can also be emitted in small quantities from building materials within the house. Examples of these would be rock fireplaces, or some drywall products. This amount of radon is generally low enough that the natural ventilation of the home will deal with this contamination source.

Exception: If high uranium containing materials, such as mill tailings from a uranium processing plant, were used during the construction of your home, consult your local health department for advice. Cases of mill tailing contamination are isolated and are generally well known by local health officials.

How are Homes Mitigated or Fixed for Radon?

Most radon problems occur in homes from the entry of soil gases from beneath them. Remember, for the home to have a radon problem a source, a pathway, and a vacuum are needed. Radon is generated in the soil beneath the home, the suction exerted on a permeable soil causes the radon to enter the home. It is not practical to excavate and replace all the soil beneath the home (that is, remove the source), nor is it practical to expect people to turn off exhaust fans and heating systems. So how is radon removed? Fortunately, the answer is that an extremely successful technique has been developed called **Active Soil Depressurization.** The following discussion describes how it works.

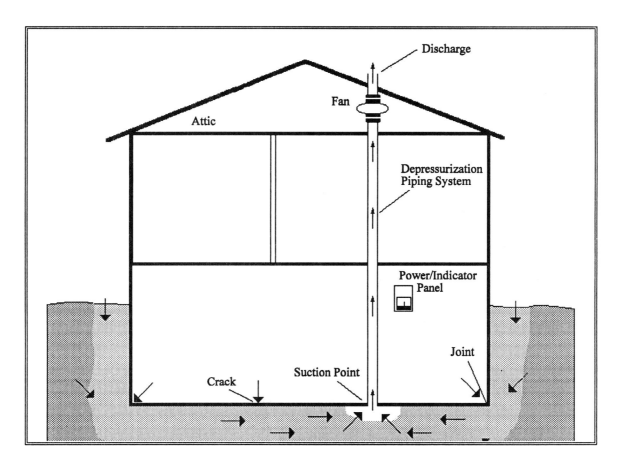

Theory Of Active Soil Depressurization

Active Soil Depressurization is a family of radon reduction techniques that mechanically creates a suction on the soil beneath the structure. This suction mechanically created on the underlying soil is greater than the suction exerted on the soil by the home. Because the suction produced by the system under the house is greater than the suction exerted by the house, the radon is vacuumed out of the soil before it has a chance to enter the home. Once it is captured by the system it can be exhausted above the home. Using a high exhaust point will prevent it from coming back into your, or your neighbors, windows.

If your house had not been built in the middle of the radon's natural pathway it would have entered the air rather than your home. Radon still enters the air but now rather than passing through the house it goes through the system to reach the air outside.

The system's vacuum is created by a special fan. The fan has the proper characteristics to create an adequate suction pressure, as well as air-flow capabilities. These fans are attached to a depressurization piping system (described in Chapter 7). The depressurization piping system is connected to the house's slab, or under a plastic sheet installed in a crawl space, or to water drainage systems. When the fan operates continuously it creates a vacuum on the radon entry points. The radon, as well as other soil gases, can be captured and safely vented away from the home.

The key to the system successfully working is in the installation details. This book will concentrate upon these details.

WHY CAN'T I JUST SEAL ALL THE OPENINGS INTO MY HOME?

Without counteracting the suction exerted on the soil by the house, radon can continue to enter through extremely small and difficult to seal leak points.

Sealing is not a reliable reduction method on its own, but it can improve the effectiveness of an active soil depressurization system.

There are many points in a home through which radon can pass. Most people consider cracks in the concrete floor as the major concern. In reality they are very small compared to other openings such as:

Concrete Joints. Expansion joints or cold joints are located where the concrete floor meets the foundation wall. These joints can be large radon entry points. Since interior finished walls are often constructed over the tops of the joints, they are generally inaccessible for good sealing even if you wanted to try to use sealing as a stand alone technique.

Utility Service Lines. There are openings around plumbing and electrical conduits where radon can enter the home from beneath slabs or through walls. These openings are also very difficult to access. Often toilets, showers and bathroom cabinets are constructed over the top of them which makes accessing these openings for proper sealing difficult.

Drainage Systems. Drainage systems built into a home that are designed to collect water can provide an easy pathway for radon entry. An example of this would be a sump pit located in the basement that allows ground water to seep in so it can be pumped away. If ground water can get into the sump, so can radon from the underlying soil.

Crawl Spaces and Exposed Earthen Areas. A very large soil opening is presented if your house is constructed over a crawl space. Even if you have crawl space vents or your builder laid down a loose sheet of plastic as a vapor barrier, the radon can still come into the home from the crawl space area. This is because of the house vacuum described earlier. This vacuum draws air from the crawl space into the living space above. There are too many openings in the flooring above the crawl space to stop the radon from entering. The crawl space vents may decrease the suction pressure but not counteract it completely. Also, the benefit that vents can provide is lost when they are closed in the winter months. Radon entry is often the highest during this period.

The direction of air flow into the house is reversed once an active soil depressurization system is installed. In fact, at locations where soil gas air used to enter a home, such as a floor crack, interior air now flows down through the crack once the depressurization system has been installed and turned on (compare the houses pictured on pages 3-2 and 3-4). Sealing of cracks will decrease this air loss and increase the strength of the vacuum. The greater the vacuum is, the better the radon reduction will be. Sealing will also reduce the loss of interior conditioned air after the system is working. Sealing against inside air loss will also greatly reduce the potential for back drafting of combustion appliances.

THIS BOOK WILL SHOW HOW AN ACTIVE DEPRESSURIZATION SYSTEM CAN BE APPLIED TO:

♦ **Homes Built Over Crawl Spaces**

♦ **Homes That Have Water Drainage Systems**

♦ **Homes Built Over Basements or Are Slab-On-Grade**

These three applications are those most commonly used by professional mitigators. Although there are other approaches, they are generally used as a supplement to the techniques listed above. By using these techniques you will most likely accomplish a reduction to below the EPA's recommended action level of 4 pCi/L. If not, then call a radon mitigation specialist to determine what additional measures may be needed. You will not be wasting your time and effort by still installing these systems. In fact, you should be able to save hundreds of dollars even if you need additional professional help after installation.

To determine which, or how many, of the techniques above will be needed for your home you will need to spend some time inspecting the foundation of your home. You will need to ask questions like: Do I have a crawl space? Do I have a basement? Do I have both crawl space and basement? Do I have a drainage system that I can use to my advantage? A "flow chart" style of the decision process is outlined (preceding Chapter 1) to assist the homeowner in deciding which, or how many, radon reduction techniques should be used.

How This Book is Organized

There are three basic types of active depressurization systems detailed in this manual which can be used by themselves or combined:

♦ Sub-membrane depressurization for crawl spaces,

♦ Depressurization systems that utilize water drainage systems,

♦ Sub-slab depressurization systems for basements and slab-on-grade homes that do not have drainage systems.

A depressurization system is the common element for these approaches. This system consists of the piping and the fan necessary to produce the vacuum for collecting the radon for each of these approaches. Therefore, Chapter 7 describing the depressurization system will apply to all of the detailed mitigation systems described in Chapters 4,5,6 and 9. Another common element is the Chapter 8 on sealing entry points that will enhance each of the applied techniques and a *very important chapter on general safety practices.*

Warning: If you only read isolated parts of this book, you will not have sufficient details to complete a radon mitigation system. This could result in poor radon reductions and serious injury.

Radon Reduction Technique Installation Process

1.	**Read Book (especially safety chapter)**
2.	**Identify Construction Features of Home**
3.	**Plan System**
4.	**Acquire Materials**
5.	**Reread Applicable Chapters**
6.	**Reread Safety Section**
7.	**Install System**
8.	**Seal Leak Points**
9.	**Have a Back Draft Test Performed**
10.	**Retest Radon Levels in Home**

To successfully perform the repairs described in this manual without harm to yourself, follow the process steps outlined above. Pay special attention to the following:

Step 6 is one the most important. Be aware that the repairs in this manual will expose you to many hazards. Some are solvent based caulking and glue, while some are physical hazards presented with any type of remodeling work. The caulks recommended in this manual are standard materials that can be found at many building supply stores. However, some people are sensitive to their use. If you are a person who is sensitive to organic vapors you may not want to continue but rather hire a professional contractor listed with the EPA's Radon Contractor's Proficiency Program. If you are not excessively sensitive to chemicals, *you take the proper precautions outlined in the safety section, and follow the manufacturers' instructions,* everything should work out well.

Step 9 is equally critical. At the conclusion of the installation you will turn on the system. Look for leaks that can be sealed to improve the efficiency of the system. If you do not look for large system leaks, you could cause your combustion appliances to back draft. This condition is rare but the effects could be life threatening. If your hot water heater or furnace back drafts, poisonous carbon monoxide gas could accumulate in the home. *Hire a professional furnace or home inspector who has the proper equipment to evaluate your combustion appliances when you have completed the system.* Proper methods for testing for carbon monoxide are varied and involved.

Radon reduction systems alone are not responsible for causing carbon monoxide poisoning. However, an incorrectly installed system by a well meaning do-it-yourselfer can cause a serious safety problem. Don't take a chance with the health and safety of your family - have a back drafting test done. Whether you install a radon system or not, it is recommended to have a back draft test done anyway.

Chapter 4

How To Reduce Radon In Homes That Are Completely Or Partially Built Over Crawl Spaces

What mitigation system will give you the best radon reduction?

What are the best materials?

How is it installed?

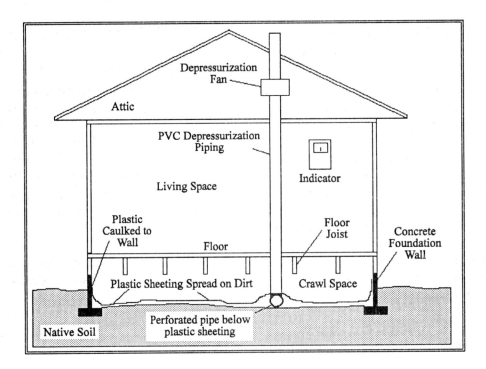

Houses Built Completely or Partially over a Crawl Space

This chapter specifically deals with how to fix radon entry from crawl spaces. If your house has a basement or a slab-on-grade portion in addition to a crawl space you need to refer to those chapters in this book as well (see Radon Reduction Flow Chart preceding Chapter 1).

Homes are often built over crawl spaces where the living area is suspended over bare earth. Crawl spaces allow for a large entry of radon into the home above even if vents to the outside were installed on the sides of the crawl space. The suction that is naturally created by the house over these crawl spaces can draw the radon, along with other soil gases, into the home. This chapter applies to homes that are constructed:

1.   Completely above a crawl space,
2.   Partially over a crawl space,
3.   Homes that have large exposed earthen areas inside of them.

Ventilating the crawl space by blowing outdoor air through it would be one reduction method. Although this can reduce radon levels, it can cause freezing problems for pipes in the crawl space of homes in cold climates. There is a more reliable method for reducing radon entry that does not present this concern, it is called **Sub-Membrane Depressurization (SMD).**

To construct a sub-membrane depressurization system a perforated pipe is laid on the ground in the crawl space. Then a strong plastic sheet is laid on the ground in the crawl space over the top of the perforated pipe. Next, the edges of the sheet are sealed to the walls of the crawl space and the seams are sealed. A fan is then connected to the perforated pipe to draw the radon from beneath the plastic. This system collects the radon as it comes up from the soil preventing it from entering the crawl space. The collected radon can then be exhausted harmlessly outdoors (see figure above).

BEFORE ATTEMPTING ANY WORK IN THIS SECTION, BE AWARE OF THE FOLLOWING:

1.	You will be spreading plastic in a crawl space. Is there enough working room for you to crawl through this area? Can you get to all of the walls? If not, STOP. You may not want to attempt this work or you may need a professional radon mitigator.

2.	Solvent containing caulks will be used to seal the plastic sheeting. *If you, or other occupants of the home are sensitive to these chemicals - do not attempt this repair.* You must ventilate the crawl space area during the installation to reduce the build up of fumes from the caulk. This can be done with a window fan. For additional ventilation, you can also run your depressurization piping into the crawl space area and turn it on.

3.	Take proper precautions to protect hands, knees and eyes. Crawl spaces can have a lot of sharp rocks and construction debris in them. Wear durable coveralls, knee pads, gloves and goggles (see safety item chart).

4.	Take proper precautions to insure that you are not exposed to other crawl space dangers. Crawl spaces often are the homes of spiders, snakes and rodents.

5.	Crawl spaces are often sprayed with pesticides. Wear proper respiratory protection when working in these areas. Wash hands and face thoroughly after working in these areas, before eating, drinking or any time you notice any skin irritation.

6.	**If your home has asbestos materials in the crawl space DO NOT ATTEMPT THIS REPAIR.** Furnace ductwork and heating pipes are often run through crawl spaces. These can be wrapped in insulation containing asbestos. This material is easily damaged and forms a dust in the air, and if inhaled, can result in serious health problems. If this is the case in your home, contact a professional who is familiar with the proper precautions that must be taken to protect your health and the health of the workmen.

How to determine if asbestos is a potential problem: Asbestos wrapped ducts may look like cloth wrapped on sheet metal duct work or a cloth wrap insulation on hot water piping. The insulation on the heat piping may also look like corrugated cardboard. If your crawl space has any material that looks like this, the chances are very good that it is asbestos and some has fallen on the dirt floor of the crawl space. If you are unsure, it is best to hire an inspector who is trained and certified in asbestos analysis.

7.	While ventilating and working in the crawl space dust will be created. A dust mask is a requirement for this job (see respiratory protection discussion in Chapter 10).

✓ Tools and safety items you will need:

Goggles		Ventilation Fan		Utility Knife	
Leather Gloves		Trouble Lights		Duct Tape	
Sturdy Coveralls		Knee Pads		Caulk Gun	
Hat		Helper		Polyurethane Caulk	
Dust Mask		Smoke Stick		Flashlight	

Planning the Sub Membrane System

This section will focus on the work that will occur in the crawl space. A depressurization system as described in Chapter 7 will also be installed.

Please refer to the flow chart preceding Chapter 1 to decide if additional areas of the house will need to be repaired to fully reduce radon levels.

Planning Step 1.   Measure the dimensions of the crawl space.

The following is a summary of the planning process that will be described in greater detail with an example for illustration.

Make a drawing: Make a sketch of the crawl space. Be sure to note all of the turns of the walls, the length of the walls and the location of any interior support posts that may be setting on concrete pads. If there are concrete pads on the floor of the crawl space, measure the location of the pads and their dimensions (all four sides) and include them on your sketch.

Estimating the plastic needed: Once you have completed a sketch of the crawl space, you can estimate the amount of plastic sheeting and caulk you will need. The plastic sheeting will be laid down to cover the entire dirt floor surface of the crawl space area. When installed properly at least 12 inches of plastic will run up the foundation walls of the crawl space. Seams need to overlap by at least 12 inches. Caulking will be used to seal the edges to the walls and also to seal all of the seams. Duct tape will be used to hold the overlapped edges of the seams together until the caulk sets up.

Type of plastic sheeting to buy: The type of plastic that is recommended is white, high density, 4 mil thick, cross laminated polyethylene. It can be most economically purchased in large 20 foot by 100 foot rolls.

> *Important:* The plastic used must be strong enough not to tear while installing it in the crawl space. Another important consideration is long-term durability as you, or others, crawl over the top of it. This could happen during future maintenance work on the home in the crawl space (e.g.: furnace repair, plumbing maintenance, etc.).

Other Considerations: Some crawl spaces have deep trenches or uneven surfaces. You must allow for enough plastic to cover the sides and bottom of the trenches when you install the plastic sheeting. When the system is turned on the plastic will be drawn down to the soil and will conform to the irregular surfaces. The plastic acts like a plastic vacuum packaging you see on small utensil packaging.

> *Important:* Allow enough plastic so when the depressurization system is turned on and the plastic is drawn down, it will not be pulled away from the walls.

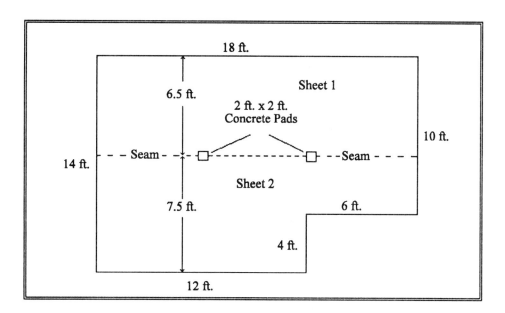

Planning Step 2.   Determine how much plastic will be needed.

Determine the best way to lay the plastic on the crawl space surface. The sketch above shows a sample crawl space. Notice that there are concrete support pads in the middle of the floor. These pads will have support posts sitting on them that support the house above. You cannot remove these support posts in order to slide the plastic over the pads. Therefore, you will have to fit the plastic around them. *Note:* Whenever an obstruction exists, such as the concrete pads shown above, it is best to plan a seam at the obstruction.

A seam line is shown on the above sketch as a dashed line going from left to right. This means that two sheets of plastic, sheet 1 and sheet 2, can be cut prior to installation. The two sheets should overlap at least 12 inches along the seam. This will make fitting the plastic around the pads much easier.

The following details are also needed to finalize the measurement of the plastic sheeting:

♦   Add at least 1 foot (both lengthwise and widthwise) for each foundation wall that the plastic will be sealed to.

♦   Add at least 1 foot of length or width to one of the sheets for each seam.

♦   Remember to add extra length if there are trenches or irregularities in the crawl space floor.

Sheet	Wall Meas.	+ Wall Seal	+ Wall Seal	+ Seam	= Total
Sheet 1 Length	18	1	1	0	20
Sheet 1 Width	6.5	1	0	1	8.5
Sheet 2 Length	18	1	1	0	20
Sheet 2 Width	7.5	1	0	(Added to sheet 1)	8.5

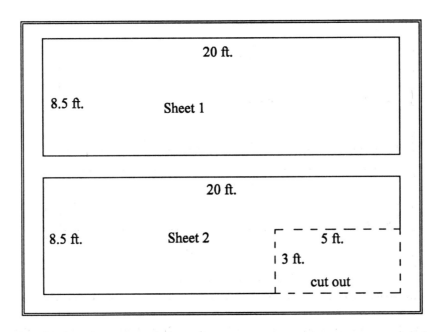

Planning Step 3.   Plan how to cut the plastic.

To use the least amount of plastic and get the best results from the sub-membrane depressurization system the above picture shows how the two sheets of plastic sheeting will be cut. It is best to cut the plastic prior to putting the plastic in the crawl space. Using a 20 foot wide roll, a length of 20 feet would be cut from the roll and then re-cut into two 10 by 20 foot strips. If you buy the plastic sheeting in a 10 foot roll, two 20 foot long strips would be cut from the roll.

Note: In the example above the width of a single sheet was determined to be 8.5 feet. If you cut the plastic into 10 foot wide strips this allows for a greater than the suggested 12 inch overlap at the seams. Remember that the minimum overlap is 12 inches - more is okay.

Note that a cut out has been shown for an indentation in the foundation.

How to make the cut-out:

1. Measure from the edge of the plastic closest to the indentation.

2. Make sure to add at least 1 foot of excess plastic to allow for sealing the plastic to the foundation walls.

*In the example above, you would measure 5 feet from the right edge and 3 feet from the bottom edge.

Interior walls:

Some crawl spaces have concrete walls inside of them to support the weight of the home. Treat internal foundation walls exactly the same as an exterior wall. Cut plastic in these areas wide enough and long enough to seal the edges of the plastic at least one foot up on these walls.

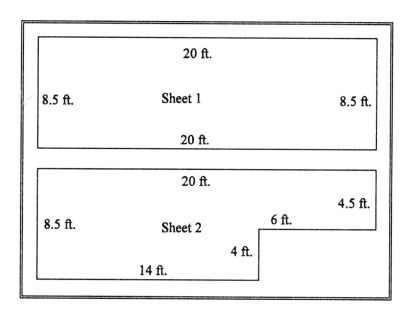

Planning Step 4. Plan how much caulk and duct tape will be needed.

The sheeting will need to be sealed at walls and seams with caulk. Duct tape will be used to temporarily hold the plastic sheeting in place until the caulk hardens. Sealing should be done at:

1. **Edges.**   Wherever the plastic will come in contact with a foundation wall of the crawl space.

2. **Internal foundation walls.**   If there are concrete walls that run through the inside of the crawl space, the plastic will also need to be sealed to these walls.

3. **Concrete pads.**   Wherever the plastic comes in contact with a concrete pad on the floor of the crawl space.

4. **Seams.**   Wherever two sheets of plastic come together, the overlapped seam must be sealed with caulk and duct tape run along the free edge to hold it in place temporarily.

Polyurethane caulking, which can be applied with a caulking gun, is used for this purpose. A good rule of thumb for estimating the amount of polyurethane caulk needed is:

♦   One 11-ounce tube of polyurethane caulk will make 8 feet of joint, seam or edge seal.

Using the previous example and assuming that the concrete pads are 1 ft. by 1 ft.

Foundation Walls	Internal walls	Pad perimeter	Seams	Total feet
8.5+20+8.5+8.5+4.5+6+4+14 =	+0	+2 pads x4 =	+20+20 =	
+74	+0	+8	40	= 122

122 ft of sealing will be needed in this example. To get the number of tubes of caulk, divide the feet by 8, or: 122/8 = 15.25. Buy at least two more tubes of caulk than needed, or in this example buy 17 tubes of polyurethane caulk. You will also need approximately 150 feet of cloth backed duct tape.

Planning Step 5.   Plan the perforated soil gas collection pipe.

As shown in the figure on page 4-2, a length of corrugated, and perforated 3 inch pipe will be laid on the crawl space floor prior to installation of the plastic sheeting. This perforated pipe is commonly referred to as ADS pipe. ADS is a specific brand name. The perforated pipe will eventually be connected to the depressurization system through a vertical riser of PVC pipe per the detail shown in a later detail (Figure on page 4-10).

The perforated pipe is laid directly on the soil with a single length of pipe running the length of the crawl space. If the crawl area is divided into sections there will be a length of pipe beneath the plastic sheeting for each section of the crawl space.

It does not matter where the pipe is laid beneath the plastic. It does not have to run through the center of the covered area. It can be run along the wall if desired. You should plan to run it through areas that would not need access for routine house maintenance. This minimizes stepping on the pipe and potentially damaging the plastic sheeting that will be laid over it.

Planning Step 6.   Plan the depressurization piping system. *(See Chapter 7)*

A depressurization piping system will need to be installed to collect the radon from beneath the plastic sheeting. This piping system and its fan are described in Chapter 7. The depressurization piping system will connect to a perforated pipe that will be laid on the crawl space floor before the plastic sheeting is installed. As a preview the depressurization piping will meet the following criteria:

♦ Pipe above plastic sheeting should be schedule 40 PVC pipe.

♦ Piping should be sloped back to the suction point which, in this case, is the point that the system connects to the plastic sheeting.

♦ The depressurization fan should be located either in an unused attic, in a garage, or outside the home. **The fan should not be in the crawl space area.**

♦ The discharge of the system (where the radon will be exhausted) should be at least ten feet above grade and ten feet away from any other openings into the home.

♦ The piping system should be labeled.

♦ The fan should be either low voltage, class 2, installed by homeowner or 120 volt hard wired by an electrician.

♦ There should be a mechanical performance indicator installed.

♦ Piping that is routed through unheated spaces in cold climates; piping may need to be insulated.

♦ Piping that is routed through a garage wall or any other fire rated wall, a fire stop must be used.

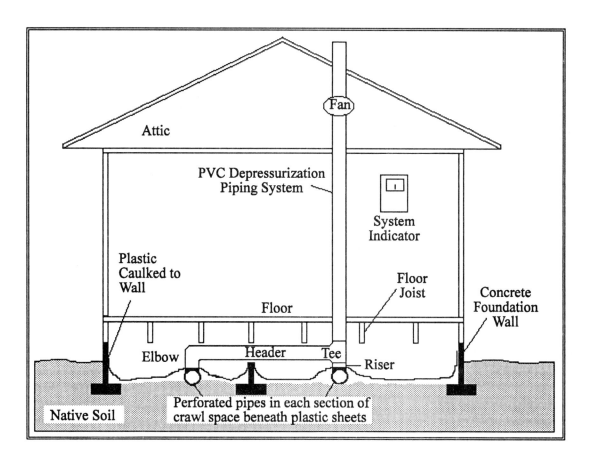

Planning Step 7.   Planning the depressurization piping system if the crawl
space is in sections.

Some crawl spaces have internal concrete foundation walls for supporting the home. If this is the case with your home, you will have to treat each section of the crawl space as a mini crawl space system.

Each section will have its own piece of plastic sheeting sealed to the concrete walls.

Each section will have a separate suction point riser that is tied to a common depressurization system (see figure above).

Each of the risers can be connected to a common length of schedule 40 PVC piping that is then routed to a single fan. This piece of pipe is referred to as a "header" with tees or elbows installed to connect it to each suction point. This header can be supported from the floor joists or on top of the intermediate foundation walls.

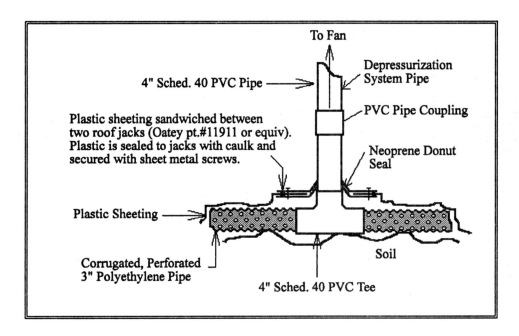

Planning Step 8.   Making the connection to the perforated piping.

As described earlier, a length of perforated pipe will be laid on the crawl space dirt before the plastic is installed. Depressurization piping will be attached later to this perforated piping. If the system riser is located in the center of a crawl space the perforated pipe is cut and a tee is installed (the illustration above shows how this is done). If the suction piping riser is to be at one end of the crawl space, a PVC elbow would be used instead of the "tee" shown in the drawing above. *Note:* If your crawl space is separated by foundation walls more than one riser is needed.

To achieve a tight seal at the point where the suction pipe passes through the sheeting, the use of roof jacks with neoprene collars (standard plumbing vent flashing) is very effective. These roof jacks are approximately 12 inches by 12 inches square with a round opening in the middle. This round opening has a flexible neoprene donut or gasket that will slide down around the PVC pipe. The neoprene gasket makes the seal around the pipe.

Two roof jacks are used to accomplish the seal for each suction riser. One is installed on the riser pipe below the plastic sheeting. The other roof jack is placed on the riser pipe above the plastic sheeting. This allows the sheeting to be sandwiched between the two flat portions of the roof jacks. A round hole is simply cut in the sheeting for the riser to pass through, and a circle of caulking is applied to both the top of the lower roof jack plate and the bottom of the upper roof jack plate. When the two plates are compressed and screwed together, a very tight seal is achieved. In addition to a little caulk, you will need the following materials for each suction point connection:

Item:	Quantity
Polyethylene roof jack for 4 inch pipe	2
4 inch PVC elbow or tee	1
12 inch long section of 4 inch PVC pipe	1
4 inch PVC coupling	1
# 8 by 3/4 inch sheet metal screws	10
3 inch corrugated and perforated pipe (ADS)	long enough to run length of crawl space

Installing the Sub-Membrane System in the Crawl Space

In this section, step by step instructions will be given for the installation of this system. Read this entire section along with the previous section regarding the planning of the system before proceeding. *Read Chapter 10 on safety before starting.*

Installation Step 1.   Assemble equipment and materials.

The following is a checklist of equipment and materials that you will need to have before starting.

Area	Item	✓
Safety		
	Goggles / safety glasses	
	Dust mask	
	Leather gloves	
	Knee pads	
	First aid kit	
	Ventilation fan	
	Assistant	
	Flashlight	
	Trouble lights	
	Heavy coveralls	
	Hat (Bump cap, skull cap, or heavy baseball cap) to protect head hitting floor joists	
Material	Plastic sheeting-4 mil, high density cross-laminated polyethylene is preferred	
	Duct tape	
	Sheet metal screws	
	caulk	
	corrugated pipe	
	roof jacks	
	Depressurization system piping and fan system (see chapter 7)	
Tools	Rake	
	Shovel	
	Utility knife and razor blades	
	Caulking gun	
	Tool bucket	
	Drill	
	Trash can	
	Rags	
	Extension cords	
	Screw driver	
	Flashlight	
	Smoke stick (see Chapter 8)	
	Wire brush	

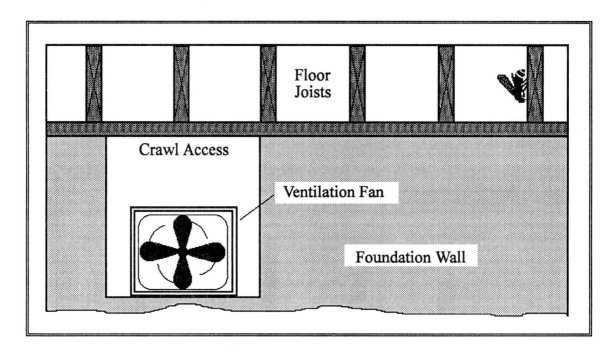

Installation Step 2.   Set up safety equipment.

DO NOT BEGIN THIS WORK IF ASBESTOS IS FOUND IN THE CRAWL SPACE OR IF CHEMICAL SPRAYS HAVE BEEN USED. IF FOUND, CEASE ALL WORK AND CONTACT A PROFESSIONAL !

The first step in this project will be to insure adequate ventilation during the work.

♦   A powered fan, as shown above, can sit in front of the crawl space access for good ventilation of the crawl space.

♦   A window fan can be used in place of a powered fan to ventilate the crawl space.

♦   MAKE SURE THAT ALL OF THE CRAWL SPACE VENTS ARE OPEN TO INSURE GOOD CROSS FLOW OF AIR.

♦   Set fans up such that they draw air from the crawl space and exhaust fumes and dusts to outside of the home.

Protective Clothing

Crawl spaces are notorious for having sharp objects such as old boards with nails, glass, sharp rocks and construction debris. You should also protect your head and eyes from wires and nails that can protrude down from the sub-flooring.

Installation Step 3.   Prepare the crawl space floor.

♦   Remove stored items from crawl space.

♦   Remove loose construction debris from crawl space floor.

♦   Remove broken glass and other sharp objects.

♦   Remove large rocks from the crawl space area or dig a pit in the crawl space and put them into it. Cover the pit over with loose dirt.

♦   Rake floor to collect small sharp objects and dispose of them.

It is not necessary to remove all pebbles and broken rocks. The plastic sheeting that is suggested for use is very strong and is resistant to puncture. However, if you plan to access the crawl space often or if you plan to use it as storage in the future, it would be wise to protect the plastic from the rocks beneath it. Protect the plastic in frequently used areas by laying some carpet scraps or pieces of cardboard on the dirt before you lay the plastic sheeting down. If you plan to store items on top of the plastic, lay carpet scraps above and below the plastic to protect it.

Installation Step 4.   Lay out perforated pipe.

Cut the length of corrugated pipe needed to run the length of the crawl space.

♦   Lay the pipe in areas away from crawl space access openings.

♦   The pipe does not have to run the exact length of the crawl space. It can be cut back a few feet from each end of the crawl space.

♦   If your system suction piping riser is to be at one end of the crawl space, run the pipe to that point where you will connect it to a 4 inch PVC elbow riser (see next installation step).

♦   If your system suction piping riser will be more centrally located, then cut the length of pipe into two pieces. Lay the two sections in the crawl space so two ends of the pipe can be connected to either side of a 4 inch PVC tee. The location of this tee should be where the suction system riser will be.

♦   If your crawl space is broken into sections (as would be the case with internal foundation walls) each crawl space will have to have a separate system of perforated pipe and suction system risers.

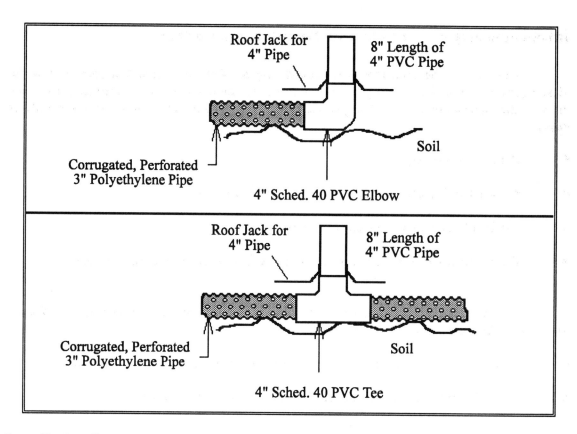

Roof Jack for 4" Pipe

8" Length of 4" PVC Pipe

Corrugated, Perforated 3" Polyethylene Pipe

Soil

4" Sched. 40 PVC Elbow

Roof Jack for 4" Pipe

8" Length of 4" PVC Pipe

Corrugated, Perforated 3" Polyethylene Pipe

Soil

4" Sched. 40 PVC Tee

Installation Step 5.   Make riser connection to perforated pipe.

At the point in the perforated pipe where the suction system riser is located, make either of the connections depicted above. If the perforated pipe is extending only in one direction from the suction piping then use the upper illustration. If the perforated pipe is to be laid in two opposite directions from the riser point, use the lower illustration.

♦   If using the upper illustration glue an eight inch length of 4 inch diameter PVC riser pipe into one end of the elbow. If using the lower illustration glue an eight inch length of 4 inch diameter PVC riser into the vertical portion of the tee. The piece of pipe will later be connected to the depressurization system and should not be less than eight inches long. Use PVC glue to make this connection. AVOID SKIN AND EYE CONTACT WITH PVC GLUE.

♦   Connect the perforated pipe to the end of the elbow as in the upper illustration or to both ends of the tee as in the lower illustration. A three inch ADS pipe will fit snugly inside of the 4 inch elbow or tee. The ends of the corrugated pipe should be pushed in 2 inches and secured with three sheet metal screws for each connection. The sheet metal screws should be run through the outside of the PVC fitting and into the ADS pipe to securely hold it into the fitting. Attach with either a drill and screw driver or use a nut driver on a variable speed electric drill. It is not important to seal this joint since it will be beneath the plastic sheeting.

♦   Slide the roof jack down over the short length of pipe so its seal is on top.

Installation Step 6.   Cut and spread plastic out on floor.

Refer back to the sketch that you made during the planning stage of this chapter. Lay the plastic out on a flat surface like a garage floor or on the lawn. Carefully measure the plastic and cut it to the dimensions that you had planned. ***Remember the old rule: Measure twice and cut once.***

♦   Use a measuring tape.

♦   A chalk line is useful in making straight lines for cutting.

♦   Cut the plastic with a sharp knife or scissors.

♦   The plastic can be oversized but not undersized. You can trim it once it is installed.

After you have cut the sheets roll them up and take them into the crawl space. Roll them out in the fashion you plan to install the sheets.

♦   Remember that you will need about 12 inches to go up each wall for a good seal.

♦   Remember that you will need about 12 inches of overlap where the sheets meet to form a seam.

♦   Spread sheeting under plumbing pipes and ductwork that may be in the crawl space.

♦   Set rocks or bricks on the plastic to stabilize it while you spread it out and work on it.

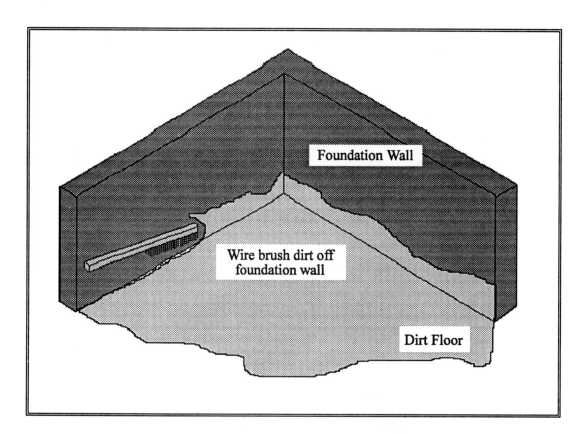

Foundation Wall

Wire brush dirt off foundation wall

Dirt Floor

Installation Step 7.   Preparing the walls for sealing.

The key to any seal is how well you prepare the surface. The polyurethane caulk that is being recommended in this manual is very durable, provided that it has been applied to a relatively clean surface.

♦   Brush the surface of the concrete walls the plastic edges will be sealed to. The key is to remove the loose surface dirt. Brush an area of the wall approximately 6 inches above the dirt level. Remember that you will next run a thick bead of caulk along this surface. So brush where you think you will be running this bead of caulk.

♦   You can prep all of the walls at one time or you can brush a portion and then caulk the plastic to it in order to minimize your movement on the plastic.

♦   If the walls are damp, this is of no consequence. The polyurethane will adhere to damp (not wet) concrete walls.

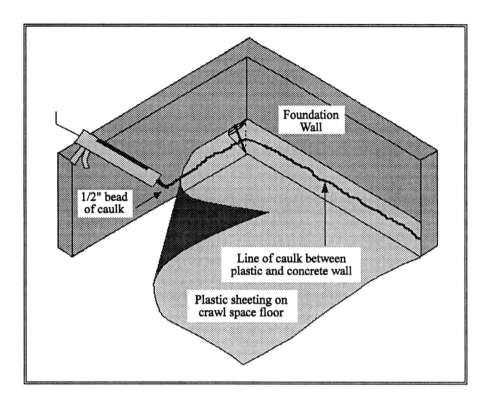

Installation Step 8:   Sealing the plastic in place.

 **Caution: Before proceeding with this step be sure that you have read the manufacturer's safety data sheet for the caulk and are familiar with the properties of this material. Be sure that your ventilation fan is operating. Some people are sensitive to the fumes from the solvents that are in these caulks. A chemical resistant respirator may be appropriate if you are sensitive or cannot get good ventilation. Do not wear a respirator unless you have the pulmonary capacity to breathe through it when you exert yourself. See Chapter 10 on safety.**

To seal the sheeting to the walls of the crawl space, a thick bead of polyurethane caulk is applied directly onto the surface of the concrete. A hand powered caulking gun works well for application.

♦   Apply a single but continuous bead of caulk on the surface of the concrete about 6 inches up on the wall. The bead should be about 1/2 inch wide. Remember, one tube should run approximately 8 feet. **DON'T SKIMP !**

♦   As soon as possible (less than 20 minutes) after applying the caulk, press the plastic onto the caulk and smooth the plastic firmly along the entire length of the bead of caulk. Set a rock or a brick on the plastic periodically to hold it in place.

♦   In corners, apply a liberal amount to the wall and the back side of the plastic and fold it into the corner (see Installation Step on page 4-20).

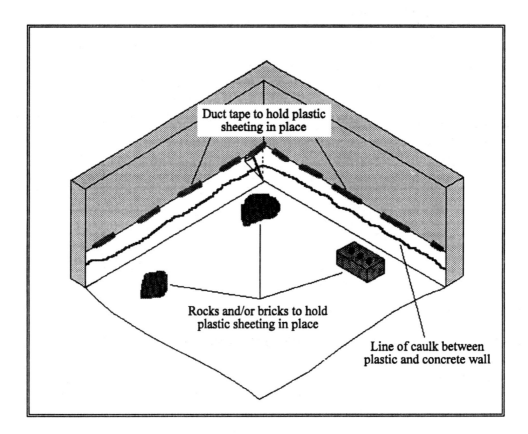

Duct tape to hold plastic
sheeting in place

Rocks and/or bricks to hold
plastic sheeting in place

Line of caulk between
plastic and concrete wall

Installation Step 9.   Temporarily securing the edges of the plastic.

Because it takes a few days for the caulk to fully cure, and you will be crawling around on the plastic, it is a good idea to secure the plastic where you have sealed it.

♦   This can be done by taping the free edge of the plastic sheeting to the wall with a high quality duct tape.

♦   It is also a good idea to set a rock or brick on the plastic near the concrete wall.

♦   If the plastic is pulled off anyway, you can always re-glue it to the wall.

♦   While securing plastic in place, this is a good time to see if you have put a continuous bead of caulk behind the plastic. If you have used the plastic and caulk recommended in this manual, you should be able to see the bead of caulk through the plastic. If not, pull the plastic back and re-caulk it.

♦   Run your hand along the plastic over the bead of caulk and press the plastic on, pushing the plastic onto the caulk on the wall to insure a good seal.

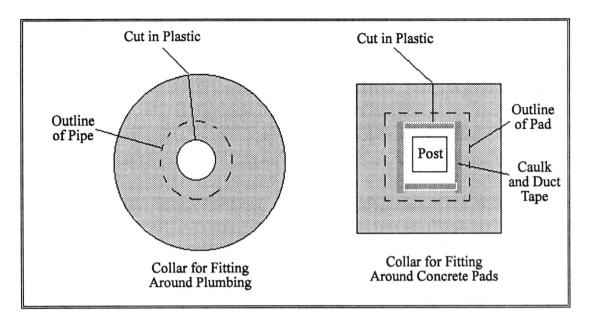

Installation Step 10.   Fitting around plumbing pipes and pads.

One of the difficult parts of installing the plastic sheeting is sealing around obstacles on the crawl space floor. Typical obstructions found are vertical plumbing pipes and concrete pads that are under house support posts.

Fitting around vertical pipes:
The cut-out shown on the left side of the figure would be made for sealing around a plumbing pipe that rises up from the crawl space floor. This circular cut-out is approximately 2 feet in diameter. A round hole cut in the center of the plastic should be at least two inches smaller than the diameter of the pipe you are going to seal around. Pipe diameter is shown as dashed line in above left figure. A cut is made from the center hole to the outside edge of the collar. This will allow you to slip the collar around the pipe. Run a 1/2 inch bead of caulk around the surface of the pipe at the point where you are going to seal it to the collar. Open the collar and place the inner circle around the pipe and wrap duct tape around it several times to hold the collar tightly against the caulk. Run a bead of caulk along the cut in the collar, overlap the two edges, press together and cover with duct tape. You should cut the main sheet of plastic so it can be placed around the pipe. The collar can be above or below the main sheet of plastic. Run a 1/2 inch bead of caulk in a circle on the face of the collar and press the main sheet of plastic onto the caulk. Seal the slit in the main sheet as you would a seam. This method will provide an excellent seal.

Fitting around pads:
The collar shown on the right hand side of the figure above is for concrete pads. The outline of the concrete pad is shown as a dashed line. Wire brush and apply a continuous 1/2 inch bead of caulk around the top surface of the pad. Fit the rectangular collar around the support post, laying the plastic on the caulk on top of the pad. Press the plastic onto the caulk to form a seal. Apply caulk the cut on the collar and tape it. Tape the free inside edge of the collar to the concrete. You should cut the main sheet of plastic so it can be placed around the pad and post. The collar can be above or below the main sheet of plastic. Run a 1/2 inch bead of caulk in a circle on the face of the collar and press the main sheet of plastic onto the caulk. Seal the slit in the main sheet as you would any seam.

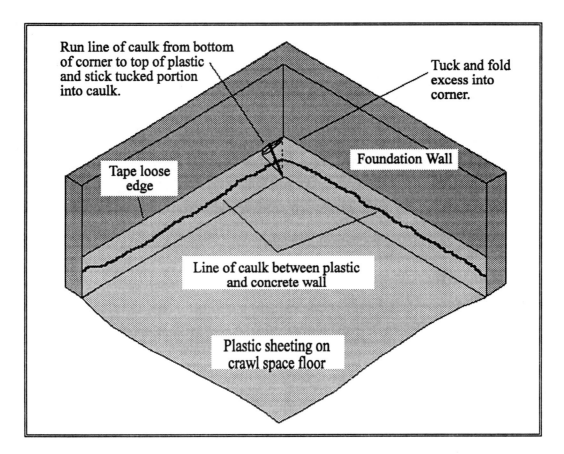

Run line of caulk from bottom of corner to top of plastic and stick tucked portion into caulk.

Tuck and fold excess into corner.

Tape loose edge

Foundation Wall

Line of caulk between plastic and concrete wall

Plastic sheeting on crawl space floor

Installation Step 11.   Fitting plastic into corners.

Sealing the plastic into corners is important for obtaining a good seal. This is especially true for areas of the crawl space that are the closest to the perforated gas collection pipe. Sealing corners is similar to wrapping presents.

Run a 1/2 inch bead of caulk along the walls for sealing the edges of the plastic. Run this bead into and around the corner. While pushing the plastic into the corner at the base of the wall press the edges of the plastic into the caulk on the walls and corner. This should leave a triangular shaped flap extending out from the corner. Run a bead of caulk on the exterior surface of the plastic, on one side of the corner and press this tuck onto it. Open the flap of the tuck and squirt some caulk into it and press it closed.

Tape the free edges of the plastic to the walls and set rocks or bricks on the plastic to hold it in place until the entire installation is completed.

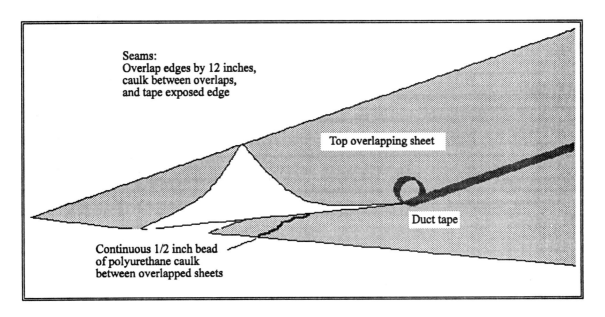

Seams:
Overlap edges by 12 inches,
caulk between overlaps,
and tape exposed edge

Top overlapping sheet

Duct tape

Continuous 1/2 inch bead
of polyurethane caulk
between overlapped sheets

Installation Step 12.   Sealing seams.

After the plastic has been fitted and sealed into the corners and around posts it is time to seal the edges.

♦   *IT IS CRITICAL THAT YOU DO NOT PULL THE PLASTIC TIGHT TOWARDS THE SEAM. LEAVE IT LOOSE WITH SEVERAL INCHES OF EXCESS IN THE PLASTIC. IF YOU MAKE A TIGHT FIT THE PLASTIC WILL BE PULLED AWAY FROM THE WALLS WHEN THE DEPRESSURIZATION SYSTEM IS TURNED ON.*

The seam seal is made by overlapping two edges by at least 12 inches. Apply a 1/2 inch wide bead of caulk on top of the sheet of plastic that will be on the bottom of the overlap. Lay the overlapping sheet on top of the bottom sheet. Using your hand, press down on the top sheet along the bead of caulk. You should be able to see through the plastic in order to see that you have a continuous bead of caulk. Using cloth backed duct tape, tape the free edge of the top sheet to the bottom sheet. This will hold the seam until the caulk sets up.

The bead of caulk does not have to be straight as long as it is continuous - don't skip sections. The bead should not be closer than 3 inches from either edge of the seam or it will squirt out and make a mess when you press the two sheets together.

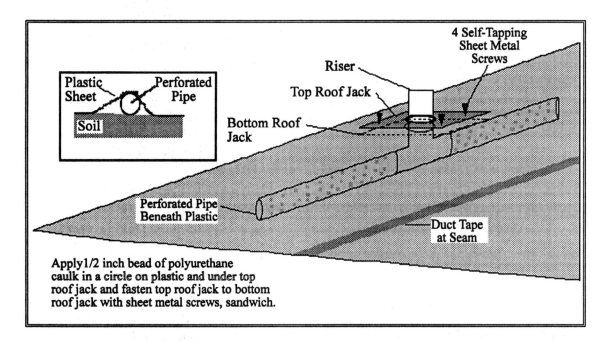

Apply 1/2 inch bead of polyurethane caulk in a circle on plastic and under top roof jack and fasten top roof jack to bottom roof jack with sheet metal screws, sandwich.

Installation Step 13.   Finish connection at riser pipe.

Return to the location where the riser attached to the perforated pipe comes through the plastic. Note that the 4 inch PVC riser should be protruding through a 6 inch circular hole in the plastic sheeting.

♦   Apply a 1/2 inch wide circle of caulk to the surface of the plastic around the 6 inch hole.

♦   Slide the roof jack down over the 4 inch PVC riser pipe and press the plate portion of the roof jack onto the caulking.

♦   Using four 1-inch #8 self tapping sheet metal screws, secure the top roof jack to the bottom roof jack beneath the plastic. Drill the four screws in so that they will penetrate through the caulking that was applied to the plastic sheeting. Tightening the screws will draw the plates together and sandwich the plastic in between. The caulk will set up and create a good seal at this critical point.

♦   Connect the depressurization piping system to the riser by using a 4 inch PVC pipe coupling (see Chapter 7).

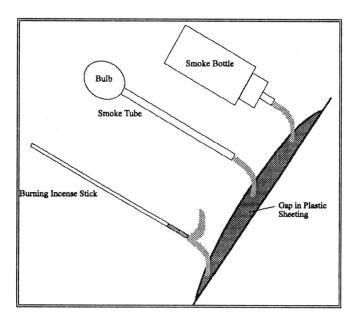

Installation Step 14.   Checking for leaks.

After the system has been turned on, a suction will be created beneath the plastic. This vacuum catches radon and other soil gas that otherwise would have entered the crawl space and eventually entered the home. The better the vacuum is, the better the radon reduction will be. A better vacuum can be produced by finding and sealing leaks in the plastic at seams, edge seals and at locations where the plastic was sealed around obstructions.

Sometimes you can hear air being drawn down through a leak. However, it is best to use some type of smoke generator to detect air being drawn down below the plastic. The picture above shows three different types of smoke generators that can be used for this purpose. A flashlight should be used to help see the direction that the smoke moves. If it goes down through an opening, use some caulk to reseal the opening until smoke is no longer seen flowing through the opening.

Burning Incense Stick: An incense stick or a "punk" can be purchased that, when lit with a match, burns slowly and produces a light smoke. This can be held close to a seam for example, to see if a leak is causing the smoke to be drawn down. If so, re-seal the seam with caulk. Because the smoke is warm, it will want to rise on its own, therefore it is as not as sensitive for finding leaks as other devices. To compensate for this, put the burning end as close to the opening as possible and shine a flashlight on the smoke and look for small wisps of smoke being drawn down.

Smoke Tube and Smoke Bottle: These are devices that can be ordered from radon catalog supply houses or sometimes from a heating and ventilating equipment supplier. They are filled with titanium tetrachloride **(do not get in eyes or on skin)**. When the bulb or bottle is gently squeezed, a small amount of the chemical is released into the air. The chemical forms a hydrochloric acid mist in the air **(do not breathe)**. These devices are more sensitive than the incense stick and more likely to find leaks. Use a flashlight with these devices as well.

For this application the incense stick is more than satisfactory.

Radon Mitigation System

Do Not Damage Plastic on Floor of Crawl Space

If plastic must be cut or removed for maintenance purposes, turn off fan located in _(location)__. Switch for fan located in _(room)__. Fan powered from breaker # _(number)_ in fuse box.

If plastic is damaged, repair with polyurethane caulk and/or duct tape. Turn system back on after repair.

Installation Step 15.   Labeling and maintenance.

After you have spent what was probably an incredibly entertaining weekend of crawling through the underbelly of your house, it would be a shame if one of your family members or a workman in the future inadvertently damaged the plastic sheeting. A label should be placed near or on the crawl space access door to warn people not to cut or remove this plastic sheeting. There may be times, however, that access may be needed beneath the plastic. This could occur if a plumber would need to work on piping beneath the home.

Access beneath the plastic is not a problem, providing the system is temporarily turned off. Turning the system off prevents the loss of a large amount of interior air which could cause back- drafting of combustion appliances (see Safety Chapter 10). After the necessary work is done, the plastic can be folded back together and re-caulked and taped. It is a good idea to make straight cuts in the plastic when this is done and to save left over plastic for such an event.

If small holes are made in the plastic, this is not a serious problem. It only means that the system will have to move a slightly larger amount of air. These small leaks can be easily fixed with a piece of duct tape placed over the top of the puncture.

If the crawl is to be used for storage, it would be a good idea to lay down a rug or scrap of carpet in these areas to prevent accidental punctures. The plastic recommended for use is actually very durable and the small punctures will need very little attention. It is the large rips and cuts that are of concern.

An example label is shown above that will help you and future homeowners maintain the quality of your work. This can be made up on a piece of paper and glued to a door, or typed on a sticky label.

♦   **Don't forget to label all visible sections of the depressurization system piping.**

Chapter 5

How to make Use of Existing Water Drainage Systems to Reduce Radon

How to make use of a sump system.

How to make use of an exterior foundation drain.

How to do use these systems without affecting their water drainage capability.

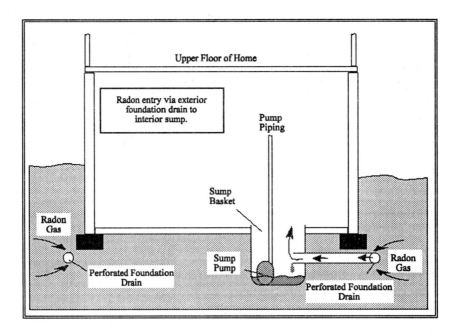

Radon Reduction Through the Depressurization of Drainage Systems

This chapter deals with how to use the water drainage system, that *may* have been installed during the construction of your home, to reduce radon. Radon reduction systems that capture radon by creating a vacuum on the drainage system itself have proven to be very effective in reducing radon. This is due to the following reasons:

The diagram above shows a water drainage system that was installed on a home with a basement. During the construction of the home a perforated pipe was placed at the bottom of the trench that was made when the footings of the home were poured. This perforated pipe forms a loop around the foundation and collects rain water that falls onto the soil above it. The loop is connected to a pipe that is routed to a sump inside of the home. This sump could be made out of concrete, steel, plastic or simply be a hole in the concrete floor. A pump is normally found in these sumps that will remove the water into the storm sewer system.

These drainage systems were installed so water could easily reach the drainage collection pipes. This factor allows radon, as a gas created in the soil, to also reach these same collection pipes. The natural vacuum that the house exerts on the soil causes a significant amount of radon to enter the home through the collection pipes, into the sump and then into the home itself. Merely sealing off the sump with a sealed lid is not a reliable solution. However, if a vacuum was applied to this same lid and the entering radon is collected and exhausted outside, a very reliable mitigation system would result. This method is referred to as "drain-tile depressurization." How this is actually done depends upon the type of drainage system that was installed on your home. Depressurization of exterior foundations not attached to a sump work equally well and are also described later in this chapter.

Important: *To utilize this approach you must have had a drainage system installed on your home during its construction. Not all homes have them. If you do not have a drainage system, then other techniques like sub-slab depressurization are more cost-effective than installing a new drainage system. Also, if you have a crawl space you should deal with that area first or simultaneously (see flow chart preceding Chapter 1.)*

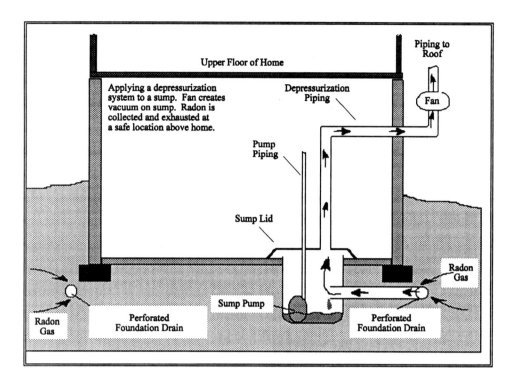

Applying a depressurization system to a sump. Fan creates vacuum on sump. Radon is collected and exhausted at a safe location above home.

How a depressurization system can use an existing drainage system to reduce radon.

The picture above shows how a depressurization system is used to collect radon from a drainage system and exhaust it harmlessly outside the home. Refer to illustration on page 5-2 where the radon was shown to enter the home through the perforated water collection piping. By creating a vacuum on the sump you not only catch radon at a major entry point but you can also catch it at other places in the soil via the vacuum created on the entire drainage system. The system shown above is more specifically referred to as "sump depressurization."

The sump depressurization system shown above was installed by first installing a cover or lid over the sump. This lid was placed on the concrete floor around the sump. It was also sealed to the floor to prevent air leakage. The depressurization system piping was attached to the lid and then routed to the depressurization fan. The fan creates a vacuum on the sump.

When a vacuum is created on the sump, a vacuum is also created on the drainage piping that is connected to the sump. Because the drainage collection system in this illustration is a perforated pipe looped completely around the foundation of the home, a large radon capture area is created. This explains the excellent reductions that are generally seen with these types of systems.

Note: In this example, the fan was located outside the house. This is acceptable, as long as the discharge is run to a safe location away from openings into the home. Alternatively, the piping could have been run up through the house, with the fan in the attic with its exhaust being through the roof. *The routing of the depressurization system is detailed in Chapter 7 and should be read as part of the overall design of these systems.* This chapter will concentrate on how depressurization systems are connected to the types of water collection systems that are most commonly found in homes.

Planning the Drainage Depressurization System

The discussion in this chapter will concentrate on how connections are made to the various types of drainage systems commonly found in homes. The depressurization system that will collect the radon from the drainage system and exhaust it outside is described in Chapter 7.

Please refer to the flow chart preceding Chapter 1 to determine if additional portions of the house will also need to be repaired to adequately reduce radon levels.

Planning Step 1. Deciding what kind of drainage system was installed on your home.

Most homes that are constructed in areas of high rainfall or are built on the sides of hills where ground water can flow into the portions of the home are constructed with some means for reducing the entry of rain water into the home. This is done by two basic methods:

1. **Sumps.** Water is routed to a sump or holding tank where a water pump is used to pump the water to a storm drain system. An illustration of this type of system was shown on the previous page. Water is often routed to the sumps, located inside of the home, by means of water collection pipes that are either in the ground outside the home or are in the soil underneath the concrete slab. If you look down into the sump basket and see pipes penetrating the side of the basket, this is probably the type you have.

Sometimes the water flows through gravel that has been laid beneath the concrete slab to get to the sump. In this case the sump basket has perforations in its side where the water can easily flow into the basket for collection.

2. **French Drains or Perimeter Drains.** These are systems where perforated pipes have been installed either around the outside of the foundation or around the inside of the foundation. These are the same types of pipes that can be found in conjunction with sump systems. However, the difference here is that rather than going to a sump, they have a leg of pipe that is routed away from the house that allows the water to be drained away from the house. The drainage away from the house generally happens by three different methods:

A. **Daylight Drain Discharge.** This is typically seen on homes that are constructed on a hillside. One or two pipes are connected to the perforated water drainage pipe and slope away from the house to a point where the pipe or pipes exit the hillside. This allows the collected water to drain down the hillside away from the house.

B. **Dry Well.** In this case a pipe is connected to the foundation drain pipe and routed away from the house to a hole that has been dug and filled with rocks or gravel. Water collected in these holes can easily drain into the water table below. This is more common with older homes.

C. Storm Sewers or Interceptors. This is where the perimeter foundation drain is connected to large pipes that are designed to collect ground water from several homes in a neighborhood. These large pipes may be connected to the storm drain system where the storm water is collected and diverted away from the subdivision. They may also be connected to large underground pipes that run off a hillside where the storm water from the subdivision is drained away.

Important: *If the drainage system of your home is connected to a storm sewer or an interceptor, this technique will not work.* You will not be able to achieve a sufficient vacuum due to the large amount of air in these underground collection systems. If you do not know if your drainage system is connected to one of these systems, ask your builder or call your local regional building department.

Before you begin this work be aware that these drainage systems were originally installed for the purpose of preventing drainage water from entering your home. They were not installed for future use as a radon reduction system. If done properly, the drainage system can be used very effectively for radon reduction while still being able to divert water from the home. The important thing to remember is that you cannot modify the drainage system in a fashion that will not allow it to function as a water drainage system, or not allow for maintenance. Some key elements are as follows:

◆ Lids placed over sumps should be sealed with gaskets and mechanical fasteners to allow for future access to the pump beneath it.

◆ If a pump is located in the sump, it cannot be removed to allow for easy installation of the cover. This is especially true if a pedestal type pump is installed in your sump. If you have a pedestal style water pump, it will have to be replaced with a submersible type.

◆ If your house has a perimeter foundation drain that drains off a hillside (drain discharge), you cannot seal off these drains in order to improve the vacuum on the radon reduction system. Special traps have been designed for this purpose. "P" traps or other types of water trap seals are not appropriate either, since they can become filled with silt and restrict the normal flow of water away from the home.

◆ The type of fan used to create the vacuum for the radon reduction system should not exceed a maximum suction pressure of 1 1/2 inches of water column. The typical radon fan described in Chapter 7 is appropriate for this application, since it is capable of moving the amounts of air needed with these systems (but not creating too large a vacuum that would effect the natural gravity flow of the water drainage). The use of higher vacuum capability fans could prevent proper water drainage away from the house.

Each of these concerns, and how to deal with them will be detailed in the balance of this section.

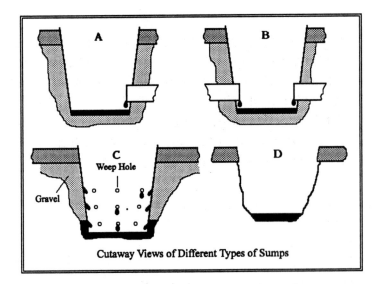

Cutaway Views of Different Types of Sumps

Planning Step 2.   Determining if you have a sump style drainage system.

The above diagram shows four types of sumps that are often found in the lowest floor of a home. Sumps are usually located in the corner of a slab. In newer homes, they are typically made out of black plastic and are set into the aggregate prior to the concrete being poured up to them. They vary from 18 to 30 inches in diameter.

First: Look down into the sump with a flashlight to see if there are one or two 3 to 4 inch diameter pipes entering the side of the sump. If there is only one pipe entering the sump, as in illustration A above, then it is probable that there is a loop of perforated drainage pipe running around the outside of the foundation with a single leg running to the sump. This will allow for the depressurization system to be attached either to a lid placed on the sump or alternatively, to the perforated pipe outside the foundation as is described in the exterior drain system described later in this chapter.

If there are two pipes entering the sump pit, as in illustration B, then it is likely that there is a loop of pipe beneath the slab inside of the foundation wall. The significance of this is that you must attach the depressurization system directly to the lid placed over the sump. You do not have the option to connect to a drainage pipe outside the home.

If your sump does not have any pipes entering it, but rather has holes through its sides as in illustration C, or is an open pit as in illustration D, then you have a sump that has no perforated piping connected to it. This is also the case if the sides of the sump are dirt or gravel, as in illustration D. In this case one can assume that the sump was set through a layer of gravel that was placed on the soil prior to the concrete slab being poured. This means that the depressurization system must be connected to a lid placed over the sump. The depressurization system will extract the radon from the gravel layer through the holes in the side of the sump basket.

Second: Determine if there are any pipes other than those for ground water drainage entering the sump. Examples of this would be floor drains, waste water from laundry machines, or pipes connected to hollow block drainage systems. If this situation exists with your sump, a depressurization will draw a significant amount of air from the inside of the home. _**This will not only hurt the efficiency of the radon reduction, but more importantly could cause the combustion appliances to backdraft and cause poisonous carbon monoxide to enter the home**_. If this is the case in your home, you will either have to reroute these pipes away from the sump or use the sub-slab depressurization methods described in Chapter 6.

DecisionPoint

If you have determined that you have a sump style drainage system, continue with this section. If you think that you may have an exterior style drainage system you may want to go to the exterior drain section of this chapter beginning with page 5-18. It is important to note that you may have a combination of sump and exterior drain so that both sections of this chapter will need to be understood.

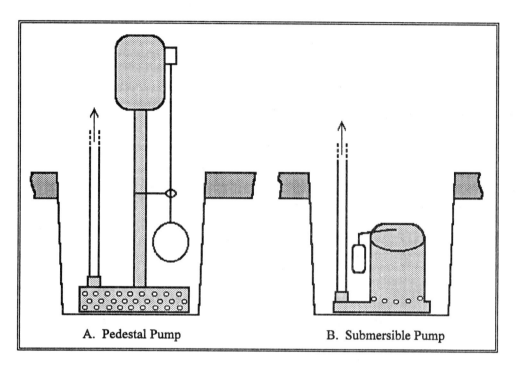

| A. Pedestal Pump | B. Submersible Pump |

Planning Step 3.   Sumps - determine what type of sump pump you have and whether it needs to be replaced.

You need to determine whether you have a submersible pump or a pedestal style pump. The importance of this is to determine how the lid will fit over the sump hole and still allow the piping and electrical cord to enter and exit through the lid.

Illustration A above depicts a pedestal style pump. This pump has an electrical motor elevated well above the sump hole. There is a rotating shaft that is connected to the actual water pump that is located down in the sump pit. It will be impossible to install a lid that will properly seal around the shaft or shaft casing. *You will have to replace this pump with a submersible type.* Purchase the new pump first or obtain sufficient information on the one you plan to purchase to determine pipe size openings for the lid.

Illustration B above depicts a submersible pump. These low profile pumps have both the electrical motor and the water pump packaged in a single unit. They are called submersible because they are sufficiently sealed to where they can be set slightly off the bottom of the sump and not be damaged by the accumulated water. These are desirable because the only penetrations that have to go though the lid are for the electrical cord and the discharge piping.

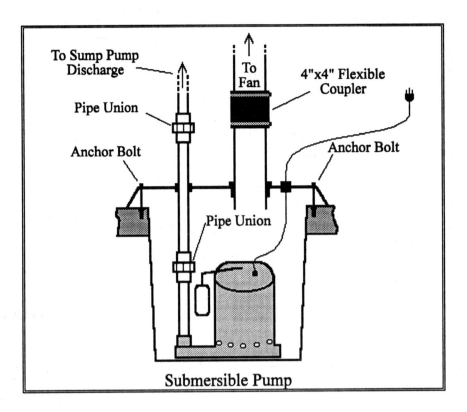

To Sump Pump Discharge

To Fan

4"x4" Flexible Coupler

Pipe Union

Anchor Bolt

Anchor Bolt

Pipe Union

Submersible Pump

Planning Step 4.   Sumps - determining how plumbing will have to be revised to accommodate lid.

Since a lid will be placed over the entire sump hole, the plumbing will have to pass through the lid. If you purchase a prefabricated sump lid for radon reduction you will have to insure that your sump pump piping will pass through the precut openings provided in the lid. If you decide to make your own lid, or the size or configuration of your sump does not allow for the use of a prefabricated lid, you will still need to plan the penetrations.

The illustration above shows the piping running through the sump lid. Note that a union has been installed on the piping above and below the lid. A union is a device for connecting two straight lengths of pipe with wrenches. The union on the discharge piping of the sump is important because this allows the piping to be disconnected from the lid. Then the lid can be disconnected from the concrete floor and slid up far enough to allow access to the lower union. Once access is obtained to the lower union, it can be disconnected and the lid moved out of the way to allow access to the sump pump. Unions can be commonly found at any plumbing hardware store.

The necessary vacuum seal is accomplished between the lid and this straight section of pipe with rubber seals that can also be obtained at plumbing supply stores. The use of the rubber seal allows the lid to slide up and down on the pipe for easy removal and access to the pump below.

If you are not comfortable with revising this piping, it may be wise to purchase the lid and hire a plumber to make these modifications.

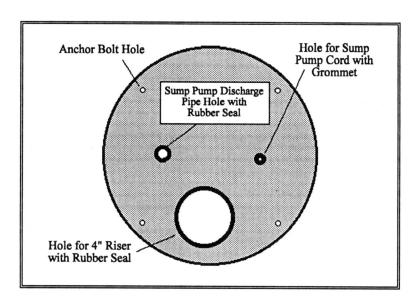

Planning Step 5.   Sumps - Determining the lid size and penetration sizes for round sumps.

Step 1:   Measure the outside diameter of the sump. This is done by using a measuring tape laid across the sump opening flush with the floor. Measure from edge to edge of the sump opening. Move the measuring tape to make sure that you come up with the largest measurement. This is the diameter. Your sump lid will need to be a minimum of 3 inches larger in diameter than the diameter of the sump opening. This will allow for the sump lid to attach to the concrete around the sump. For example, if the diameter of the sump is measured to be 18 inches, the lid will need to be 21 inches or larger to allow for a minimum 1 1/2 inch overlap over each side of the opening.

Step 2:   Measure the outside diameter of the discharge piping of the submersible pump. Do this by holding the measuring tape up against the pipe and at a right angle to it. Consult the following chart to determine the proper size of pipe.

If outside diameter of pipe in inches is:	Then pipe size in inches (schedule 40) is:
7/8	1/2
1 1/16	3/4
1 5/16	1
1 11/16	1 1/4
1 15/16	1 1/2
2 3/8	2
2 7/8	2 1/2
3 1/2	3

Step 3:   Fill out the following table. Contact a radon equipment supplier and provide this information to them. Many plumbing supply houses also have access to these covers as well.

Minimum lid diameter (actual measurement plus 3 inches)	
Sump pump piping hole diameter	
Depressurization piping hole size	4 1/2 to 5 inches (for 4 inch pipe)
Electrical cord for sump pump hole size:	1 1/2 to 2 inches with rubber seal for standard cord

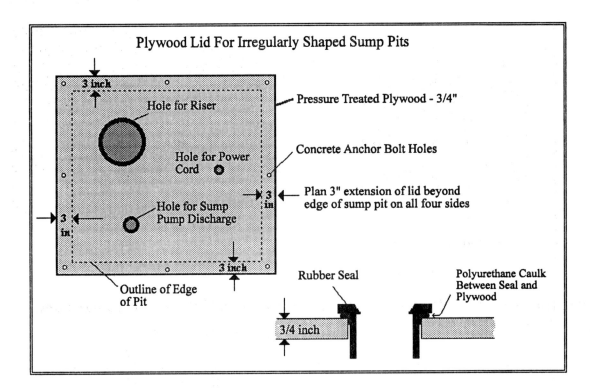

Plywood Lid For Irregularly Shaped Sump Pits

Hole for Riser

Hole for Power Cord

Hole for Sump Pump Discharge

Outline of Edge of Pit

3 inch

3 in

3 inch

Pressure Treated Plywood - 3/4"

Concrete Anchor Bolt Holes

Plan 3" extension of lid beyond edge of sump pit on all four sides

Rubber Seal

Polyurethane Caulk Between Seal and Plywood

3/4 inch

Planning Step 6.   Sumps - Making your own lid.

In some cases you will not be able to find a prefabricated lid to fit over your sump hole. This can happen if your sump is rectangular rather than circular. You can make your own lid and purchase and install the rubber seals for the plumbing penetrations yourself. This will also have to be done if you are planning a sub-slab depressurization system as is described in Chapter 6 (in this particular case, you would be sealing the hole to prevent loss of vacuum and a riser hole will not be needed).

Step 1.   Measure the dimensions of the sump hole. Your home-made lid will have to be at least 3 inches wider on *each* side of the sump opening. Measure the sump pump piping diameter (see Planning Step 5).

Step 2.   On a piece of paper layout the dimensions of the lid. Don't forget to add three inches for the overlap on each side. Lay out where the penetrations for the piping and electrical cord should be. Plan a hole for the 4 inch schedule 40 PVC depressurization pipe.

Step 3.   Purchase appropriately sized rubber seals for each of the lid penetrations from a plumbing supply store. Uniseal is a brand name commonly used for this purpose. A 1/2 thick bead of silicone caulk will be run under the lip of the seal and then pushed into place (see Chapter 8 on sealing).

Step 4.   Purchase the lid material. The lid material that you purchase must be of suitable strength to support a 250 pound person who might stand on top of it. Plywood is typically used for this purpose. The plywood should be 3/4 inch thick and suitable for outdoor use (pressure treated). The wood should be painted on all sides with a marine paint to reduce potential damage from the sump moisture. If the opening that the lid will cover is greater than 2 feet, the lid should be reinforced by attaching 2 by 2 inch boards wood screwed to the bottom side of the lid. Place on 12 inch centers, and make sure that these braces do not sit on the concrete. That is, when the lid is set down the braces fit up to the inside edge of the sump.

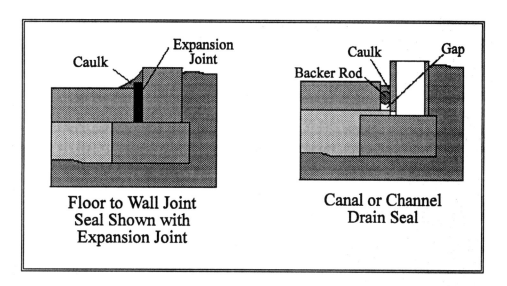

Floor to Wall Joint
Seal Shown with
Expansion Joint

Canal or Channel
Drain Seal

Planning Step 7.   Determine what slab openings will need to be caulked and sealed. Refer to Chapter 8 for more on sealing slab openings.

Because sumps are often located in corners and near outside walls, special attention needs to be paid to sealing the floor to wall joints, especially the ones nearest the sump itself.

The floor to wall joint area could be just a simple crack (cold joint) between the floor and the wall. If so, this should be wire brushed and caulked with polyurethane caulk as described in Chapter 8. Use the guidance detailed in that chapter as to the amount of caulking that will be needed.

Be sure to follow the ventilation and safety precautions when using this caulking as detailed in Chapters 8 and 10.

The floor to wall joint area could also be what is referred to as a "canal drain." These are wide channels in the concrete floor (typically 2 inches wide) that run along the outside edge of the basement floor. These are intended to collect drainage water that then seeps into the gravel under the slab. These cannot be completely sealed without impacting the home's drainage system. They need to be filled with a backer rod that is squeezed halfway down into the channel (see illustration B above). Caulking is then applied on top of the backer rod. Although this is described in more detail in Chapter 8, it is important to plan for this and to make sure that the pathway to the sump for the collected drainage water is not disrupted.

Be sure to follow the ventilation and safety precautions when using this caulking as detailed in Chapters 8 and 10.

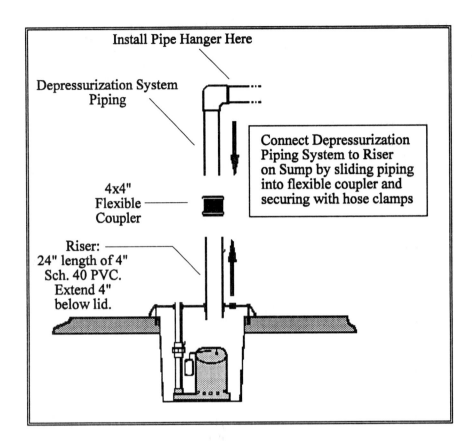

Install Pipe Hanger Here

Depressurization System Piping

Connect Depressurization Piping System to Riser on Sump by sliding piping into flexible coupler and securing with hose clamps

4x4" Flexible Coupler

Riser: 24" length of 4" Sch. 40 PVC. Extend 4" below lid.

Planning Step 8.   Planning the depressurization piping system connection to the sump lid.

The most appropriate size and type of depressurization system pipe to be used for this method is 4 inch schedule 40 PVC. The connection of the piping to the lid should be made by inserting a minimum 24 inch length of 4 inch pipe through the rubber seal on the lid. This riser should be inserted at least 4 inches down through the lid. The rubber seal should fit snugly around the outside edge of the pipe.

The depressurization piping described in Chapter 7 will connect to this riser with a 4 inch rubber or neoprene hose clamp style coupler. This coupler is designed to slip over the outside of the two pipes that are butted together. A seal on either end is accomplished with hose clamps that tighten the flexible neoprene onto the pipe. These couplers can be purchased from most plumbing supply stores and some of the radon equipment supply houses. The purpose of using a connector here as opposed to gluing the PVC piping together is so this connection can be loosened and the sump lid removed for maintenance purposes.

Planning Step 9.   Planning the depressurization system piping.
[Also See Chapter 7]

A depressurization piping system will need to be installed to collect the radon from the sump. This piping system and fan are described in Chapter 7. The depressurization piping system will connect to the 24 inch long, 4 inch PVC riser on the lid with the flexible pipe coupling described in the previous step. As a preview, the depressurization piping should follow the following criteria:

♦   Pipe should be schedule 40 PVC pipe.

♦   Piping should be sloped back to the sump to allow condensed water to flow back to the sump.

♦   The depressurization fan should be located either in an unused attic, in a garage or outside the home. *The fan should not be inside the home or inside the sump itself.*

♦   The discharge of the system, where the radon will be exhausted, should be at least ten feet above grade and ten feet away from any other openings into the home.

♦   The piping system should be labeled.

♦   The fan should be either low voltage, class 2, installed by homeowner or 110 volt hard wired by an electrician.

♦   There should be a mechanical performance indicator installed.

♦   Piping routed through unheated spaces in cold climates, piping may need to be insulated.

♦   For piping routed through a garage wall or any other fire rated wall, a fire stop must be used.

Installing the Sump Depressurization Systems

This section is devoted to the installation of a depressurization system that will be attached to a sump inside the house. If you are attaching the depressurization system to an exterior drain you can skip to that section of this chapter (page 5-18). Read this section along with Chapter 7 on Depressurization Systems, Chapter 10 on Safety, and Chapter 8 on Caulking and Sealing before proceeding with this work. You should also read the "Finishing Touches" section at the end of this chapter.

Sump Installation Step 1.   Assemble Equipment and Materials

The following is a checklist of equipment and material that you will need to gather before starting:

Area	Item	√
Safety	Goggles/safety glasses	
	Dust mask	
	Leather gloves	
	First aid kit	
	Ventilation fan	
	Flashlight	
	Coveralls or old clothing	
Material	**Prefabricated Sump Lid Materials**	
	Prefabricated lid with rubber seals	
	Four 1 inch long by 1/4 inch concrete anchor bolts and anchors (should be supplied with lid)	
	Home-Made Lid	
	3/4 inch plywood	
	Marine grade paint and brush	
	Four 1 1/2 in. long by 1/4 inch concrete anchor bolts and anchors	
	Rubber seals for pipe and electrical penetrations	
	Other Materials:	
	1 tube of silicone caulking	
	4 inch flexible pipe coupling	
	Two pipe unions of appropriate size for sump pump piping	
	Necessary piping for retrofitting the sump pump piping	
	Polyurethane caulking for sealing concrete openings (see Chapter 8)	
Tools	Electric drill or hammer drill	
	Carbide tipped drill bit, sized for concrete anchors	
	Caulking gun	
	Rags	
	Trash can	
	Extension cords	
	Wire brush	
	Wrench for concrete anchor bolts	
	Smoke stick (see Chapter 8)	

Step 2. Clean the sump. This may be your last chance to remove the dirt and lost toys that have accumulated in the sump over the years. For some reason these areas seem to be the final resting places for super balls and small toys from the local hamburger stand. After you put on the lid you will not want to remove it to fix a sump pump clogged by these. Scoop this stuff up and dispose of it. Wire brush the top of the concrete around the sump that your lid will contact. *Watch out for spiders!*

Modifying the plumbing system:

Discuss this modification with a knowledgeable person at a plumbing supply store or hire a plumber to do this work. Refer back to illustration in Planning Step 4.

Step 3.　If you have a pedestal style pump - remove it and replace it with a new submersible pump.

Step 4.　Cut the sump discharge piping at the location where you plan to install the upper piping union.

Step 5.　Remove the sump pump and cut the discharge piping approximately 3 inches above the discharge port of the pump and install the lower piping union.

Step 6.　Insert the appropriate length of sump pump piping through the seal in the lid you either bought or had made. Install the matching parts of the unions on the two ends of this pipe after it has been inserted. Use the appropriate pipe cements as recommended by your plumbing supply store if PVC pipe is used. If metal pipe was originally installed either have the pipe ends threaded for steel pipe or replace this section with schedule 40 PVC pipe rated for at least 125 pound pressure service.

Step 7.　Line the lid up over the pump so the stub of pipe runs through the lid and lines up with both the discharge of the sump pump and the rest of the sump piping. Take a pencil and insert it through each of the holes on the side of the lid to mark on the concrete the locations for the anchor bolts.

Step 8.　Set the lid off to the side and drill the concrete slab using a carbide tipped concrete drill bit or a hammer drill. Use the bit size recommended on the packaging of the concrete anchors you purchase. Vacuum out the concrete dust and the surface of the concrete that the lid will set on.

Step 9.　Remove the rubber seal in the lid for the electrical service cord. This seal should have a split in it. Route the plug end of the cord up through the hole in the lid. Place the split rubber seal around the cord and reinsert into the hole in the cover. Pull the desired length of cord up through the rubber seal.

Step 10.　Set the lid back in place and connect the sump pump piping. Tightly fasten the lid to the concrete with the anchor bolts.

Step 11.　Plug in the pump and run water into the sump with a garden hose inserted through the large hole that will be used for the depressurization piping. The sump pump should turn on and begin pumping this water away. Check for water leaks at your two union connections. If they leak, remake the joints. If not, proceed to the next step.

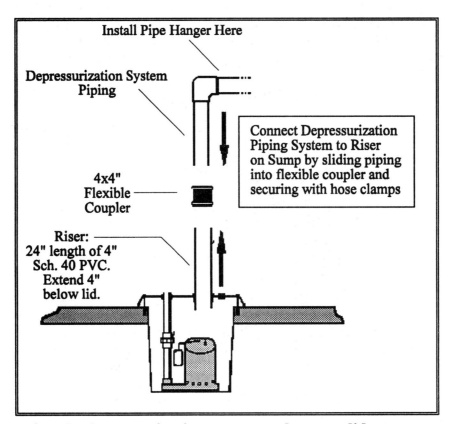

Install Pipe Hanger Here

Depressurization System Piping

Connect Depressurization Piping System to Riser on Sump by sliding piping into flexible coupler and securing with hose clamps

4x4" Flexible Coupler

Riser:
24" length of 4"
Sch. 40 PVC.
Extend 4"
below lid.

Connecting the depressurization system to the sump lid.

Step 12. Insert the riser (4 inches in diameter, with a minimum 24 inch long PVC pipe) through the large rubber seal in the lid. The pipe may need to be lubricated with some soapy water to help fit it through the rubber seal. The pipe should extend at least 4 inches down through the sump lid. Measure the vertical distance from the lid up to the top of the riser pipe and write this dimension down.

Step 13. Install the depressurization piping system per the methods described in Chapter 7. Plan to run the depressurization piping down towards the riser on the lid so the end of the depressurization piping stops 1 1/2 inches above the top of the sump riser, with the measurement made in step 12 above.

Step 14. Take the 4 inch flexible rubber coupling and apply a soapy solution to the inside surface, if necessary. Loosen the hose clamps fully. Slide one end of the coupling over the end of the depressurization system piping. Slide it up about 3 inches on the pipe. Line the riser pipe up with the depressurization piping and pull up on the riser so it is about 1 inch from the open end of the depressurization piping. Slide the rubber coupling down over the riser and position it on the riser and the depressurization piping so the hose clamps will tighten up on each pipe to make a good air tight connection.

Step 15. Turn the system on and check for leaks and have the draft of your combustion flues checked.

Step 16. Turn to the "Finishing Touches" section of this chapter for labeling and other helpful hints.

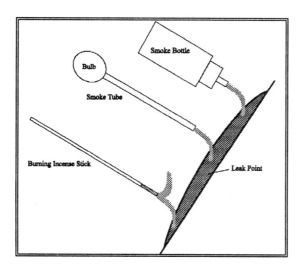

Sump Installation Step 17.   Check for leaks.

After the system has been turned on a suction will be created in the sump and, in turn, in the soil under and around the home. This vacuum catches the radon and other soil gas that otherwise would have entered the home. The better the vacuum is, the better the radon reduction will be. A better vacuum can be produced by finding and sealing leaks around the lid and at the pipe penetrations. You should also check the floor to wall joints and other slab joints at this time (see Chapter 8 on sealing floor cracks and joints).

Sometimes you can hear air being drawn down through a leak in order to find it. However, it is best to use some type of smoke generator to detect air being drawn down through the leak. The picture above shows three different types of smoke generators that can be used for this purpose. A flashlight should be used to help see the direction that the smoke moves. If it goes down through an opening, use some caulk to reseal the opening until smoke is no longer flowing down. *The type of caulking to be used on the lid to floor joint or around the pipe penetrations should be silicone and not polyurethane.* Silicone will allow for future access to the plumbing system, whereas polyurethane will not. You should, however, use polyurethane on the concrete cracks and floor to wall joint areas as described in Chapter 8.

Burning Incense Stick: An incense stick or a "punk" can be purchased and when lit burns slowly. It produces a light smoke. This can be held close to a suspected leak area to see if the smoke is drawn down. If so, re-seal the seam with caulk. Because the punk's smoke is warm it will want to rise on its own. Therefore, it is as not as sensitive for finding leaks as the other devices. To compensate for this put the burning end as close to the opening as possible and shine a flashlight on the smoke and look for small wisps of smoke being drawn down into the crack or leak.

Smoke Tube and Smoke Bottle: These are devices that can be ordered from a radon catalog supply house or possibly from a heating and ventilating equipment supplier. They are filled with titanium tetrachloride (*do not get in eyes or on skin*). When the bulb or bottle is gently squeezed a small amount of the chemical is released into the air. The chemical forms a hydrochloric acid mist in the air (*do not breathe*). These devices are more sensitive and more likely to find leaks. Use a flashlight with these devices as well.

For this application the incense stick is satisfactory.

Planning the Exterior Drain Depressurization System

If you have determined that you have an exterior drainage water collection system from the information provided earlier in this chapter, this section will assist you in how to attach a depressurization system to the exterior drain.

Planning Step 1. Understanding exterior drain tile systems.

This technique is used where perforated pipes have been installed for water collection either around the outside or inside of a foundation. These are the same types of pipes that can be found in conjunction with sump systems. However, the difference here is that rather than going to a sump, they have a leg of pipe that is routed away from the house. This allows the water to be drained away from the house rather than being collected.

The perforated drain pipe can be a corrugated 3 inch or 4 inch flexible black polyethylene pipe. It could also be a white PVC 3 inch or 4 inch rigid pipe with holes drilled in it. Regardless of the type of pipe, these are generally laid in the ground just below and beside the bottom of the foundation footing. This would have been installed during the construction of the home and is not something that would be specifically installed cost effectively for radon reduction. If you do not have either an internal or external drainage system, refer to other methods described in this book.

Generally there are three different methods for draining the water away from the house:

A. **Daylight Drain Discharge.** This is typically seen on homes that are constructed on a hillside. This is where one or two pipes are connected to the perforated water drainage pipe and slope away from the house to a point where the pipe or pipes exit the hillside. This allows the collected water to drain down the hillside away from the house.

B. **Dry Well.** In this case a pipe is connected to the foundation drain pipe and routed away from the house to a hole that has been dug and filled with rocks or gravel. Water collected in these holes can easily drain into the water table below. This is more common with older homes.

C. **Storm Sewers or Interceptors** This is where the perimeter foundation drain is connected to large pipes that are designed to collect ground water from several homes in a neighborhood. These large pipes may be connected to the storm drain system where the storm water is collected and diverted away from the subdivision. They may also be connected to large underground pipes that run off a hillside where the storm water from the subdivision is drained away.

> **Important:** *If the drainage system of your home is connected to a storm sewer or an interceptor, this technique will not work.* You will not be able to achieve a sufficient vacuum due to the large amount of air in these underground collection systems. If you do not know if your drainage system is connected to one of these systems, ask your builder or call your local regional building department.

Before you begin this work be aware that these drainage systems were originally installed for the purpose of preventing drainage water from entering your home. They were not installed for future use as a radon reduction system. If done properly, the drainage system can be used effectively for radon reduction while still being able to divert water from the home. The important thing to remember is that you cannot modify the drainage system in a fashion that will not allow it to function, or not allow for maintenance. Some key elements are as follows:

♦ If you have an exterior drain that has been routed to an interior sump you have the choice of creating a vacuum on the drainage system by connecting the depressurization system either to a sump lid or directly to the exterior drain pipe itself.

Regardless of which method is used for connecting to the system, if the drain is connected to an interior sump the sump pit must be sealed with a lid. Failure to do so may not only affect radon reduction <u>but could cause combustion appliance backdrafting and carbon monoxide poisoning.</u>

♦ A perimeter foundation drain that drains off a hillside (discharge) may have openings that will have to be sealed to accomplish the desired vacuum. If done correctly, you can close them off without affecting the ability of your drainage system to work properly. Special traps have been designed for this purpose. "P" traps or other of types water trap seals are not appropriate since they fill with silt and, over time, will restrict the normal flow of water away from the home.

♦ The type of fan used to create the vacuum for the radon reduction system should not exceed a maximum suction pressure of 1 1/2 inches of water column. The typical radon fan described in Chapter 7 on depressurization systems is appropriate for this application, since it has the capability to move the large amounts of air needed with these systems, while not creating so much vacuum to affect the natural gravity flow of the water drainage. The use of higher vacuum capability fans could prevent proper water drainage away from the house.

Each of these concerns, and how to deal with them, will be detailed in the balance of this section.

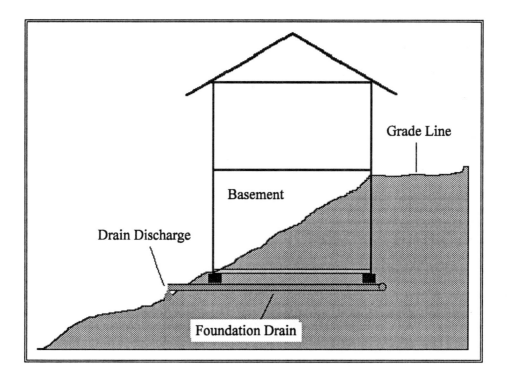

Planning Step 2.   Determine if you have a drain discharge.

Drain discharges are where the water, which is collected by the exterior foundation drain, can drain naturally off a hillside. They are often found on homes that have been built into a hillside as the illustration above shows. These drain discharges are open ends of the perforated piping system. These pipes often stick out the hillside. Made out of black corrugated pipe or white PVC pipe, they are generally 3 or 4 inches in diameter.

Sometimes the builder will connect the same type of corrugated pipe to the downspouts of the gutter and run them off the hillside as well. You may find several pipes coming out of the side of the hill. If this is the case, you will have to figure out which one is which.

1.   Count the number of downspouts that have pipes connected to them that also go down below the ground.

2.   Count the number of pipes that come out of the back of the hillside.

If the number of pipes coming out of the hillside is 1 or 2 more than the number of downspouts, you probably have that number of drain discharges rather than a dry well. Now the trick is to determine which is which.

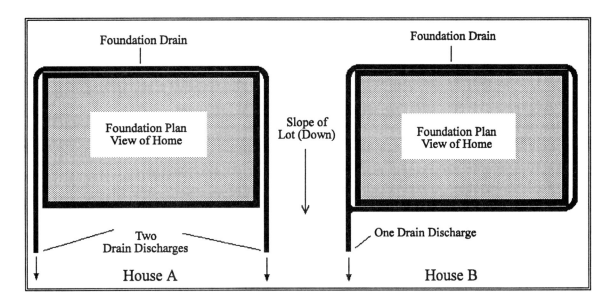

Foundation Drain | Foundation Drain

Foundation Plan View of Home

Slope of Lot (Down)

Foundation Plan View of Home

Two Drain Discharges

One Drain Discharge

House A | House B

Planning Step 3.   Identifying the drain discharges.

It is important to find the drain discharges in order to achieve a vacuum. Exterior foundation drains that go to drain discharges are generally installed one of two ways:

1.   They can be laid around the foundation on three sides in the shape of a horseshoe (see House A in the illustration above). The side that would not have a drain pipe along it would be on the outside of the house where the elevation of the ground is the lowest. In this case there are two drain discharges that would extend out from the hillside. These can generally be found coming off two corners from the home directly toward the low side of the lot.

2.   A continuous loop of foundation pipe can also run around the house (see House B in the illustration above). In this case there is only one drain discharge coming off the house. This drain discharge generally will be off one corner of the home and run directly toward the lowest point of the lot. Look for a pipe at this location.

If your downspouts have pipes attached to them for drainage, as described previously, you will have to:

1.   Look at each of the downspout pipes and draw a direct mental line from where it penetrates the ground to the hillside. Chances are you will find a pipe penetration there. This is the downspout. Repeat this for all of the downspouts.

2.   If you find one or two pipes coming off the corners of the house that cannot be accounted for (after eliminating all of the downspout pipes), you have found the drain discharge or drain discharges.

At this stage, note the number of drain discharges that you think you have. This will be confirmed either by the next step or when you actually install the system. Measure the diameter of the drain discharge ends to determine the pipe size of the drain pipe. It will be either 3 or 4 inches in diameter.

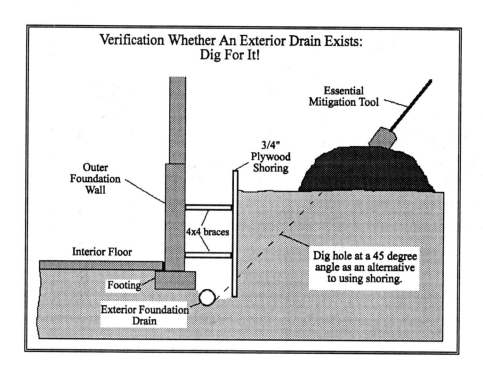

**Verification Whether An Exterior Drain Exists:
Dig For It!**

Essential
Mitigation Tool

3/4"
Plywood
Shoring

Outer
Foundation
Wall

4x4 braces

Interior Floor

Dig hole at a 45 degree
angle as an alternative
to using shoring.

Footing

Exterior Foundation
Drain

Planning Step 4.   Confirming that you have an exterior foundation drain.

The sure fire method to confirm the existence of the exterior drain and the location of at least one drain discharge is to dig down and find it. This might seem like a lot of work in the planning stage but if you dig it correctly, and have allotted sufficient time to do so, you can make the radon system connection and fill the hole back in at the same time.

Before you dig the hole plan exactly how you intend to run the depressurization piping system. Typically, depressurization systems attached to exterior foundation drains are run totally outside the house. Pick a location on a side of the house that would be an appropriate spot for the depressurization fan and piping to be located (see Chapter 7). Do not pick a location on the downhill side of the house since the drain may be in a horseshoe shape rather than a loop. Don't pick a spot outside a garage wall either, since drains are generally not routed around garage foundations. *Before digging, read Installation Step 2 on page 5-28 of this chapter.*

Once the foundation drain is exposed you can get its exact size. You can also cut a small hole into it and insert a garden hose. Turn it on and look for water coming out of an open end of a pipe. Let the water run fully open for several minutes. The end of the drain could also be covered over by dirt and rocks. In this case you may see a wet spot. If you do not see any evidence of water, and you have checked with the local building department to make sure that you are not connected to a storm sewer or an interceptor, you can assume that either the drain discharge runs to a dry well in the ground or it is well covered over. In this case, you won't need to seal it. Methods for sealing exposed drain discharges will be discussed later.

<u>*Important:*</u>   *When you dig the hole you must provide shoring to keep the side of the hole from caving in, or dig a much larger hole so the sides are at a 45 degree angle. You must take these precautions to keep the dirt from caving in, especially if the hole is greater than 3 feet deep. Don't ignore this. People have suffocated to death when dirt has caved in on them. Also when you dig the hole it should not be left open for someone to fall into. Cover it with a sheet of plywood and rope it off.*

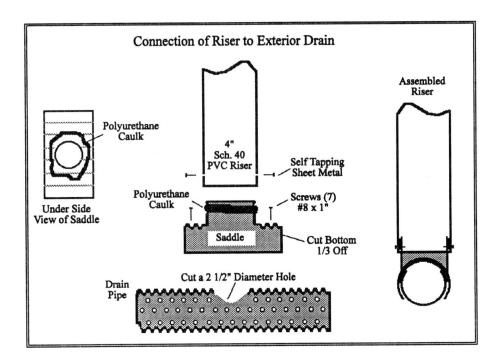

Connection of Riser to Exterior Drain

Planning Step 5.   Planning the riser connection.

One of the critical parts of this system is the connection of the riser to the exterior drain pipe. Basically, you have two options:

Option 1 - Saddle Connection.   The illustration above shows an easy method for attaching the system riser to the drain pipe. You can purchase a "tee" that is made for flexible and corrugated piping systems from your local plumbing supply house. This type of tee is made by ADS or may be referred to as an "irrigation piping fitting". If you cut off the bottom third of the straight section of the tee, you end up with a saddle that will snap over the existing drain pipe. This allows for an easier connection than cutting out a section of the existing pipe and inserting a tee. This riser connection can be made during the planning stage if you dig down to the drain to verify its existence, or later when you plan to install the entire system.

Note: If you plan to make the connection before finishing the system, make sure you read the portion of the installation steps that covers back-filling the hole. Also, if you plan to leave the riser open to the atmosphere for a while, be sure to tape over the discharge to keep out debris. The connection can be carried out in the following two methods:

Step 1.   Cut the appropriate length of riser. This riser should be 4 inch diameter schedule 40 PVC pipe. The length of the riser should be long enough to extend from the exterior foundation drain vertically, to about 2 feet above grade.

Step 2.   Apply a 1/2 inch wide bead of polyurethane caulk around the outside surface of the throat of the saddle. Slide this up into the end of the riser and screw three 1/4 inch by 1 inch long self tapping sheet metal screws to hold the saddle securely in place. A variable speed drill with a nut driver works well for this. If you do not have one, insert the un-caulked saddle into the pipe and pre-drill three pilot holes through both the riser and the top of the saddle. Then caulk it and screw the assembly together.

Step 3.   Cut a 2 1/2 inch diameter hole in the top of the exterior drain pipe with a utility knife. This hole should be at the location where the riser is going to connect to the drain.

Step 4.   Apply a 1/2 inch wide bead of caulk continuously around the underside of the saddle (see figure on previous page).

Step 5.   Carefully set the saddle onto the drain pipe with the riser located directly over the top of the hole that was cut in the previous step.   Push down on the riser and snap it into place. Using 4 self tapping sheet metal screws, 1/4 inch by 1 inch, screw the sides of the saddle into the drain.   Having a person hold this vertical while it is screwed into place is very helpful. Also, if you do not have the variable speed drill and nut driver as described in Step 2, you will need to place the riser on the drain before caulking the under side of the saddle, and pre-drill the holes.   After this is done caulk the underside of the saddle, snap into place and screw the two pieces together.

This method of attachment can be used for flexible and corrugated pipe as well as PVC pipe drain systems.   This method has the advantage of not requiring the drain pipe to be cut entirely into two pieces to allow for the insertion of a tee fitting.

Option 2 - Inserted Tee.   Another method for securing the riser to the drain would be to actually cut a full section out of the drain pipe and insert a tee. Subsequently, the riser can be glued into the top opening of the tee. Methods for gluing pipe are thoroughly described in Chapter 7.   It is difficult to move the drain pipe around enough to insert the tee with this method.   A great deal of difficulty can be encountered in trying to keep loose dirt and rocks out of the drain pipe.   Generally the first method described, with the saddle, results in the cleanest connection.

Important: *Regardless of the method for connecting the riser to the drain pipe, it is important to make sure that no gravel or dirt enters the drain pipe or the riser when it is exposed. If debris enters the pipe it can block the normal flow of drainage water and also cause the radon system not to function.*

After the connection is made, you can immediately refill the hole. You do not need to wait for the caulk to cure on its own. It will cure underground just as easily as above ground. If there was gravel around the drain when you uncovered it replace it before you begin refilling the hole.

As you fill in the hole, hold the pipe vertical, stop every 6 inches and tamp the dirt down by stomping on it. Pack the soil thoroughly as the hole is filled to reduce the amount of vacuum lost due to outside air leaking down to the connection point. This will improve the performance of the radon system.

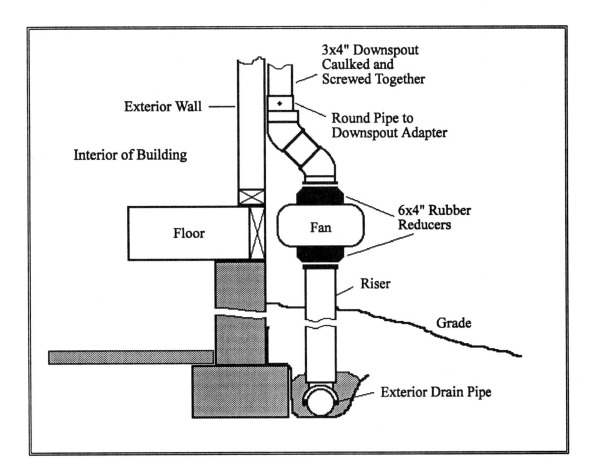

3x4" Downspout Caulked and Screwed Together

Exterior Wall

Round Pipe to Downspout Adapter

Interior of Building

6x4" Rubber Reducers

Floor

Fan

Riser

Grade

Exterior Drain Pipe

Planning Step 5.   Location of the depressurization fan.

As is discussed in more detail in Chapter 7, the location of the fan must be outside the living envelope of the home. Since the riser for this mitigation approach is outside the home, it is logical to choose a totally exterior piping system. The diagram above shows this method. Please refer to the chapter on depressurization piping systems for a more detailed description of piping system components.

If you live in a climate that has freezing temperatures in the winter time you are advised to:

1.   Try to place the fan and discharge piping on the southern exposure of the home to minimize ice build-up in the fan and piping.

2.   Use a water separation device to shunt the collected water away from the fan (see Chapter 7).

These recommendations are valid for all depressurization systems, but are the most critical to observe when depressurizing drainage systems.

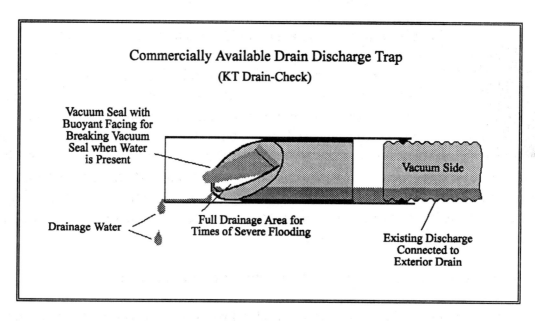

Commercially Available Drain Discharge Trap
(KT Drain-Check)

Vacuum Seal with Buoyant Facing for Breaking Vacuum Seal when Water is Present

Vacuum Side

Drainage Water

Full Drainage Area for Times of Severe Flooding

Existing Discharge Connected to Exterior Drain

Planning Step 6. Sealing major leak points and the drain discharge ends.

When the depressurization system is finally connected to the riser (which is in turn attached to the drain system), a vacuum will be created. The stronger the vacuum is, the better the radon reduction will be. Air leakage into the system will cause the vacuum to be less than desirable. Major air leaks to consider are:

◆ Floor wall joints inside the home (see Chapter 8 and Planning Step 7 on page 5-11 of the sump section of this chapter for proper sealing).

◆ Sump holes where the drain does not go to a daylight end but rather drains to a sump inside the home (see the earlier section of this chapter on installing sump pit lids).

◆ Discharge ends of the drain system.

During the previous steps of this section you should have determined the drain discharges for the drain system. You also should have determined the number and size of these pipes.

Note: It is possible that your drain discharges were buried under landscaping or they alternatively went to a gravel pit under the soil. If your drain discharges are not exposed, you may not need to be concerned with these until after you install the system.

The above illustration shows a commercially available drain discharge end trap that has been designed specifically for radon reduction. These are designed in different sizes for different sized drain discharge pipes. The design of these is such that the daylight end can be glued and screwed into these traps. The large area of the flapper, along with the seal, allows for a tight seal when the depressurization system is operating. The angled design of the flapper allows for the full, unobstructed flow of water out of the end of them during rainy periods. Determine the size and number of these which will be needed and order them from catalog supply houses listed in the appendix.

Important: *Do not seal off these daylight ends or put traps on them that can fill with dirt or rodent nests. These drain discharges must be allowed to drain freely.*

Installing the Exterior Drain Depressurization System

This section is devoted to the installation of a depressurization system that will be attached to an existing exterior foundation drain. You should read the previous section on planning the exterior drain system along with the first section of this chapter on sump systems. If your drain is connected to an interior sump the details for sealing these sumps are contained in the sump section of this chapter. Read this section along with the Chapters 7,8, & 10 on Depressurization Systems, Sealing and General Safety Precautions before proceeding with this work. You should also read the "Finishing Touches" section at the end of this chapter.

Sump Installation Step 1.   Assemble equipment and materials.

The following is a checklist of equipment and material that you will need to gather before starting:

Area	Item	√
Safety	Goggles/safety glasses	
	Dust mask	
	Leather gloves	
	First aid kit	
	Ventilation fan	
	Flashlight	
	Coveralls or old clothing	
	Helper or observer	
Material	Materials for sealing interior sump - if needed.	
	Shoring materials for stabilizing excavation (see Planning Step 4)	
	Piece of plywood, wood stakes, rope, cloth strips for covering hole and warning kids away from hole if it is to be left open for a period of time	
	1 tube of polyurethane caulking	
	1 ADS saddle tee	
	10 foot length of 4 inch, sch. 40 PVC pipe (riser)	
	1 inch #8 self-tapping sheet-metal screws (7)	
	Drain - check for drain discharge ends (see Planning Step 6)	
	Duct tape or cap for temporarily sealing off riser	
	Material needed for depressurization system (see Chapter 7)	
	10x 10 sheet of plastic or drop cloth	
Tools	Electric drill - cordless or powered	
	Screw driver or 1/4 inch nut driver	
	Caulking gun	
	Rags	
	Sharp utility knife	
	Extension cords	
	Shovel and other digging tools	
	Wire brush	
	PVC saw	
	Smoke stick (see Chapter 8)	

Installation Step 2.   Dig down to the drain.

At the location where you plan to install the riser, lay out a sheet of plastic or a drop cloth on the ground where you can put the excavated dirt. This will make it easier to clean up the loose dirt when you refill the hole. Begin digging the hole out with shovel, pick, etc. *If the hole is going to be deeper than 3 feet, you must make provisions to insure that the hole does not cave in.* You have two options for preventing the hole from caving in: (see Planning Step 4.)

1.   Dig the hole as wide as deep. This makes the sides of the hole at a 45 degree angle to prevent caving in. You get a bigger hole but it is certainly a smaller hole than the one that they will bury you in if the hole caves in on you.

2.   You can dig a smaller hole than described above, if you use 3/4 inch plywood on the sides of the hole and brace them against the side of the house with 4 by 4 pieces of wood toe nailed to the plywood. As you dig deeper a brace should be located every 2 foot below the grade (see figure on page 5-22).

The authors will agree that digging large holes is a lot of work and the use of shoring may save some excavation but working in a hole with wood bracing in the way is not easy either. We recommend following the first method - dig a large hole!

Important: As you dig be careful of breaking gas lines, sprinkler lines, and exterior buried conduit that may be located around your home. The existence of these interferences should not prevent you from digging at these locations as long as caution is exercised so they are not damaged. This is why we do not recommend the use of power digging equipment like back-hoes, jack hammers and powered augers. Another reason for not using this equipment, is the potential for damage to the side of the house. Use a shovel and other hand tools.

The drains are generally just below the foundation footing. They will be laid right next to the footing. You may have to dig a little deeper than the top of the footing to find it. You will recognize that you are getting close when you encounter gravel or a fibrous cloth. If you run into this cloth uncover the cloth with your hands. *Do not rip the cloth out.* Carefully cut the cloth with a knife and fold the cloth back out of the way.

Once the cloth has been moved out of the way, scoop out the gravel that is between the cloth and the drain pipe. Place this gravel in a separate pile or a bucket for later use. As the gravel is removed the drain should be exposed. Remove a sufficient amount of gravel to allow you to make the riser connection. If you have already assembled the necessary materials for connecting the riser move onto the next step.

If you have dug down to the drain to confirm its existence and to make the necessary measurements for drain size and discharge location, perform that work now (see Planning Step 4). If you are planning to leave the hole open long enough to obtain the necessary riser connection materials, you should replace the gravel around the exposed pipe, lay the fiber cloth back over and close it with duct tape (this keeps dirt from getting into the drain). Place a large sheet of 3/4 inch plywood over the hole. Place stakes around the opening and run a rope along the stakes and attach the ends to the house. Tie some white strips of cloth to the rope. The plywood sheet and warning rope is to warn burglars not to step into the hole at night and sue you.

Installation Step 3.   Make the riser connection.

After you have exposed the drain and assembled the necessary parts for the riser connection refer back to the step by step instructions detailed in Planning Step 5. This would be a good time to have a helper with you to hand things to you and to hold the pipe as you backfill the hole. Make the connection. *Be sure to follow the safety instructions on the side of the tube of caulk.*

After making the connection, place the gravel back around the pipe that you removed in the previous step. Lay the fiber cloth back over the gravel. Seal the two edges of the cloth with some of the polyurethane caulk that you used to make the drain connection. Tape the edges together with duct tape so they will stay in place as you fill the hole.

Backfill the hole with the dirt. Be careful not to disturb the riser connection or the fiber cloth that you repaired. Also have your assistant hold the pipe vertically as the hole is filled. As the hole fills up, stop every six inches and stomp on the dirt to compact it. Repeat this filling and compaction process until the hole is filled.

Installation Step 4a.   Install the drain discharge checks.

Install the drain checks described in Planning Step 6. Be sure to follow the manufacturers' instructions. Since polyurethane caulks or PVC glues will be used to make this connection, follow safety procedures provided with the material and the general safety procedures described in the safety section of this manual (see Chapter 10).

When installing these devices be sure to locate them at the end of the drain discharges. Make sure that they are oriented in a manner so when the flapper opens it will hinge up vertically. If needed, put some dirt beneath them for support.

If desired, dig back along the drain discharge pipe into the hillside and cut off a portion of the pipe. Then attach the drain check so the end of it will stick out of the hillside when the dirt is replaced.

It is important to install these so water can continue to flow out of them unobstructed and in a location where they will be protected from lawn mowers and where gradual hillside erosion will not cover them over.

Installation Step 4b.   Cover sump if needed.

If your drainage system did not have drain discharge but rather was attached to an internal sump, install the sump lid (see the first section of this chapter).

Installation Step 5.   Install the depressurization system.

Install the depressurization piping system as planned earlier in this section and in Chapter 7.

Installation Step 6.   Check for air leaks.

After installing the system turn it on and check for air leaks. This is done with a smoke stick as is described in Planning Step 3 in Chapter 8 on sealing. Some key areas to check are:

- ◆ The drain discharges to see if the flappers are seating well (note some leakage may occur at this point; it is one of the major leaks you will be concerned with). If found, make sure that no dirt is lodged between the flapper and the inside of the trap.

- ◆ Check other pipes that come out of the hillside to see if smoke is drawn into them. If so, then there is an additional discharge that needs a drain check - install it.

- ◆ If you have an interior sump and you attached a lid to it, check for leaks around the lid as is described in Installation Step 15 in the sump section in this chapter.

- ◆ Check the floor to wall joints and cracks in the slab of the home. Check around plumbing and electrical penetrations through the interior floor and walls. If smoke is drawn through these openings, seal them per the techniques shown in Chapter 8.

Installation Step 7.   Check flues for backdrafting.

Contact a competent inspector to test these devices. Do not run system until this test has been completed (see Chapter 10).

Finishing Touches

After the sump suction or the exterior foundation system has been installed, run through the following check list to make sure you have done everything:

Item		√
Checked for air leaks at:		
	Sump lid	
	Sump lid penetrations	
	Floor to wall joints	
	Floor cracks	
	Drain discharge	
Checked the drafting of your combustion appliances See Safety Chapter 10		
Installed a system performance indicator		
Labeled the piping system at all visible locations		
Installed a system label (see next section)		
Painted exterior metal parts		
Re-tested the home for radon		

Finishing Touches (cont.)

Install at least one system label describing the system.

In at least one location a label should be placed to tell workman and future homeowners about the system you have installed. This is to insure that radon reductions are maintained and that serious health concerns are not encountered if the systems are improperly disconnected for maintenance work. The key concern is if the system is opened up and the depressurization fan is left on. This could cause large amounts of air to be drawn from the house and could cause combustion appliances to backdraft. These labels can be made on paper and glued to an appropriate location or better yet typed on an adhesive backed label.

Here is a sample label for a depressurization system on sumps. This can be used for a strict sump system as well as an exterior foundation drain system that goes to an interior sump.

Radon Mitigation System

Do not remove sump lid without shutting off system

If lid is to be removed for maintenance purposes, turn off fan located at____. Switch for fan is located in_____. Fan powered from breaker # ___ in fuse panel. After maintenance has been performed, all pipe connections should be remade, sump cover resealed with silicone caulking, and fan turned back on.

Below is a sample label for exterior foundation drain depressurization system with drain discharge. Note that since this label is outside, you should write it on a plastic label with an indelible marker, or glue it inside a sealable plastic envelope and attach it to the fan.

Radon Mitigation System Fan

This fan is connected to the exterior foundation drain.

If work is to be done on the foundation drain, this fan can be shut off by disconnect located _____. The fan is powered from breaker # ___ in the electrical breaker panel.
There are also ____ # of drain check assemblies located on the hillside on the ___ side of the home. If these are to be temporarily removed for service work, they should be reinstalled after the work has been completed.

Chapter 6

Sub-Slab Depressurization Systems

How to reduce radon in slab-on-grade or basement homes that do not have crawl spaces or existing drainage systems.

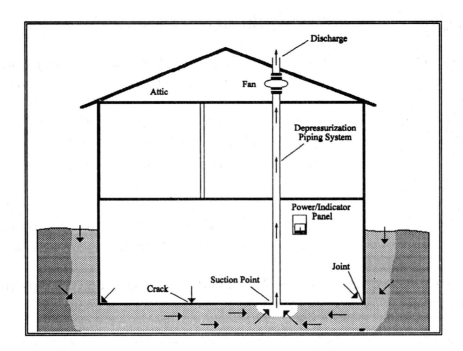

Sub-Slab Depressurization (SSD)

The illustration above shows a sub-slab suction system. A hole is cut through the concrete slab. A cavity is formed in the soil beneath the hole. A PVC pipe fitting is set into the hole and attached to the depressurization system. The depressurization system creates a vacuum near the hole, if not entirely under the slab. The vacuum created at the hole under the slab causes the radon, as well as other soil gases, to move toward the suction point where it is collected and exhausted safely above the home.

The success of the SSD system depends on how porous the soil is beneath the slab. If the slab was poured on top of gravel or washed rock, the potential for collecting radon from beneath the entire slab is very good. However, in cases where the soil is tightly compacted only a small area of the slab will be under vacuum. In these "tight soil" cases, additional suction points will be needed to adequately reduce the radon. Professional mitigators have methods for estimating the number of suction points before an installation. However, a suitable compromise for the homeowner is to install a system with one suction point. Then perform some tests to see if the system needs to be expanded. It is actually rare to need more than two suction points in a home.

When do I need to use sub-slab suction?

Use sub-slab suction on homes that have concrete slab floors resting directly on the soil and if they do not have water drainage systems associated with the house. Drainage systems often work better than a single sub-slab suction point system. This is because the vacuum created by the drainage system approach extends around several sides of the house or beneath the entire slab itself.

If your house is built over a crawl space this technique will **not** apply. Your home could also have a crawl space and a basement foundation type in which you may need to apply both sub-slab and sub-membrane depressurization systems and connect them to a common depressurization piping system (see Chapter 9). Sub-slab suction is a frequently used technique and, in many areas of the country, is the only radon reduction method used.

Planning the Sub-Slab Suction System

Before beginning the installation, the safety information in Chapter 8 should be thoroughly reviewed. This chapter will provide information on the location and installation of the actual suction point. The result of the work in this chapter will be a 4 inch PVC riser from the concrete floor. To complete the system, you will have to install the depressurization piping system described in Chapter 7.

Consult the flow chart preceding Chapter 1 to determine if additional approaches also need to be considered.

Planning Step 1. Confirming that sub-slab suction is appropriate or if you need assistance from a professional mitigator.

Sub-slab suction systems are used as a first option under the various conditions shown below:

	Question	NO	If YES, then:
1	Is the house built totally over a crawl space?	Proceed with this chapter	Consult Chapter 4 instead.
2	Does the house have both crawl space and concrete slab?	Proceed with this chapter	Consult the details in Chapter 4 and 9 as well as this chapter.
3	Is there a sump or an exterior drain system on the home?	Proceed with this chapter	Consult Chapter 5.
4	Is the native soil permeable? An example would be decomposed granite/gravel.	Go to next question	Proceed with this chapter.
5	Is the native soil impermeable but had gravel placed beneath the slab during construction?	Go to next question	Proceed with this chapter.
6	Is slab setting on clays with no gravel beneath it?	Go to next question	Call a professional radon mitigator.
7	Are you unsure of soil permeability beneath slab?	Proceed with this chapter	Read through the planning steps in this chapter to help with this question.
8	Do you have ductwork for your forced air furnace or air conditioner beneath the slab?	Proceed with this chapter	Call a professional radon mitigator.
9	Do you have a hydronic heating system (a grid of hot water pipes beneath the slab)?	Proceed with this chapter	Call a professional radon mitigator.
10	Do you have a thermal or solar heating system with ductwork, piping or open spaces that distribute soil air into the home?	Proceed with this chapter	Call a professional radon mitigator.

Note: Before giving up read the following planning steps.

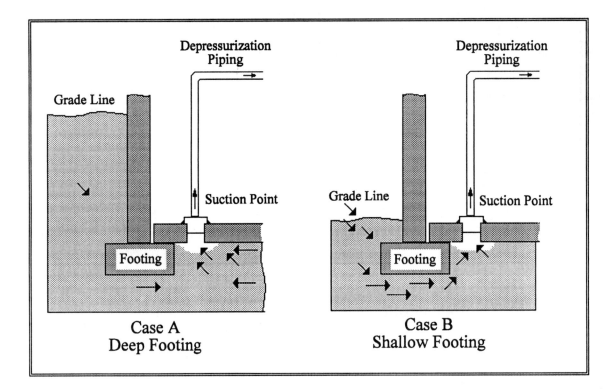

Case A
Deep Footing

Case B
Shallow Footing

Planning Step 2. Determining relative location of a suction point.

The first step is to determine whether you can place the suction points near an outside wall.

Typically it is best to locate the suction point next to an outside foundation wall. We know this is contrary to common sense that would put it in the middle of the floor. Better vacuum is typically achieved with a sidewall location because:

1. The soil is generally looser under this portion of the slab.

2. The vacuum is applied to the floor wall joint which is a large radon entry point.

3. The adjacent wall provides a convenient support surface for piping attachment.

A concern with an outside foundation wall suction point location is if the vacuum will be defeated by outside air being drawn in rather than air from beneath the slab. Refer to the figure above. In Case A a suction point has been installed in a slab of the basement (or a slab on grade home) where the footing is well below grade due to frost codes (2 1/2 to 3 feet or more). Most of the air in Case A is being drawn to the suction point through the soil beneath the slab -- this is good. In Case B the footing is close to the surface of the soil. When the footing is close to the surface of the outside grade, a lot of outside air can be drawn in, thereby reducing the sub-slab vacuum and the system's efficiency.

Shallow footings are generally found in parts of the world where frost does not form in the ground. An example would be southern Arizona. If you have shallow footings, you will have to choose a more centrally located suction point location for the most optimal radon reduction. However, for the most part deep footings are found. This is why the suction point is commonly located next to an exterior foundation wall.

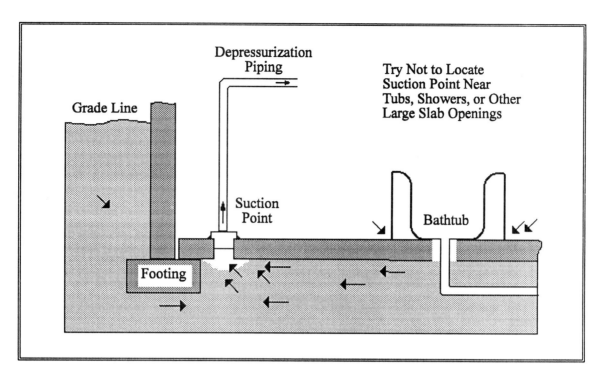

Planning Step 3.   Avoiding potential problems by eliminating certain suction point locations.

When selecting a suction point pick a location that is convenient and where the "suction field" or "radon capture zone" will extend as far as possible beneath the slab. A large opening in a slab can prevent a vacuum from being extended beyond the opening. An example of this is shown above where a suction point was located near a bath tub. There is generally a 12 inch by 12 inch opening in the slab beneath the tub for plumbing. A similar opening in the concrete can be found beneath showers, and toilets. When a suction point is very close to these openings, air from inside the room is drawn down through the opening location rather than from beneath the slab. This presents two problems:

1. The suction field can be stopped at these locations, thus requiring the addition of more suction points to obtain full coverage of the area under the slab.

2. Excess air is drawn from inside the house. This will increase the potential for backdrafting combustion appliances and increase the heating cost of the home.

Try to select locations for the suction points as far away from these locations as possible. If you must locate a suction point near these large openings, be prepared to get involved with significant sealing efforts.

Also, in selecting a location near an outside wall, the suction point should be next to a floor wall joint. These are significant leak points also. However, these can be easily sealed if they are accessible. Therefore, try to select an area of the floor where the walls are not furred out and finished. This will allow you to access those critical joints which are closest to the suction point. Pick an unfinished utility room or laundry room for this reason.

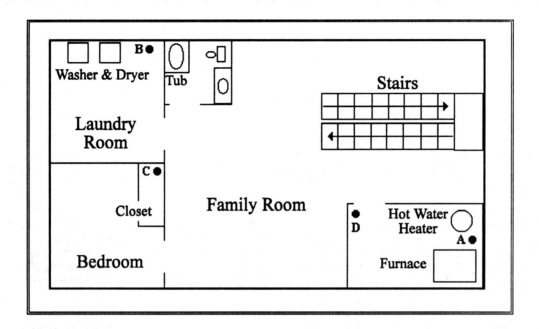

Planning Step 4.   Choosing potential suction points.

Running your depressurization system piping through a home, although a great conversation piece, is not very attractive. A suction point is generally most effective when placed next to an outside wall. This also allows the piping to be concealed.

First, walk through the basement and look for unfinished areas that you do not plan to remodel. At the same time, think of how you might route the depressurization piping either through the house or to the outside and up along the side of the house to the roof. See Chapter 7 on piping systems to help with the planning process.

Pick a suction point using the criteria described in the previous steps. Balance that with the easiest and most direct route for running your depressurization system piping. Once you have selected a suction point where it would be the most convenient to install, move on to the next planning step.

The illustration above provides an example of a basement floor plan. If the footings are deep (over 2 1/2 feet below grade), point B in the laundry room or point A in the furnace room would be convenient choices for suction points. However, point A will probably work better than point B because it is further from the bathroom / tub area (see previous Step 3 for discussion). Select point A, in this case as your prime location, and point B as your backup location.

On the other hand, if the footings are very shallow, one might select point C or D since they are more centrally located. Select closets or inside corners of unfinished areas, if possible, to conceal the piping. Because some air noise can be heard through these pipes, try to keep them out of frequently used rooms. If you have shallow footings, select point D as your first suction point location and point C as your back-up choice.

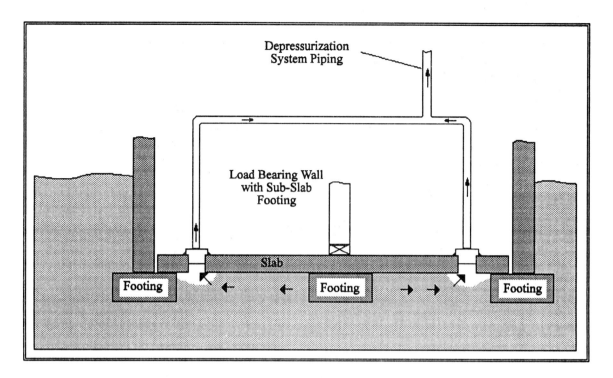

Planning Step 5.   Obstacles that may interrupt suction field extension.

One suction point may be able to impact the entire area under the slab if the underlying soil is uniformly permeable. An example of this would be where gravel had been laid completely under the slab when the house was built. Sometimes there can be obstacles to the movement of soil gas beneath the slab even when the soil is permeable. One common example of an obstacle is when a footing runs under the middle of the slab.

An intermediate foundation footing or grade beam is often run under a slab to support a load bearing wall (generally running through the center of the room). One way to tell if you have a load bearing wall is to look at a wall in the center of a room. If the ends of the upper floor joists set on top of this wall, it could be a load bearing wall with a footing beneath the slab. Sometimes the floor joists are set on a beam held up by support posts that are on small pads beneath the concrete. The small pads will not disrupt the suction field as would a continuous concrete footing running the length of the basement. One method for overcoming an obstacle (like a continuous intermediate footing) is to place a suction point on both sides of the intermediate footing as shown above.

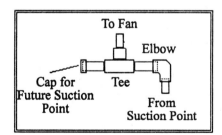

It is always a good idea when locating your primary suction point that a second suction point could be attached to it as conveniently as possible. Generally a tee is installed in the piping system at the point where a second suction point could be connected. This tee would be installed with a short length of capped PVC pipe. The pipe could be cut at a later time for connection to a second suction point, if needed.

As discussed in the following step, a second suction point is not always necessary.

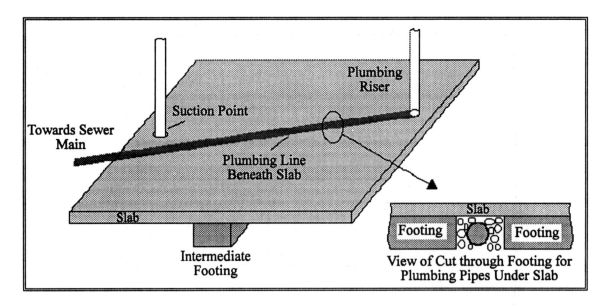

Towards Sewer Main

Suction Point

Plumbing Riser

Plumbing Line Beneath Slab

Slab

Intermediate Footing

Slab

Footing | Footing

View of Cut through Footing for Plumbing Pipes Under Slab

Planning Step 6.   Suction point location -- using plumbing trenches.

To overcome obstacles to the vacuum field, a trick that many professionals use is to locate a suction point near an existing underground plumbing line. This could be a water pipe or, more commonly, a sewer line. The above figure illustrates this.

When plumbing is installed before the slab is poured, it is laid in trenches. These trenches are loosely backfilled before the concrete is poured. Also, if there are intermediate foundations for bearing walls, as was described in the previous planning step, these plumbing lines and trenches pass underneath or through a notch in the foundation footing. If you create a vacuum along the side of one of these trenches it is possible to extend the suction field along it. This is especially helpful where an intermediate footing would otherwise be an obstacle to the suction field. When this technique is used the vacuum can often be extended beyond the footing and to the opposite end of the slab.

The best way to decide if plumbing trenches will help is to locate the riser on your sewer piping. These risers are generally found in your utility room or furnace room. Note the riser's location. Next, locate where the sewer main is by finding the manholes. Manholes are typically in the street in front of your house but in some instances could be in an alley. Draw a mental line from the point the sewer riser comes through the slab in the basement to where the manhole is. If this cuts across a large portion of the basement slab or if it crosses where you think an intermediate footing for a bearing wall is, this location could be a good primary suction point.

Important: When you cut through the concrete for the installation of the suction point do not cut through the concrete directly above the plumbing trench. Rather than drilling directly above the trench, drill down along the side and dig sideways under the slab (by hand) until you reach the pipe. Take your time here because if you break a pipe under the slab it could be very costly to repair. This will require caution in drilling the concrete but could save you the trouble of making more than one suction point.

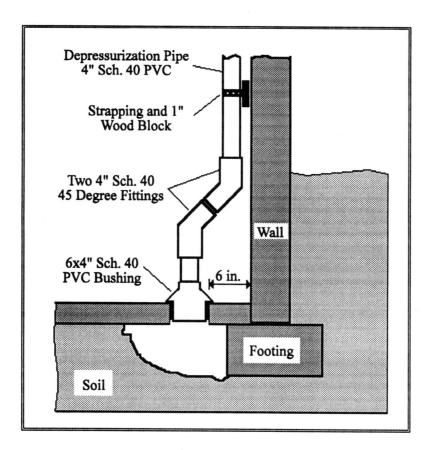

Depressurization Pipe
4" Sch. 40 PVC

Strapping and 1"
Wood Block

Two 4" Sch. 40
45 Degree Fittings

6x4" Sch. 40
PVC Bushing

6 in.

Wall

Footing

Soil

Planning Step 7.   Planning the suction point location.

The above figure illustrates how the actual suction point core and pit will look like if it is installed next to an exterior wall. A suction point located near an interior wall will look the same. One of the criteria in choosing a suction point is the limitations that the piping system will place on its location. The following discussion provides some details that will help you locate the hole. How to cut the actual hole and install the fitting through the floor will be discussed later in this chapter.

Note that a 1 inch thick block of wood has been shown between the vertical portion of the depressurization piping and the wall. This will be used to support the piping. See Chapter 7 for more details. The installation detail above shows two 45 degree fittings glued together with a short section of pipe in between them. In this example the pipe stub between the two 45's is no longer than 3 1/2 inches so the two 45's butt up against each other. With these conditions the closest edge will be 6 inches away from the wall. Of course it can be farther away from the wall if the section of pipe between the elbows is made longer. You may have to extend the distance away from the wall if you have wider than normal footings.

The technique of putting two 45 degree fittings together allows for the pipe to be firmly attached to the wall near the suction point. It also minimizes the amount of lost living space that you will experience.

Note: This same minimum distance also applies if you are locating a suction point near an interior wall.

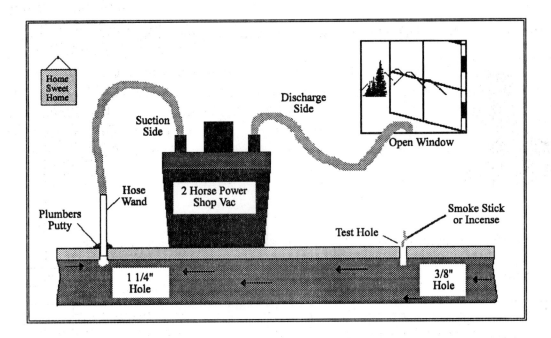

Planning Step 8.   Confirming that you have selected a good suction point.

Let's assume that you have picked a convenient and appropriate suction point location. By using the previously listed criteria you have chosen a primary suction point location. Now let's see if you chose wisely. What you are about to do is to simulate a sub-slab system. You will be using a highly technical piece of equipment you may already own, called a sub-slab suction simulator, otherwise known as a big vacuum cleaner.

You should perform this step. Although you could go ahead and install the system and hope for the best. Actually, all of the tools needed for this suction test will be needed for the installation of the actual system anyway. Besides, you have been looking for a reason to buy a big shop vacuum anyway.

Concept of the suction test:

Drill a 1 1/4 inch hole through the concrete and about 8 inches into the soil at the location of the primary suction hole (see previous planning step). *Watch out for sub-slab pipes.* Drill a few 3/8 inch diameter holes, called test holes, through remote parts of the slab. After inserting the wand of the vacuum cleaner suction hose down into the hole and sealing with plumbers putty, *run a length of vacuum hose attached to the discharge out a window.* Next, you will turn on the vacuum. With a smoke or incense stick you will observe if smoke is drawn down the smaller test holes when the vacuum is turned on and off. If the smoke is pulled down a test hole **only** when the vacuum cleaner is on, you know that the sub-slab suction system is impacting that portion of the slab between the vacuum hole and the 3/8 inch test hole. Repeat this for other test holes at various locations around the slab to convince yourself that the vacuum can impact the entire slab area.

If there are parts of the slab that you cannot impact, pick a secondary sub-slab hole using all of the criteria listed before. Repeat the process with the vacuum cleaner suction attached to this secondary hole. Perform this process until you have identified the number and location of suction points that will be needed to create a vacuum under the entire slab. A more detailed description is given on the following pages.

Planning Step 9.   Sub-slab suction simulation diagnostics.

This step is to determine the number and location of the suction points that will be necessary to create a suction field beneath the concrete slab area. Before beginning this work assemble the following tools and safety equipment. You should also read the general safety practices described in Chapter 10 of this manual before commencing the work.

The following is a checklist of equipment and materials you will need before starting.

Area	Item	✓
Safety		
	Safety eye goggles	
	Dust mask	
	Leather gloves	
	First aid kit	
	Assistant	
	Ear protection for you and your assistant	
Material		
	Jar of plumbers putty	
	Duct tape	
	6 in. by 4 in. PVC schedule 40 reducing bushing	
Tools		
	Shop vacuum (2 horsepower or greater)	
	2 inch vacuum cleaner suction hose Two lengths of hose at least 6 foot long each	
	Length of flexible dryer vent - long enough to attach from vacuum cleaner discharge hose to the nearest operable window and out of the window at least two feet.	
	Vacuum wand -- 1 1/2 in. on one end and 2 inch on other end. This is a normal accessory when you buy shop vac hose.	
	Electric hammer drill (1 1/2 inch -- not your typical hand drill; these can usually be rented along with bits from most tool rental houses)	
	1 1/4 inch by 12 inch bit for hammer drill	
	3/8 inch by 12 inch bit for hammer drill	
	Heavy duty extension cord (three prong)	
	Flashlight	
	Smoke stick (see Chapter 8)	

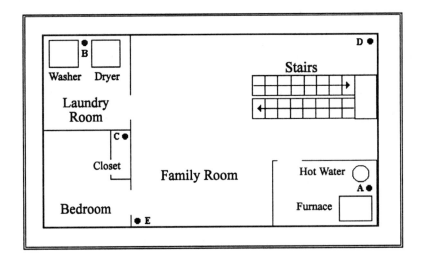

Planning Step 10.   Performing the sub-slab simulation.

The following is a step-by-step procedure for performing the sub-slab simulation as was briefly described in the previous planning step.

Step 1. Make a sketch of the concrete floor area. Mark your preferred suction point location. In this example, we will choose point A in the furnace room. We did this because it is near an outside wall and would be in an area that would be the least obtrusive. We are hoping that this one suction point will be sufficient to impact the soil under the entire slab. This process will prove or disprove this assumption.

Step 2. Using the dimension provided in Planning Step 7, or according to your own piping installation design (see Chapter 7), set the 6 inch by 4 inch reducer on the concrete floor in the exact location that you plan to install it. Mark a circle on the concrete floor with a marking pen or grease pencil, using the outside circular edge of the 6 by 4 reducer as a guide. Make an "x" mark in the approximate center of the circle.

Step 3. Put the suction hose on your shop vac and plug it in. Tape the suction hose to the floor so it is within a couple of inches of your "x" mark. This is to catch the dust you will be making when you drill through the concrete at the "x" mark. Run the discharge hose out of the window because some fine concrete will get through the filter of the vacuum and make a mess if you don't run it outside.

Step 4. Attach the 1 1/4 inch bit to the hammer drill and set the drill to the rotary hammer setting.

Step 5. Put on your eye, ear and respiratory protection and turn on the vacuum cleaner.

Step 6. Drill a 1 1/4 inch hole <u>straight</u> down through the concrete at the location in the center of the circle that you had marked with an "x." Be careful! These hammer drills can bind up on a piece of reinforcing wire in the concrete. When the drill binds up it can deliver quite a twist. Make sure you are standing in a position so when this happens you will not be caught between the drill and the wall or have the handle whack you in the knee cap. Stand out from the drill with the drill between you and the wall. To reduce the chance of binding up the drill, hold the drill as vertically as you can. Pull the bit out frequently as it is turning in order to clear the hole of concrete dust. *Note:* **Do not push down on the drill**. The weight of the drill alone is enough to drive the bit through the concrete. If you get anxious and try to make things happen faster by pushing it, you will only cause undue stress on your wrists and elbows and increase the chance of the bit binding up.

Drilling through the concrete should only take 3 to 4 minutes unless you hit something. Generally the drill bit will cut through reinforcing wire in the concrete. Sometimes it won't. If you have drilled at a location where you cannot get through the concrete, move a couple inches away from your "x" mark and try again.

If you bind the drill up in the hole and cannot pull it back out with the drill then remove the bit from the drill. Extract the bit from the floor by taking a pipe wrench and secure it to the bit near the floor. Put a block of wood between the wrench and the floor. By twisting the drill bit and using the leverage provided by the wood block you should be able to free it up. **Don't put your wrench on the splined portion of the bit!**

Take your time. As you get close to the bottom of the slab take it easy. *Caution:* Once the drill goes through the bottom of the slab, it could drop very quickly and hit a plumbing line that you didn't know was there. Once you get through the slab, look down into the hole with a flashlight to make sure nothing is in the way. Drill further down, look frequently to make sure you don't hit a pipe. Keep drilling until you have drilled as deeply as you can, at least 6 inches below the slab.

Note what happens as the bit goes through the concrete.

- ♦ Does it drop sharply? This could mean there is a cavity under the slab. This is good.

- ♦ Are rocks or pea gravel visible at the bottom of the hole or are drawn up along side of the bit? This indicates loose permeable fill beneath the slab. This is excellent!

- ♦ Is the dirt at the bottom of the hole or on the bit a damp plastic like clay material? This means that the soil may be impermeable and difficult for air to flow through it. Don't stop though; go on to the next step because you make get lucky and still be able to create a decent vacuum field beneath the slab.

Step 7. After the hole has been drilled, vacuum up the dust around the hole. *Don't put the hose down into the hole yet.*

Step 8. Change the bit in the hammer drill from the 1 1/4 to the 3/8 inch bit. Go to opposite corners and ends of the slab. Look for inconspicuous places to drill these test holes through the concrete. Corners of closets are good. Corners of rooms are good even if they are carpeted. You can always pull up a corner of the carpet with a pair of square nose pliers, and pound it back into place with a block of wood and a hammer -- *don't drill through carpet.*

Step 9. Drill the pilot holes with the same technique described above for the big hole. Locate them approximately 6 inches out from the walls to avoid spread footings. If the drill does not drop through the bottom of the concrete, drill at an alternate location. Mark the location of the test holes on your drawing. In our example we have drilled pilot holes at points B, C, D and E on the preceding sketch.

Step 10. After cleaning the dust around the small holes, take the shop vacuum back to the location of the big hole. Attach the second length of vacuum hose to the discharge port of the vacuum cleaner and run it out an open window.

Warning: **If you do not exhaust the vacuum out the window you could be exposed to high levels of radon gas.** If the length of hose is insufficient to reach the window, stick it in one side of a cheap flexible dryer vent hose. Tape this connection together with duct tape so it is tight. Then run the dryer vent hose to and out the window.

Step 11. Attach the 1 1/4 inch wand to the end of the vacuum cleaner suction hose and stick it down into the large hole (hole A). Seal the wand to the hole by pressing plumber's putty all around the side of the wand where it meets the top of the concrete.

Step 12. Get your incense stick (or smoke device) and flashlight (see Chapter 8 on sealing) and go to one of the test holes. With the vacuum cleaner "off" observe which way the smoke moves when held right next to the hole. It should rise into the room. Now have your assistant turn the vacuum cleaner "on." Is the smoke now being pulled down through the hole? Use your flashlight to be able to see this subtle change in direction. Turn the vacuum cleaner "on" and "off" several times to confirm that you are seeing the effect of the vacuum cleaner rather than the kids opening and closing doors upstairs.

If the smoke is drawn down a hole when the vacuum cleaner is turned on, you can conclude that a suction point installed at the location of the vacuum cleaner hole (point A) would positively impact the area beneath the slab between the vacuum hole and the particular small test hole.

Step 13. Repeat this testing procedure at each of the small holes that you drilled. Note the results either on your sketch or on a table such as the one below:

Vacuum Cleaner on Hole ID:____	Test Hole:__ Smoke ↑ or ↓ Vac **Off**	Test Hole:__ Smoke ↑ or ↓ Vac **On**	Test Hole:__ Smoke ↑ or ↓ Vac **Off**	Test Hole:__ Smoke ↑ or ↓ Vac **On**	Test Hole:__ Smoke ↑ or ↓ Vac **Off**	Test Hole:__ Smoke ↑ or ↓ Vac **On**	Test Hole:__ Smoke ↑ or ↓ Vac **Off**	Test Hole:__ Smoke ↑ or ↓ Vac **On**

For example, assume the following data was obtained for the house plan illustrated on page 6-12:

Vacuum Cleaner on Hole ID:____	Test Hole:__ Smoke ↑ or ↓ Vac **Off**	Test Hole:__ Smoke ↑ or ↓ Vac **On**	Test Hole:__ Smoke ↑ or ↓ Vac **Off**	Test Hole:__ Smoke ↑ or ↓ Vac **On**	Test Hole:__ Smoke ↑ or ↓ Vac **Off**	Test Hole:__ Smoke ↑ or ↓ Vac **On**	Test Hole:__ Smoke ↑ or ↓ Vac **Off**	Test Hole:__ Smoke ↑ or ↓ Vac **On**
	B	B	C	C	D	D	E	E
A	↑	↓	↑	↓	↑	↓	↑	↓

This data would indicate that the vacuum cleaner hooked to suction point A was able to cause the direction of smoke to be reversed at all test hole locations (shown by the arrows pointing down at test holes B, C, D and E). This means that a single suction point located at point A would work well, and that we can assume one suction point is all that is needed.

On the other hand, what if the data had turned out as follows:

Vacuum Cleaner on Hole:__	Test Hole:__ Smoke ↑ or ↓ Vac Off	Test Hole:__ Smoke ↑ or ↓ Vac On	Test Hole:__ Smoke ↑ or ↓ Vac Off	Test Hole:__ Smoke ↑ or ↓ Vac On	Test Hole:__ Smoke ↑ or ↓ Vac Off	Test Hole:__ Smoke ↑ or ↓ Vac On	Test Hole:__ Smoke ↑ or ↓ Vac Off	Test Hole:__ Smoke ↑ or ↓ Vac On
	B	B	C	C	D	D	E	E
A	↑	↑	↑	↓	↑	↑	↑	↓

You can see that the vacuum cleaner was able to reverse the direction of the smoke at points C and E, but **not** at B and D. This means that a suction point located at A will only affect the soil under half of the slab. What do we do now?

If the primary suction point does not impact the entire slab, you may have to install more than one suction point. To confirm the location of a second suction point move the vacuum cleaner to that location. Drill an 1 1/4 inch hole, and stick the suction hose and wand into this hole and repeat your test. *Be sure to follow all of the steps describing drilling these holes, especially exhausting the shop-vac outside.* One of the test holes that was drilled previously is re-drilled with the larger bit to become the second vacuum test point. Lets assume in our example that point B was chosen as the secondary suction hole and the preceding table now looks like this:

Vacuum Cleaner on Hole:__	Test Hole:__ Smoke ↑ or ↓ Vac Off	Test Hole:__ Smoke ↑ or ↓ Vac On	Test Hole:__ Smoke ↑ or ↓ Vac Off	Test Hole:__ Smoke ↑ or ↓ Vac On	Test Hole:__ Smoke ↑ or ↓ Vac Off	Test Hole:__ Smoke ↑ or ↓ Vac On	Test Hole:__ Smoke ↑ or ↓ Vac Off	Test Hole:__ Smoke ↑ or ↓ Vac On
	B	B	C	C	D	D	E	E
A	↑	↑	↑	↓	↑	↑	↑	↓
	A	A	C	C	D	D	E	E
B	↑	↑	↑	↑	↑	↓	↑	↑

The data would now show that a suction point at location B will positively effect point D but not C, E or A. However, from the previous testing we saw that a suction point located at point A positively influenced points C and E. **Conclusion:** A vacuum simultaneously drawn on both points A and B would treat all areas of the slab. This would mean that two suction points would be installed at points A and B. One can install both suction points or just one and plan to add the second one if your post-mitigation test results are not satisfactory. There are times that full coverage is not always necessary. However, the amount of reduction will be better with full sub-slab coverage. It is a good idea to design and install the depressurization piping system with the option of being able to add an additional suction point (see Planning Step 5).

Important: If you find that more than three suction points are required you probably have very impermeable soils and you should consider calling a professional mitigator.

After you have determined the location of the suction points you can either fill the small holes up with plumbers putty or tape over them. Since you have already rented the hammer drill for the day, enlarge the hole in the concrete for the suction point. Proceed with all or part of the installation section following the planning section of this chapter.

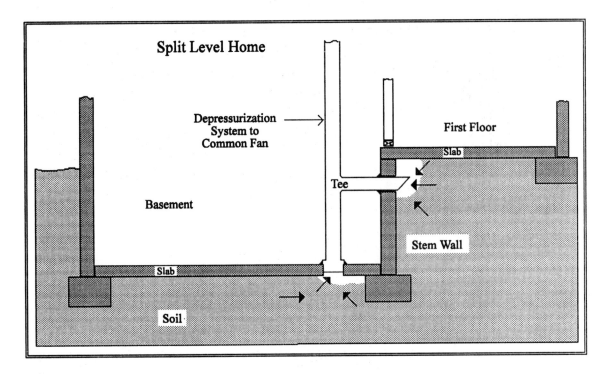

Split Level Home

Depressurization System to Common Fan

First Floor

Slab

Tee

Basement

Stem Wall

Slab

Soil

Planning Step 11.   How to handle multiple slabs in a single home.

Some homes have more than one portion built on isolated slabs. A common example of this is a split level home. The figure above illustrates such a home. You could install separate suction points on each slab and connect them to a common fan or to independent depressurization systems.

The split level home shown above has two slab areas that are separated by a stem wall. This style of construction is common with multi-level homes. The furnace or utility room is generally located in the center of the home in the lowest level and adjacent to the stem wall. This makes the utility or furnace room an excellent place for the primary suction point since they are also good places to hide suction points. Establish the location of your primary suction so it is next to the stem wall. Plan to install a tee in the depressurization piping system that can be connected to a pipe which will penetrate the stem wall.   You should be able to treat both the lowest and the adjacent slab area with two suction points in the utility room.

To test how this will work repeat the previous diagnostic test with the vacuum cleaner. However in this case you will drill your vacuum cleaner hole through the stem wall and drill your test holes through the floor above. After following all the precautions and methods detailed in step 10 you can determine whether or not this stem wall suction point will be able to treat the upper slab area.

Plan the location of this stem wall penetration to be on a vertical line with the depressurization system riser. Instead of inserting a 6 by 4 inch reducer into the wall, use a 4 inch diameter pipe inserted through a hole drilled in the wall. At least two 5 gallon buckets of soil should be removed. Insert the pipe into the hole (minimum of 6 inches past the back side of the concrete). Use expansive foam or non-shrink grout to seal the gap between the wall and the pipe (see Chapter 8 on sealing techniques). Note that the end of the pipe has been cut at a 45 degree angle with the long side up to avoid having it fill with soil. If the stem wall is hollow block, be sure to extend the pipe **completely** through the block, and completely foam the void of the hollow block around the penetrating pipe to avoid losing the vacuum at this point.

Installation Step 1.   Making the suction hole and installing the riser.

In this section you'll cut concrete. A pit will be dug. A fitting will be sealed into the opening. A riser will be attached to the fitting. Later the depressurization system piping will be attached to this riser. Before proceeding with this work, read Chapter 10 on safety and Chapter 7 on depressurization piping systems. At the conclusion of the installation the technique described in the Chapter 8 on sealing should be followed.

Before starting this work assemble the following materials and equipment:

Area	Item	✓
Safety		
	Goggles	
	Dust mask	
	Leather gloves	
	First aid kit	
	Assistant	
	Ear protection for you and your assistant	
	Ventilation fan (window fan)	
	Coveralls	
Material		
	Can of expanding urethane foam	
	Duct tape	
	6 in. by 4 in. PVC schedule 40 reducing bushing (one for each suction point planned)	
	tube of polyurethane caulk	
Tools		
	Shop vacuum (2 horsepower or larger)	
	2 inch vacuum cleaner suction hose at least 6 foot long	
	5 gallon bucket or pail	
	Hand spade or other small hand digging tools	
	Crow bar	
	Heavy wire cutters	
	Electric hammer drill that can function both as a rotary hammer and an electric chisel (1 1/2 inch -- not your typical hand drill, these can typically be rented along with bits from most tool rental houses)	
	3/8 inch by 12 inch bit for hammer drill	
	Heavy duty extension cord (three prong), with ground fault interrupter	
	Caulking gun	
	Rags	
	Chisel bit for hammer drill	

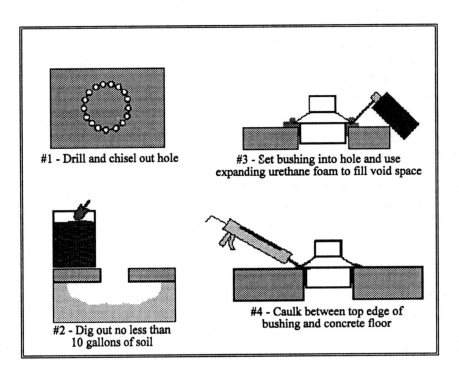

#1 - Drill and chisel out hole

#3 - Set bushing into hole and use expanding urethane foam to fill void space

#2 - Dig out no less than 10 gallons of soil

#4 - Caulk between top edge of bushing and concrete floor

Installation Step 2.   Making the suction hole and piping connection.

Warning: Wear your safety goggles, ear protection and gloves! Failure to do so can result in permanent injury.

Step 1.   Draw a circle on the floor with a magic marker or a grease marker around the 6 by 4 inch schedule 40 PVC bushing that will later be inserted into the hole (see Planning Step 7 and Chapter 7 for guidance on placement). Using the hammer drill with a 3/8 inch bit, drill several holes along the line of the circle. Check to make sure that when the bushing sets down into the hole the lip on the bushing will cover the jagged parts of the hole. Replace the drill bit with the chisel bit and change the setting on the drill to "chisel." Use the chisel to bust out the center and smooth the edges. Keep chiseling until the bushing sits down into the hole with the flange resting on the top of the concrete slab.

Step 2.   Set up a window ventilation fan to blow fresh air into the room you are working in. This will reduce your exposure to high radon levels that can be released when large openings into soil are made. Plus, it helps evaporate the sweat you will be generating. Wear leather gloves to dig out a pit beneath the opening. Dig out at least 2 five-gallon buckets of dirt. Don't skimp! This is a critical detail. The harder it is to dig, the more important it is to get the full amount of dirt out. If you find reinforcing wire cut it or bend it back and forth several times until it breaks. It is better to dig the pit wider than deep.

Step 3.   After you have removed the soil, clean up the mess with the shop vac. Insert the bushing into the hole and apply the expanding urethane foam into the voids around the bushing. Don't add so much that it fills the pit! (See Chapter 8 regarding sealants.)

Step 4.   After the foam has cured for several hours cut the excess away from the top. Apply a 1/2 wide bead of caulk to the edge of the bushing where it meets the top of the concrete. Using a piece of cardboard, smooth the caulk into the joint between the bushing and the floor in a continuous circular motion all the way around the bushing. Let this set for several hours before proceeding.

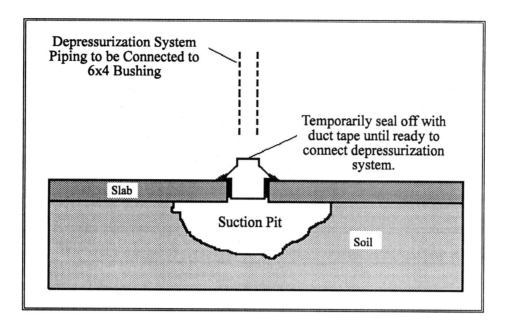

Depressurization System Piping to be Connected to 6x4 Bushing

Temporarily seal off with duct tape until ready to connect depressurization system.

Slab

Suction Pit

Soil

Installation Step 3. Connect the suction point to the depressurization system.

Now you can install the depressurization piping as described in Chapter 7. If you have installed the 6 inch by 4 inch bushing as part of your planning exercise and have not acquired all of the necessary piping yet, tape off the top of the bushing so kids do not "accidentally" throw something down into it or mice don't find a new home to live in. When you are ready to run the depressurization piping, remove the tape and glue your 4 inch PVC pipe into the bushing's throat.

If during the vacuum cleaner suction test you found that greater than three points were going to be needed and you called a professional mitigator, he will be able to connect to the 6 inch by 4 inch bushing for this system. What the professional mitigator will do is install a higher vacuum fan than is typically required. This will be done because you have unusually tight soils. The system the mitigator installs will probably use different size piping than the standard 4 inch. This isn't a problem since the bushing throat is a standard pipe size and that fittings are available to adapt to other pipe sizes.

Installation Step 4. Check for air leaks.

After you have completed the installation of the depressurization piping, turn on the system and look for air leaks through concrete cracks, floor joints and at the suction hole. Do this by using a smoke stick and a flashlight and the techniques described in Chapter 8. If you find leaks, seal them by following the methods in Chapter 8.

Installation Step 5. Backdraft test.

Schedule an inspector or a knowledgeable furnace mechanic to come to your home to insure that the drafting ability of your combustion appliances has not been changed by the radon system you have installed. It is rare that these systems will cause backdrafting. This is especially true if you have done a thorough job of locating and sealing air leaks. *However, the consequences of carbon monoxide poisoning are severe*. So turn off the system until you have the combustion flues tested by a professional. Test this with the radon system both on and off.

ACTIVE RADON VENT SYSTEM

An active sub-slab depressurization system has been installed on this home. It is designed to draw Radon from beneath the concrete slab. Suction points are located _____,_____,_____.
These are attached to a fan located _____.
If the system must be disconnected for any reason, turn off fan. The shut off for the fan is located:_____.
The fan is powered from breaker #____ in the power panel.

Installation Step 6. Label system and re-test home.

After you have performed the air leak tests and have had the combustion appliance flues tested for backdrafting it is time for some finishing touches.

Label your piping system at all visible sections of pipe.

Place a system label at each of the suction points. If there is more than one suction pipe, place a label on each section of pipe as it comes out of the floor. Make sure you list all of the suction points on the label. This is important in case someone cuts one of the pipes and does not turn off the fan. This could seriously effect radon reductions, heating costs and, most hazardous of all, an increased potential of backdrafting.

Finally, re-test the home for radon. Be sure to follow the EPA testing procedures described in Chapter 2. It is best to determine how well your system is working by placing the test device in the same location as your original tests.

Chapter 7

Depressurization System

Fan and Piping

How to install the piping and fan for sub-membrane, drainage and sub-slab depressurization systems.

Depressurization System - Deciding How Much You Can or Want to Do

This chapter will describe how the piping and fan system is to be installed. In each of the previous radon reduction chapters, individual risers or connection points were detailed. This chapter will describe the piping system that will be attached to these connection points and continued on to a safe location outside of the house.

You have a basic decision to make now. Assuming that you have either made the attachment to the sump or drain, or have laid the plastic sheeting in the crawl space, or you have installed the suction points in the concrete slab, you will have a stub of pipe to which the depressurization system will attach. You can proceed to install the piping system or you can call a plumber who could install it for you.

In making your decision whether to do this yourself or hire a plumber be aware of the following:

If you do this yourself you would be:

◆   Using PVC glue to attach plastic pipe together.

◆   Cutting precise lengths of pipe.

◆   Cutting holes through ceilings, floors, and roofs.

◆   Crawling through attic spaces filled with insulation.

If you hire a plumber be aware of the following:

Most plumbers are not familiar with some of the key elements of installing radon systems, such as proper locations of discharge points. However, if the information in this chapter is shared with the plumber, they should have no problem complying with the specific needs of a radon system.

Decision on Fan Installation

The fan that will cause the depressurization of the system is described within this chapter. Be aware that this is an electrical device. You have two choices:

1. Either you hire an electrician to install it, or

2. You purchase a packaged low voltage system that is wired similar to alarm systems or stereo speakers and install it yourself.

Unless you opt for the low voltage systems, it is not recommended that you hard wire 120 volt fans yourself.

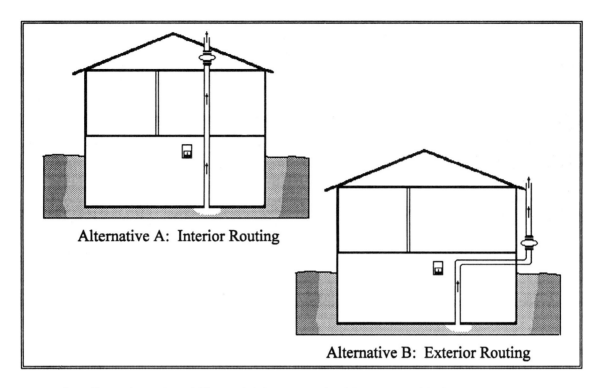

Alternative A: Interior Routing

Alternative B: Exterior Routing

Planning Step 1.   Deciding which path - inside or outside?

The piping and fan system can follow two basic routes, either up through the house or up along the outside of the house. The important criteria is that the discharge of the system must be at a location that does not allow the exhausted gases to re-enter the building through window, doors, skylights, or fresh air make-up vents. It is also important that it does not discharge into an area where people may spend time such as a sandbox or a patio. It is equally important that the discharge does not enter or affect neighboring properties as well. The U.S. EPA has generated some very specific guidance on discharge points. These should be followed specifically and are as follows:

Discharge Points Shall Be:

♦ **Minimum of 10 feet above ground level**

♦ **Minimum of 10 feet away from any opening
    that is less than 2 feet below the discharge**

♦ **Minimum of 10 feet from any private or public access**

♦ **Minimum of 10 feet from any adjacent building**

Ref. U.S. EPA Interim Mitigation Standards dated December 15, 1991

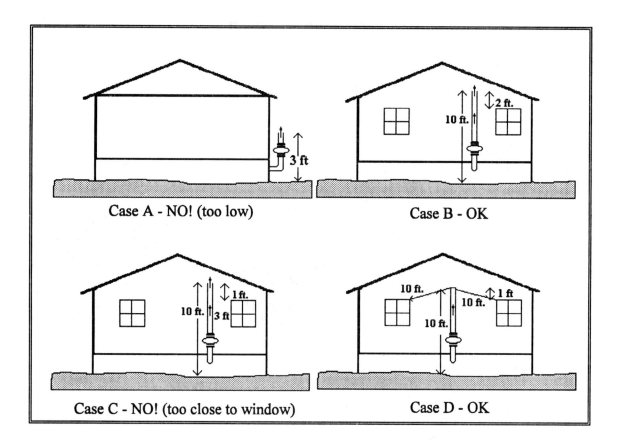

Case A - NO! (too low)

Case B - OK

Case C - NO! (too close to window)

Case D - OK

Planning Step 2.   More on picking a discharge point.

The above figure shows four examples of discharge point locations. According to the guidelines presented on the previous page the following statements can be made about the above examples:

Case A.   This is an incorrect location because it is too close to the ground. The potential for the discharge gases entering the home via a window or even through the side of the house is too great. This is a "trick" that some people use to unethically cut costs. This is unacceptable and unwise. You may cause radon to be reintroduced into the home.

Case B.   This follows the guidelines. Ten feet above the ground. Even though it is closer than ten feet from the window on the right this is acceptable because the window is 2 feet below the discharge of the pipe when a vertical measurement is made from the top of the window and an imaginary horizontal line drawn from the discharge point. *Note: This assumes the discharge is straight up. Do not turn down or use a rain cap. See discussion later on regarding rain caps.*

Case C.   This is an incorrect location because it is too close to the window. It is less than 10 feet away from a window that is less than two feet from the imaginary horizontal line made by the end of the pipe.

Case D.   This is acceptable even though the window is only 1 foot lower than the discharge, because the discharge is ten feet away from the windows, and ten feet above ground level.

Running the piping up through the attic reduces these discharges concerns. However, this routing can involve more work. Don't discharge through a low roof on a multi-level home that has an adjacent wall with windows in it.

Protecting Your Home From Radon

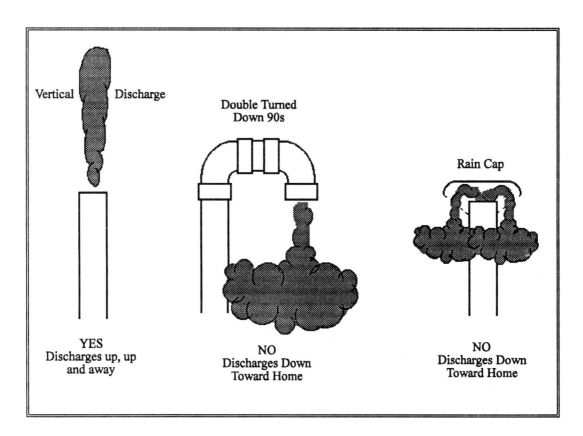

Planning Step 3.   Planning the end of the discharge.

One of the things that people invariably want to do is to put something on the discharge of the piping system to prevent rain from falling in. Rain does not present a concern for two reasons. First the air coming out the pipe blows the rain away. Secondly, the cross sectional area of the pipe is only 12 square inches. Even if the rain fell straight down and the air stream did not eject it only collect 1 gallon of water would be collected if your average rainfall is 20 inches per year. So there really is no need to utilize rain caps and, in fact, they could cause problems with the system.

If you put a rain cap on or install some type of rain diverter on the discharge you will:

♦   Cause the exhaust gas to be blown down towards the home. This will increase the potential for the exhausted gas to re-enter the home. If this happens you will not be able to recognize it. The above figure illustrates the direction of air flow of three different discharge configurations. (Note that for the purposes of the illustration an exhaust stream is shown, in reality you cannot see the exhaust.)

♦   Increase the likelihood of condensate from the system to freeze and form an ice ball on the end of the pipe, thus causing the system to malfunction.

♦   Decrease the operating vacuum of the fan and effect your system's ability to reduce radon.

Just put a rodent/bird screen in the end, and point it up and away from the home.

Fan Location Criteria

**The fan should not be located inside of the home
or in areas where fan leakage would allow radon to enter home.**

Good Locations:

> **Unoccupied attics**
> **Outside of the house**
> **In garage**

Bad Locations:

> **In crawl space beneath house**
> **In basement**
> **In occupied attic**

U.S. EPA Interim Mitigation Standards dated December 1991

Planning Step 4.   Determining where the fan will be placed.

The fan you will be using is installed as part of the piping system itself. Therefore, as you are planning your pipe routing you need to determine a suitable fan location.

Because the system you are installing is virtually mining the radon from the soil, the concentration of radon inside the piping system can be very high. Any leak in the depressurization system, on the pressure side of the fan and inside the home, can introduce significant levels of radon into the living area. Fan housings for the fans recommended later in this chapter have been designed to minimize this potential. However, the U.S. EPA's <u>Interim Mitigation Standards</u> recommend that the fan be located outside of the living space to avoid potential leak hazards.

The above figure lists both good and bad locations. Choose a location for the fan before you plan the exact routing your piping system. Here are a few other considerations:

1.   If you put the fan in the attic, locate it so it is easy to get at. Select a location with a minimum of 30 inches between the top of ceiling joist and the underside of the roof decking. *The fan must be installed vertically.*

2.   If you put the fan outside, make sure that it is rated for outdoor installations.

3.   Special precautions will have to be taken if you put the fan in an attached garage and penetrate the fire resistive wall between the garage and the house (see fire barrier discussion on page 7-12.)

```
┌─────────────────────────────────────────────────────────────┐
│                        Piping                                │
│                                                              │
│   What type of pipe?              PVC or ABS                 │
│   What thickness of pipe?         Schedule 40                │
│   What pipe standard?             DWV                        │
│   What size of pipe?              4 inch diameter            │
│                                                              │
└─────────────────────────────────────────────────────────────┘
```

Planning Step 5.   Type and size of pipe to be used.

The air stream that will be running through the pipe will be very humid and, at times, will have water condensing inside of it. Therefore, the piping material should be resistant to water damage. Plastic pipe is very suitable for this purpose. There are two materials of plastic pipe construction that can be found in local plumbing supply houses. They are PVC and ABS solvent welded piping. *Note:* **You should choose one or the other, based on cost and availability.** Don't mix piping types - do not glue pieces of PVC to pieces of ABS. When you purchase the pipe be sure to also purchase the appropriate cleaner and cement for that type of pipe.

The durability of the pipe is also important. Kids like to hang on these pipes or do whatever kids do to try to wreak havoc in your home. The strength of the pipe is a function of it's Schedule number. The Schedule number refers to the thickness of the wall of the pipe. Schedule 40 is the minimum pipe wall thickness that should be considered.

There are different service ratings given to pipe. These ratings are a function of the interior pressure that one expects to see within the pipe. Since the system you are installing does not need to withstand high pressures, a non-pressure rated pipe is adequate. The rating that is the most cost effective yet durable is Drain and Waste Vent or DWV. This is the same kind of pipe that your plumbing vent stack is most likely made of. It is also sometimes referred to as foam core. Some code designations that may help you identify necessary pipe are:

Pipe Material	ASTM Numbers	NSF Designation
PVC	D-2665 or F891-91	NSF-dwv
ABS	F-628 or D-2661	NSF-dwv

Four inch diameter pipe is the size that seems to work the most universally. If you install smaller diameter pipe you are running the risk of not having sufficient capacity for the radon to be removed from the soil. Pipe smaller than 4 inch may also create a whistling noise in the pipe. This can be very objectionable if you like a quiet home. If the air volume to be removed by your system turns out to be rather small and a smaller pipe could have been used, you have only lost the small incremental cost between 4 inch and 3 inch. On the other hand, if you had undersized the pipe, you would have no recourse other than to rip it out and start again or buy a more expensive fan to overcome the restriction presented by the smaller pipe.

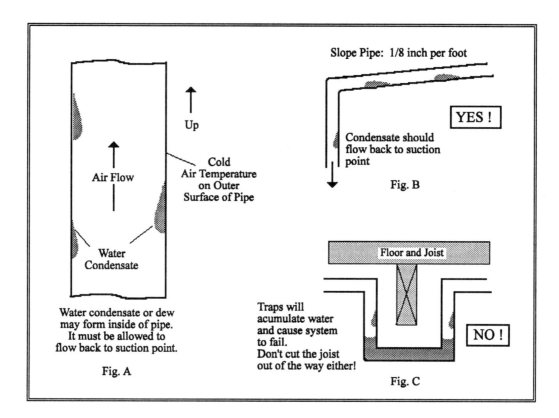

Fig. A

Fig. B

Fig. C

Planning Step 6. Allowing for condensation within the piping.

Active soil depressurization systems draw other soil gases besides radon from beneath the home, one of which is water vapor. The air in the soil beneath a home can be high in humidity. The potential for water vapor condensation exists when this humid air passes through a section of the piping system in a cold part of the home, or is routed outside. Figure A above depicts the formation of water droplets on the inside of the pipe. The majority of the condensation occurs inside of the portion the piping that is on the discharge side of the fan. The following factors increase the amount of condensation that occurs:

♦　As moisture content of the soil increases. Some parts of the country are more humid than others. The authors have seen as much as a half gallon of water per day produced from these systems.

♦　With outside temperature variations. As the temperature drops outside, the temperature of the pipe wall also drops, thus increasing the amount of condensation.

♦　When the length of cold pipe varies. The more pipe that runs through a cold attic or up the outside, the larger the condensation surface area. This also increases the contact time the air has inside the cold pipe to condense.

Note: The piping system must be installed so when the moisture condenses the water can drain back to the suction point. Do not install low spots in the piping where the water can accumulate. Figure C above depicts a common mistake that people make. Plan your piping so it slopes back to the suction point. Plan a slope of 1 inch per 8 feet of pipe or 1/8 inch per foot (see Figure B). It is just like running sewage lines.

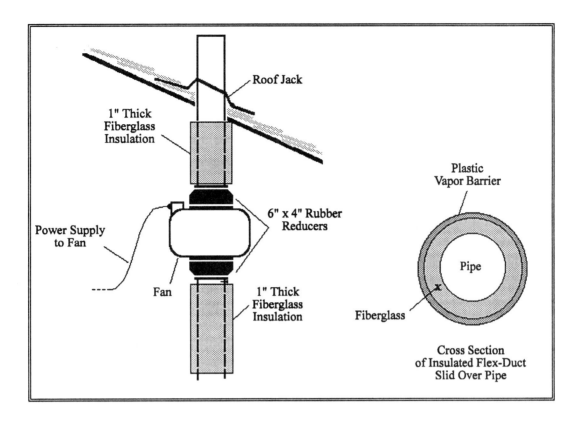

Roof Jack

1" Thick Fiberglass Insulation

6" x 4" Rubber Reducers

Power Supply to Fan

Fan

1" Thick Fiberglass Insulation

Plastic Vapor Barrier

Pipe

Fiberglass

Cross Section of Insulated Flex-Duct Slid Over Pipe

Planning Step 7.   Insulating pipes.

One of the ways to reduce the amount of condensation that occurs inside of the pipe is to prevent the wall of the pipe from getting too cold. This is especially important in very cold climates where the surface of the pipe gets so cold that the condensed water will actually freeze inside the pipe. This ice can build up and restrict, or completely choke off the desired air flow.

Insulate the outside of the pipe where it goes through cold areas. The figure above illustrates how this was done on the piping inside of a cold attic space. The easiest material to use is an insulated flex duct. This is typically used by heating and ventilating contractors for heating or air conditioning ductwork. This material has a 1 inch layer of fiberglass wrapped around a flexible plastic tube. There is also a plastic jacket around the outside of the fiberglass that can serve as a vapor barrier. It also makes the installation a lot neater. This material can be purchased in 25 foot lengths. For ease of installation, the insulated ductwork can be cut and slid over the piping *before the joints or fittings are glued together.*

Use insulated ductwork also as a jacket around the piping inside the home to reduce the noise caused by air flowing through the piping. If you buy a 25 foot length of the ductwork and only use a few feet in the attic for insulation, use the rest on the piping to dampen noise where it runs through the house. It makes for a quieter installation.

Another reason for insulating the ductwork inside of the house would be if you live in a warm, humid climate. The air temperature in the pipe could be cooler than the temperature in the home. When this occurs condensation could form on the exterior surface of the piping. The insulation will reduce this "rain making" effect inside your home. Carefully seal the jacket of the insulation to the surface of the pipe and tape any punctures in the jacket to insure a good moisture barrier, which could soak and ruin the insulation.

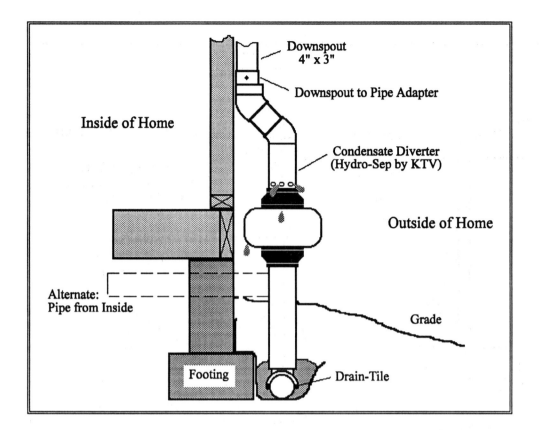

Labels in figure:
- Downspout 4" x 3"
- Downspout to Pipe Adapter
- Inside of Home
- Condensate Diverter (Hydro-Sep by KTV)
- Outside of Home
- Alternate: Pipe from Inside
- Grade
- Footing
- Drain-Tile

Planning Step 8.   Dealing with condensation on exterior fan locations.

The figure above illustrates an exterior location of a depressurization fan. Mounting the fan outside is often done if you connect to an exterior foundation drain. It is also an option for connecting the depressurization system to a sump, crawl space, or sub-slab suction system. Exterior piping is also used where it is difficult to route the piping through the home.

Condensation can occur in the outdoor piping systems. It is critical to slope these piping systems back to their respective suction points. In areas where freezing temperatures are often encountered, the water can actually freeze inside the fan housing. This causes uneven wear on the bearings, resulting in premature failure of the fan. ***Note: Moisture does not hurt the fans but the ice build up can.***

<u>Solutions:</u>

1.   Mount the fan and piping on the southern, sunny side of the home. This is of only marginal help if you live in Alaska where the sun does not shine much during the winter.

2.   Insulate and enclose the pipe and fan. Fan shrouds are commercially available. **Do not wrap with fiberglass and leave insulation exposed to the elements.**

3.   Install a water diverter that will allow the condensate to drain out onto the ground rather than accumulating in the fan housing. This device significantly reduces water and ice accumulation and is thought to extend the life of the fan. **Do not simply drill holes in the side of the pipe.** This will cause radon gas to be emitted at low elevations. *Using the proper device will separate the water but not allow the gas to escape.*

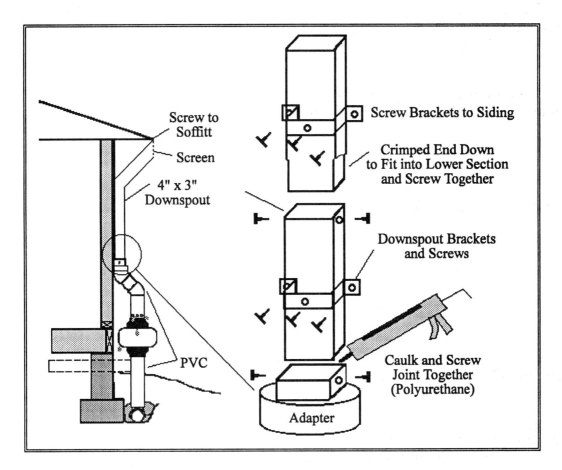

Planning Step 9.   Using downspout on exterior pipe sections.

Downspouts are often used for the exterior portion of the depressurization system. This is because the downspout looks more natural on the side of your house than a 4 inch PVC pipe. It can be plastic or metal which can be painted to match the color of your other downspouts. If you plan to do this you need to keep the following things in mind:

1.   A downspout should **only** be on the discharge side of the fan.
2.   It should never be run inside of the house.
3.   If you use metal downspout the potential for ice build up in cold climates is greater than
      if you use PVC. *Hint:* **See previous step on the use of water separators.**
4.   The downspout joints should be caulked and screwed together to minimize leakage.
5.   Try to locate it on the sunny side of the house.

Note in the illustration above that round PVC piping is used from the discharge side of the fan through two 45 degree elbows. Use PVC pipe for this due to the physical stress that can be placed on the system at this point. After you have reached the side of the house, install a round pipe to rectangular downspout adapter. Cosmetic enclosures are also available for the fan that allow for an offset to occur inside of the housing.

Be sure to use 3 by 4 inch downspout. This is a larger size than what is typically seen on homes. Use of a smaller downspout can severely restrict the air flow and decrease efficiency of the system.

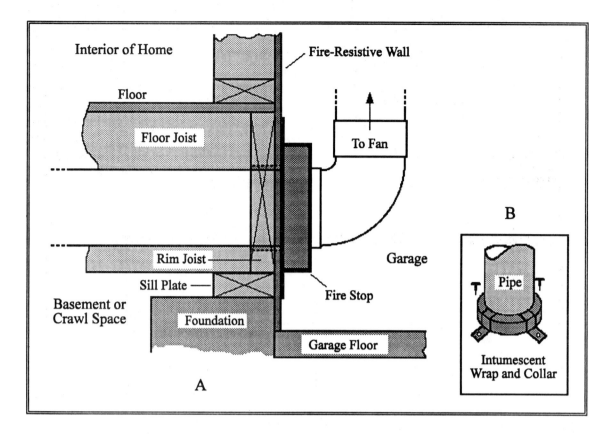

Interior of Home — Fire-Resistive Wall

Floor

Floor Joist

To Fan

B

Rim Joist

Garage

Sill Plate

Fire Stop

Pipe

Basement or
Crawl Space

Foundation

Garage Floor

Intumescent
Wrap and Collar

A

Planning Step 10.   Penetrating firewalls and fire ceilings.

As you plan your routing be aware that you cannot cut a hole through just any wall to run the piping through. Some walls and even ceilings are constructed in a manner to retard the spread of fire from one area of the house to the next. A common example of this would be if you plan to run your piping into an attached garage where the fan can be located. The wall separating the garage from the house is a fire resistive wall. This is in accordance with building codes.

If the fire resistive wall does not extend up to the roof, the ceiling of an attached garage is a fire rated ceiling. Partition walls between units and condominiums, townhouses and duplexes should also be fire rated walls. If the fire walls between separate housing units do not extend to the roof, then the ceiling of an individual unit is a fire ceiling also. Fire rated ceilings require fire stops just as much as fire walls do when running PVC pipe through them.

You may penetrate fire resistive walls, provided you install a "fire stop". A fire stop is a device that will close off the pipe should there be a fire and not allow the fire to spread through the opening. The device that is the most suitable for radon piping is the intumescent style fire barrier. Figure A, in the illustration above, shows how a penetration is made into a garage. The fire barrier itself is a series of strips of material that are wrapped around the exterior of the pipe. A sheet metal collar is then placed over the top of the strips and screwed into the wall. **Only one of these assemblies is needed on one side of the wall per penetration of a fire wall.** Figure B illustrates the pipe with the collar attached. *Note: The barrier and collar must be installed on the side of the wall that presents the greatest fire hazard and must be mounted directly on the wall.* In the case of a garage wall penetration, the assembly would be on the garage side of the wall as shown in Figure A above. These devices are readily available. To order from the suppliers listed in the appendix or from a building supply store, you must specify the pipe size you are fitting over and the fire rating desired (typically 1 hour).

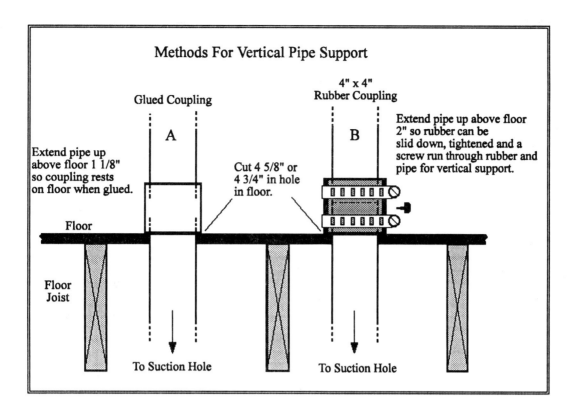

Planning Step 11.   Planning your vertical supports.

If you are running the pipe up through the house you will need to support the pipe vertically as well as horizontally. Other support methods will be described on the next page; however, approaches often used for vertical support are shown above.

You will probably be running the pipe up through a floor at some point. You will feed the pipe either up or down through an opening that you cut in the floor and connect two pieces of pipe together at that location. If you plan it correctly, the pipe coupling can rest on the floor and serve as the support. The following are two suggestions that are often used by professional mitigators.

Glued Coupling - Method A above. In this case the pipe coming up from the floor below should extend 1 1/8 inches above the top of the floor. When the coupling is glued and pushed down on the pipe it will seat against the floor. This method is more exacting than the rubber adapter described next. On the other hand it is more resistant to tampering.

Rubber Adapter - Method B above. In this case the pipe coming up from the floor below should extend at least 1 1/8 inches above the top of the floor. The rubber adapter will slide down over the lower pipe and is secured by tightening the hose clamp. To insure that the weight of the piping system does not pull the pipe out from the adapter a 1 inch long, a #8 sheet metal screw should be run in through the rubber coupling and into the PVC pipe to provide some additional vertical support. This method is more forgiving when you install the piping but could be tampered with in the future.

In both cases a round hole should be cut with a hole saw that is no smaller than 4 5/8 inch and no bigger than 4 3/4 inches. *If you are not careful when you use a hole saw, it may bind up and give you a good, sharp kick (see Chapter 10 on safety).*

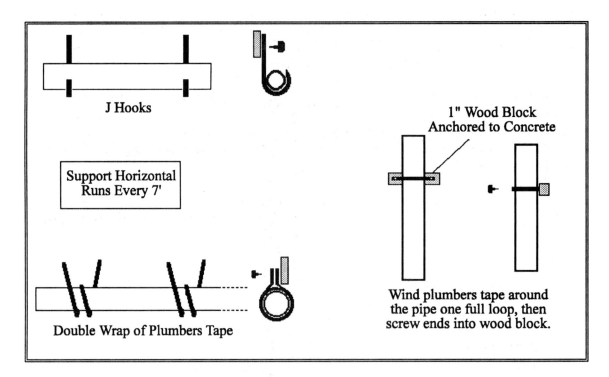

J Hooks

Support Horizontal
Runs Every 7'

Double Wrap of Plumbers Tape

1" Wood Block
Anchored to Concrete

Wind plumbers tape around
the pipe one full loop, then
screw ends into wood block.

Planning Step 12.   Planning your horizontal pipe supports.

As the pipe will be routed through the home it will have to be well supported. Even though it will only be full of air and not contain much weight - kids love to hang on them or people are known to hang deer on them (all true stories). Therefore pipes need to be well supported so they do not crack or break. A broken pipe could cause serious depressurization within the home. This could also cause the combustion appliances to backdraft. Poisonous carbon monoxide gas can accumulate when backdrafting occurs. The figure above shows three methods of pipe support.

Horizontal pipe is often supported with either "J"-Hooks or "Plumbers Tape". Regardless of the method used, the pipe should be supported every 7 feet. Don't forget to slope the pipe.

J Hooks: J hooks are plastic hooks that can be nailed or screwed into a wall or floor joist. The pipe snaps into the open end of the hook. There are several holes on the straight section of the hook with numbers on them to help you mount the hooks at different elevations. This is helpful in making sure you have the proper slope to the pipe (1 inch per 10 feet).

Plumbers Tape: Plumber's tape is a 3/4 inch wide metal or plastic tape that has had holes pre-punched into it. It can be purchased in rolls. Just uncoil as much as is needed and cut it with tin snips. Make sure that you cut enough off so you can wrap it completely around the pipe once and screw the two ends to the wall or floor joist. Actually, the plastic plumber's tape is a lot easier to work with and has adequate strength.

For providing lateral support for vertical pipes, attach a 1 inch by 1 inch by 8 inch block of wood to the wall. Use wood screws if you are attaching to a wood wall and anchors if you are attaching to masonry or dry wall. Wrap plumbers tape completely around the pipe, fasten one end to the wood block, take up the slack with the free end and screw it to the block as well.

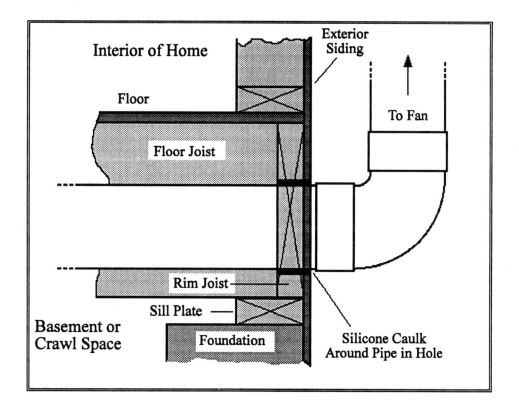

Planning Step 13.   Planning exterior wall penetrations.

You may prefer to run the piping through an outside wall and avoid the difficulties of running pipe through the interior of the house. If you are depressurizing a basement sump, or installing a sub-slab suction system in a basement, or you are depressurizing a plastic barrier on a crawl space floor - exterior piping can be used. The figure above shows how this is done.

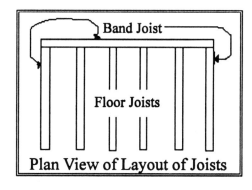

The penetration should be through the band joist. It should run through the board that sets on edge on the foundation wall. **Do not cut floor joists or run through wall at a location below grade.**

Do not cut holes through structural members or through the foundation wall below grade. Do not cut a hole through a basement wall below grade unless you want water in your basement (another true story).
Use a 4 5/8 inch hole saw or a reciprocating saw (saws-all) to make the hole. Drill a pilot hole with a small but long drill bit to make sure of the location. Seal around the pipe with silicone caulk (see Chapter 10 on safety).

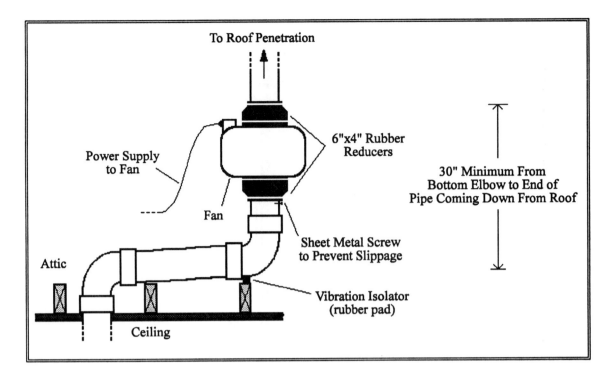

Planning Step 14.   Fan mounting.

The fan that creates the needed vacuum must be installed either outside of the home, in the garage or in the attic. The above figure illustrates a fan mounting for an attic. Regardless of the location for the fan it must be installed in the following manner:

◆   It must be mounted vertically to allow condensed water to drain down through the casing.

◆   There must be a way to remove the fan from the piping system. The best way to do this is to use 6 inch by 4 inch rubber reducers with hose clamps. These can be loosened so the fan can be slid out of the piping system. Note the screw that is shown in the drawing just below the bottom reducer. This screw is a # 8 self tapping sheet metal screw that is run into the pipe just below the bottom rubber reducer. This prevents the fan from accidentally sliding down onto the pipe. In hot attics, or for other reasons, the rubber reducer could loosen up. If this were to occur and allow the fan to slide down - the lower pipe would stick into the fan blades. This will stop the fan dead, and probably ruin it. So be sure to install the screw in the pipe below the reducer.

Note the way the horizontal piping has been run from the ceiling penetration to the fan. The pipe is being supported by the ceiling joists. A piece of rubber has been placed between the joist and the pipe to both isolate any vibration from the joist and to provide the proper slope to the fan.

The rubber 6 by 4 inch reducers also help isolate fan noise from the piping system and the rest of the home.

Important: Do not mount the fan at any orientation other than vertical, and do not glue the fan directly to the piping. Use rubber couplings.

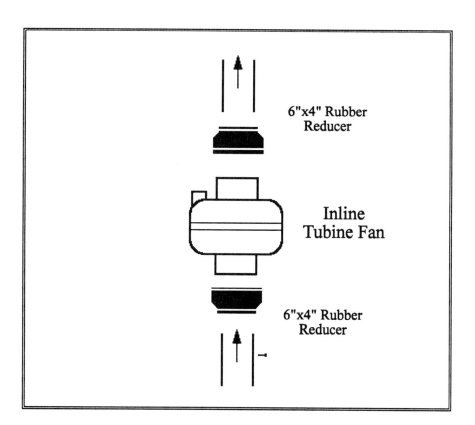

6"x4" Rubber Reducer

Inline Tubine Fan

6"x4" Rubber Reducer

Planning Step 15.   Fan selection.

In-line duct fans have proven to be the most universally applicable fan for the types of radon reduction systems described in this book. People have tried duct booster fans, wafer fans and various other types of fans. These have not shown the satisfactory results for radon reduction and durability as the in-line fans have. In-line fans set directly in the air flow of the pipe and are supported by the pipe. Their inlet and discharge opening sizes are 6 inches in diameter. There are several manufacturers of the fan units to choose from. The following is some technical data regarding some of the fans:

Manufacturer	Model #	Comments	Max. Watts	Max. flow	Max.Vac in. W.C.
Fantech	FR 150	Order FR150 for exterior use	90	270	1.5
KTV, Inc.	KTA	Low voltage, Class 2 wiring, built in indicator	90	270	1.5
Kanaflakt	K6, & T2		90	270	1.5
Rosenburg	R150		90	270	1.5

The table above shows a maximum power usage of 90 watts. Most systems actually draw approximately 60 watts or less. There are smaller sizes as well as higher vacuum fans available. However, for the systems described in this manual, this size of fan is adequate. If the sub-slab simulation test described in Chapter 6 should indicate very tight soils, then the homeowner should follow the recommendation to call a radon professional to size an alternate fan in this unusual instance.

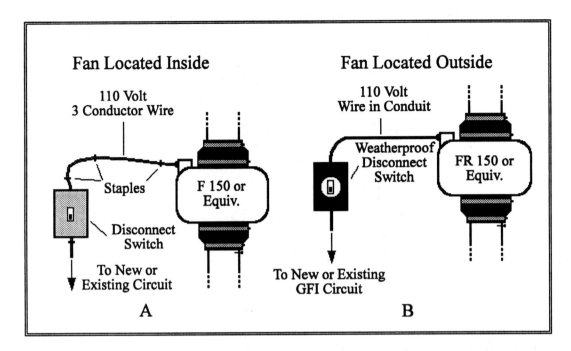

Fan Located Inside

110 Volt
3 Conductor Wire

Staples

F 150 or
Equiv.

Disconnect
Switch

To New or
Existing Circuit

A

Fan Located Outside

110 Volt
Wire in Conduit

Weatherproof
Disconnect
Switch

FR 150 or
Equiv.

To New or Existing
GFI Circuit

B

Planning Step 16.   Electrical requirements for the fans.

Of the fans listed on the previous page all but one, the KTA 150, requires running a 110 volt power supply to its remote location. The fan location will be in the garage, attic, or outdoors. You cannot attach an electrical cord to a fan and plug it in to an outdoor circuit. If you plan to purchase a 110 volt fan, plan to hire an electrician to install it. The National Electric Code is very specific on how wiring is to be accomplished. Some code jurisdictions have even gone so far as to recommend that the 110 volt fans have a dedicated circuit run from the breaker panel. The next page will discuss the alternatives provided by the low voltage system.

Here are some of the elements of most electrical codes that apply to the electrical installation (refer to the illustrations above):

Interior Locations (attic) - Figure A:

The power can be run with 14-3 wire (ROMEX), unless it is on a 20 amp circuit which requires 12-3 wire.

A disconnect switch for turning the power off to the fan must be within direct line of sight from the fan. This allows removal of the fan without electrical shock.

Exterior Locations - Figure B:

The 110 volt power is to be run in weather tight conduit on the portion of the wiring that is outside. Note that the weather tight conduit can end once it enters the home. The wiring must also be connected to a circuit that has a ground fault interrupter on it.

A disconnect switch for turning the power off to the fan must be within direct line of sight from the fan. This allows for removal of the fan without electrical shock.

The fan itself must be rated for exterior locations.

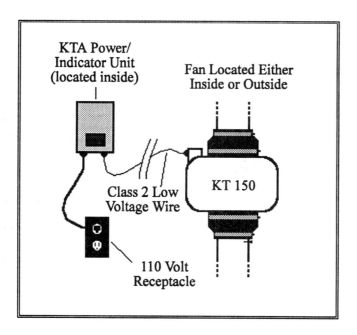

Planning Step 17.   Packaged low voltage fan systems.

An alternative fan system that has the same volumetric and suction capacity as the 110 volt fans is a unit that can be plugged in to an available receptacle. The voltage is reduced to 24 volts so it can be run in an inexpensive cable to the fan up to 50 feet away. The cable that should be used with this system is 18 gauge two conductor "sprinkler" cable. The use of sprinkler cable allows for the wiring to be run to the fan without conduit to an exterior fan location. The power supply is modified within the fan so it operates within the air flow range required.

The obvious advantage is it can be plugged in and the power cable strung like one might run a speaker wire or a sprinkler wire. Although you still need to follow certain precautions:

♦   The cable should be supported with cable staples.

♦   The power supply box **must be located** indoors and at a location where it can be observed since the power supply box has the system performance indicator incorporated into it.

Another advantage to this low voltage fan system is that the indicator system is electronic, and a pressure indication system is not needed. This can overcome the humidity and freezing problems often seen with pressure tubing (see Planning Step 19).

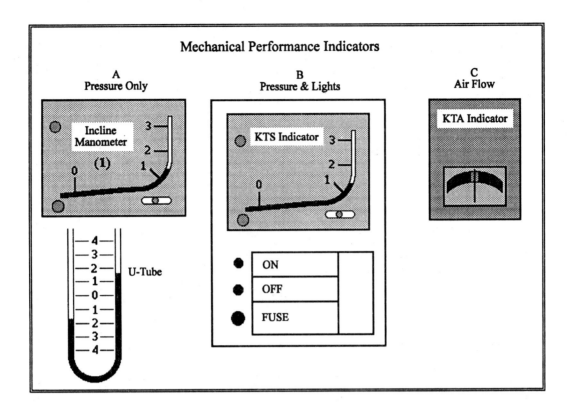

Mechanical Performance Indicators

Planning Step 18.   Types of system indicators.

As part of the installation of a depressurization system, an indicator must be installed which will tell the homeowner if something has changed the performance of the system. This is in addition to re-testing the home for radon after the installation and repeating this test at least once every two years (see Chapter 2). You could purchase a continuous radon monitor. However, the state-of-the-art in the mitigation industry is to install a mechanical indicator that will inform the occupant that either the vacuum characteristics or the air flow characteristics of the system have changed. A fan stall, a pluggage in the pipe, or a breach in the system could cause this to happen. There are two basic types of indicators as follows:

Pressure Based. The above figure illustrates several indicators available. The two under the letter A are pressure measurement devices. They are called manometers. When a 1/4 inch tube is run from the "low" side of the manometer to a portion on the suction side of the piping system and the "high" side port is left open, the liquid level will change as the vacuum of the system changes. This allows you to identify fluctuations in the radon capture efficiency of the system. This can also be accomplished by the use of a pressure switch which will sense the vacuum in the tube and turn on warning lights as the device marked B above will. The manometer and the pressure switch styles rely upon a vacuum measurement within the piping. Both require a certain amount of interpretation and generally only detect major changes in system performance. Pressure based indicators have the potential to falsely indicate problems because of condensation or freezing within the 1/4 inch pressure sensing tubing.

Air Flow Based. The device marked C senses subtle changes in air flow of the system. It does this electronically by monitoring the current draw of the fan. Slight changes in air flow due to small leaks, or piping blockages that can develop in the system, are indicated. These electronic monitors are more sensitive to problems and also do not require pressure sensing tubing, thus eliminating false signals with condensation and freezing.

Protecting Your Home From Radon

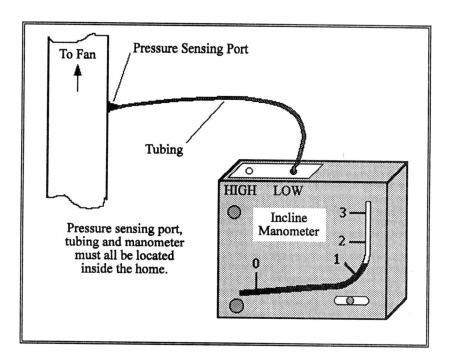

To Fan

Pressure Sensing Port

Tubing

Pressure sensing port,
tubing and manometer
must all be located
inside the home.

HIGH LOW

Incline
Manometer

3
2
1
0

Planning Step 19.   Planning the location of the pressure port if you plan to use a pressure based performance indicator.

Note: This step is not needed if the air flow style of indicator is used.

If you plan to use a manometer or pressure switch device rather than the air flow style indicator, you must carefully plan where you will make the connection to the piping system.

The manometer must be located on a wall in a portion of the home where you will frequently see it. A laundry room or a garage wall are examples of good locations. You will have to run a 1/4 inch tube from the manometer to a location on the "suction" side of the depressurization system below the fan.

Caution: **No portion of this tube should be routed outdoors or through a cold attic space**.
The reason for this is even though the tube will be on the suction side of the piping, moist air can enter the tube and condense. When liquid condenses inside of the tube, a plug of water will be formed which will give you erroneous readings and cannot be removed without dismantling or blowing out the tube. Sometimes it must be replaced completely. You will need to purchase an appropriate length of 1/4 inch tubing. It can be any length. The tubing most commonly used is 1/4 inch sprinkler or drip irrigation tubing since it is inexpensive and durable.

The manometer is generally packaged with a brass pipe to hose adapter. The pipe can be drilled with a 3/8 inch drill bit. The adapter can then be threaded into the soft wall of the PVC pipe to make the connection. The tubing is then pushed over the serrated end of the adapter to make the connection. The location this adapter should meet the following criteria:

◆   Mount it as far away from the fan as possible on the suction piping - this will improve the sensitivity of the measurement.

◆   Mount it either in a vertical portion of the piping or on the top of a horizontal run to minimize water entry into the tube.

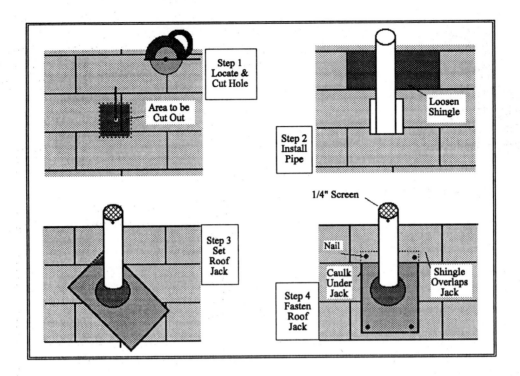

Planning Step 20.   How to penetrate the roof, if you plan an internal routing.

You have a choice of running your piping either up the outside of the house, or up through the house and through the roof. If you choose to go through the roof, you will need to cut a hole in the roof for the pipe and to repair the hole so the roof does not leak. For those roofs that have asphalt shingles or shakes, the process is relatively straightforward. If it is a flat roof, or a clay tile roof, or if the shingles contain asbestos, the repair is more involved and probably should be done by a roofing professional. The above figure illustrates how a shingle roof penetration is made with a roof jack.

1.   From inside of the attic, drill a pilot hole to mark the center of where you intend the pipe to go through the roof. Push a stick up through the roof, so you can find the pilot hole from the roof. With a circular saw or a sawsall, cut a hole that is 6 1/2 inches by 6 1/2 inches, or a circular hole that is 6 1/2 inches in diameter. *Warning: Wear safety glasses, gloves, and use a fully grounded extension cord. Failure to do so can result in permanent injury. Before cutting the hole, be in a secure position on the roof, or rope yourself off. The chance of hitting a roofing nail is pretty high, and the saw will kick.* Also the fine rocks in the shingles will spray when cut and will probably dull your blade. Use an old blade.

2.   Install the pipe and secure it both laterally and vertically as described previously in this chapter. With a flat bar or putty knife, loosen the shingle uphill from the pipe. Slide the roof jack down over the pipe with the seal side up. Run two concentric beads of caulk around the under side of the jack where it will set on the roof.

3.   Tuck one of the upper corners of the roof jack and rotate it under the shingles that were loosened above.

4.   Drive a roofing nail into each of the four corners. Place a 1/4 inch wire screen in discharge and use three #8 sheet metal screws to secure the screen.

If you plan to install the piping system yourself, be sure you are familiar with the items in the safety chapter and that you follow the instructions for the glues and caulks you will be using. Don't get PVC cement in your eyes. If you decide to use the 110 volt fans, arrange for an electrician to wire the fan.

Installation Step 1.   Assemble the materials for installing the depressurization system.

The following is a table that lists many of the items that you may need for the installation of the system.

Safety		QTY	✓
	Goggles, safety glasses, i.e. eye protection		
	Ventilation fan		
	Gloves		
	First aid kit		
Materials			
	PVC Pipe-Schedule 40 DWV or ABS Schedule 40 DWV Feet:		
	4 inch 90 degree elbows-PVC or ABS		
	4 inch 45 degree elbows-PVC or ABS		
	4 inch tees PVC or ABS		
	4 inch 221/2 degree fittings		
	Pipe solvent and cement - compatible for pipe material used		
	4 inch by 4 inch rubber couplings		
	4 inch PVC or ABS couplings		
	Roof jack		
	Tube of roofing caulk (Blackjack)		
	Plumbers tape		
	# 8 self tapping screws (at least 50)		
	1 square foot of 1/4 inch hardware cloth		
	Rubber vibration isolation strips		
	Flexible duct insulation		
	Duct tape		
	6 inch by 4 inch rubber adapters	2	
	3 in by 4 in. downspout		
	Type A downspout elbows (turn out)		
	Type B downspout elbows (turn right or left)		
	Downspout to pipe adapter		
	Downspout straps		
	110 Volt Fan Option		
	Fan		
	Electrician		
	Pressure style indicator		
	1/4 inch tubing		
	Cable staples		

		Low Voltage Fan Option	7-24	
		Integral power supply / indicator with matching fan		
		Two conductor sprinkler cable		
	Cable staples			
	Wood blocks			
Equipment				
	Extension ladder for roof			
	Step ladder (6 foot)			
	Cordless drill with 1/4 inch nut driver			
	Flashlight			
	Extension cord			
	Hole saw (4 5/8 inch) and drill (right angle with torque control is safest)			
	Circular saw or reciprocating saw			
	Rags			
	Hack saw or PVC saw (PVC saw works best)			
	Measuring tape			
	Marker			
	Plumb bob or weight on a string			
	Level			
	Hammer			

Considerations:

♦ <u>Before</u> you start this work - think carefully about how you will run the piping system. Try to run the pipe through closets and unoccupied spaces as much as possible.

♦ Make sure you pick a good weather day to do this work if you are planning to get up on the roof and cut a hole.

♦ You will need a helper for this work. Someone to hold onto the other end of the pipe is very helpful.

♦ Don't attempt electrical wiring of the 110 volt systems unless you are trained and licensed to do so.

♦ Wear your safety glasses. PVC glue is a solvent that glues the pipe together by dissolving the plastic. It will also dissolve your cornea if it gets into your eye.

♦ *ABSOLUTELY NO CONTACT LENSES* while doing this work.

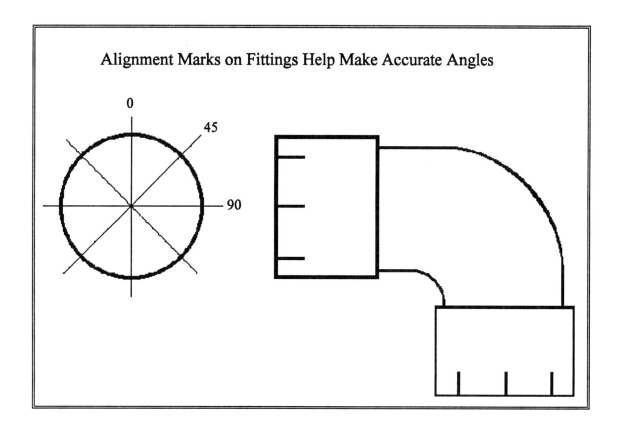

Alignment Marks on Fittings Help Make Accurate Angles

Fitting and Cutting Pipe Together

Measure twice and cut once. Refer back to the planning steps to calculate how far pipes should extend through ceilings, depending on which method of support you decided to use.

One method that even professional mitigators use is to "dry fit" the pipe. That is cut the pipe and push the fittings on without glue. This can help with the layout of the piping. If you do this, be careful that you allow for at least an extra half inch on each side of a fitting. This is because you cannot push the fitting on a dry pipe as far as you will be able to when you apply the glue.

The above illustration depicts how some fittings have marks on their sides to show increments of 22.5 degrees. When these marks are lined up on opposing fittings a perfect 45 or 90 degree angle can be made.

Mark the pipe with a marking pen and cut it with a hand saw. There are special PVC saws that work best but a hack saw will also work for this. After you have made a cut, remove the debris from inside of the pipe with a utility knife or a file.

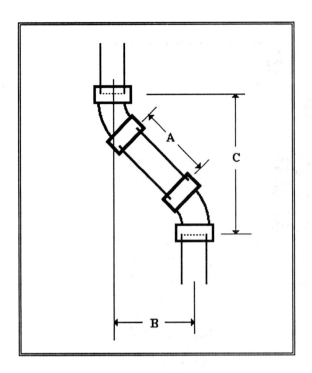

The figure above and the table below may be of some assistance in calculating vertical and horizontal offsets with 45 degree elbows. Dry fitting pipe is a good method as well.

A	B	C
Pipe Length	**Lateral Offset**	**Vertical**
between	between	distance between
two 45 degree	centerlines	pipes assuming
fittings	of vertical pipes	1 3/4 insertion
		for each pipe
inches	inches	inches
0	6.00	10.00
1	6.53	10.85
2	7.05	11.70
3	7.58	12.55
4	8.10	13.40
5	8.63	14.25
6	9.15	15.11
7	9.68	15.96
8	10.20	16.81
9	10.73	17.66
10	11.25	18.51
11	11.78	19.36
12	12.30	20.21

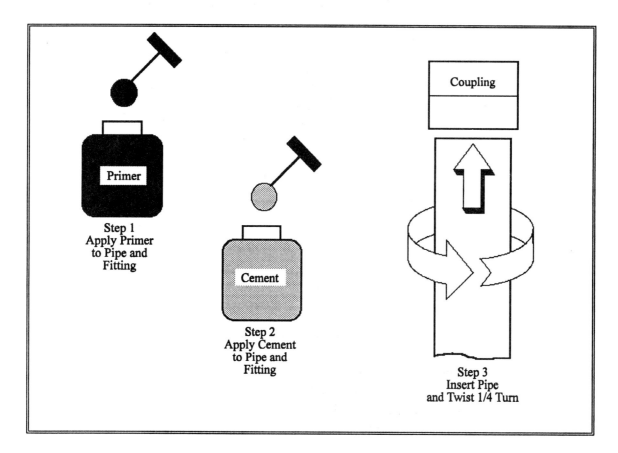

Step 1
Apply Primer
to Pipe and
Fitting

Step 2
Apply Cement
to Pipe and
Fitting

Coupling

Step 3
Insert Pipe
and Twist 1/4 Turn

Gluing Pipe

Once you have cut the pipe, you are ready to begin putting it together. The fittings are designed to slip over the pipe to form the connection within the socket of the fitting. The bond is achieved by melting both the pipe and the fitting with a solvent chemical. **WEAR YOUR GOGGLES SO AS NOT TO GET THIS SOLVENT IN YOUR EYES!**

Follow the specific instructions from the supplier of the glue. Once you apply the glue you should be prepared to immediately make the connection. Some general procedures are as follows:

Step 1. After removing debris on the pipe or the fitting, swab a solvent pipe cleaner on the inside of the fitting and on the outer edge of the pipe where it will be inserted into the fitting.

Step 2. Apply the cement all around the outside edge of the pipe and inside the socket of the fitting that the pipe will slide into.

Step 3. Push the pipe into the fitting as far as you can, 1 3/4 inches, and give it a 1/4 turn so the glue smears inside the fitting. The connection will set in just a few minutes, so you can continue on with the next fitting.

Sequence of Installation

The sequence of installing the pipe is dependent upon the layout of your home. It is generally easier to start at the suction point or riser for the system and work up. Sometimes it is convenient to make the cut through the roof and feed pipe down. Regardless of the method you use, the following general sequence will apply:

Step 1. Install the main depressurization system, whether it be the plastic sheeting in the crawl space, or the suction holes in the floor or the connection to the sump or drain tile.

Step 2. Install the piping system including the fan and insulation where it passes through cold areas but do not install the rodent screen on the discharge of the pipe until later.

Step 3. Turn on the fan and let the system run for at least five minutes to allow it to blow out any debris that may be in the pipe (e.g., plastic burrs and insulation).

Step 4. Install the rodent screen, a 1/4 inch hardware screen inserted into end of pipe and screwed into place.

Step 5. Check system for leaks and seal them (see Chapter 8).

Step 6. Adjust pressure or air flow indicator per manufacturer's instructions.

Step 7. Label the pipe on all visible portions. Labels can be purchased or you can make one of your own. An example label is shown below:

RADON VENT PIPE
DO NOT CUT OR DAMAGE

A fan is attached to this pipe and is located _____.
If this pipe must be removed for maintenance purposes,
turn off the fan. A switch for the fan is located_____,
and is connected to circuit #____ in the power panel.
After repairs have been made turn fan back on.

Step 8. Shut off the system until you have your combustion appliances (hot water heater, furnace) checked for backdrafting with and without the system on. If it backdrafts, get the flue repaired. If it doesn't, turn the system on and let it run continuously.

Step 9. Re-test radon levels in home.

Chapter 8

Sealing

How to Improve the Performance of Active Soil Depressurization Systems by Caulking and Sealing Air Leakage Points.

What is the Value of Caulking and Sealing?

When it was first determined that radon could easily enter into a home via floor cracks, around plumbing penetrations, through block walls, etc., it was theorized that one could seal all of these openings to prevent radon from seeping in. It was a good theory, but did not work in practice. Caulking and sealing cannot be relied on as a stand alone mitigation technique.

The reason that one cannot fully seal out radon is because it takes only a very small opening to account for the radon entering a home. Many openings are not readily accessible and therefore cannot be adequately sealed. Examples are beneath showers, tubs, toilets, floor to wall joints behind finished walls, etc. Granted you can get at some of the openings; however, think of radon like a balloon. If you squeeze it in one place it will bulge in another spot. If you seal at one location more radon can be forced through the openings you cannot access and seal easily.

There is still some value in caulking and sealing. The more a concrete slab can be sealed for example, the less interior air will be drawn down through the concrete slab by the depressurization system. The reduction of this lost air has many benefits:

♦   It reduces the potential for backdrafting combustion appliances.

♦   It improves the vacuum created by the depressurization system.

♦   It reduces the loss of household air which would otherwise increase the heating or air-conditioning load on the home.

♦   It reduces the electrical cost of running the fan.

All of the reasons listed above make caulking and sealing very desirable and, in the case of the backdrafting concern, mandatory. Seal at the most accessible openings and those which will have the greatest benefit.

Determining which openings and cracks should be sealed is actually very easy. You simply install the depressurization system and turn it on. Using a smoke stick and a flashlight you can see where air is being drawn into the system through openings. Once you have located these points seal them and re-check with the smoke stick.

Although some of the caulking needs will be determined after the radon system is installed, there are some areas that you can visually determine to help plan your material needs. These are:

♦   The edges and seams of a sub-membrane depressurization system (see Chapter 4).

♦   The suction points of a sub-slab depressurization system (see Chapter 6).

♦   The lid of a sump or where the depressurization piping system attaches to a drain (see Chapter 5).

♦   The exposed floor to wall joints and concrete cracks greater than 1/16 of an inch (see next section).

This chapter is devoted to methods of sealing openings in the slab that hurt the operation of an active soil depressurization system. Special sealing activities associated with the specific radon system installed are covered in the chapters describing those systems.

Note: Because caulking materials contain solvents that can generate harmful vapors, proper ventilation must be used during this operation. If you are especially sensitive to chemical fumes, you should seek the assistance of a professional. Read Chapter 10 and the Material Safety Data Sheets

Planning Step 1.   Determine what areas will probably need to be sealed.

The areas of greatest need for sealing are ranked as follows and in order of their importance:

1.   Floor to wall joint in areas nearest the suction point location.

2.   Floor cracks greater than 1/16 inch within a 5 foot radius of the suction point.

3.   Floor to wall joint areas on the far end of slab.

4.   Floor cracks greater than 1/16 inch further than 5 feet from suction points.

5.   Concrete slab control joint cracks and where separate pours of a concrete slab adjoin each other.

6.   Hollow block walls near floor suction points.

7.   Floor drains.

One should assume that when dealing with an unfinished slab area, items 1 through 5 will be necessary.

Open areas beneath bath tubs and showers are major leakage areas. These often do not need to be addressed if you have planned your system so the suction points are as far as possible from them. If they cause a concern, **silicone** caulk can be used to seal the bases to the floor to minimize the loss and still allow access to the fixtures.

When dealing with a finished area where access is limited by furred out walls and carpeting, item 1 is usually not practical. After the system is installed, the reduction of radon achieved and whether or not the drafting of the flues in the home have been affected will determine the need for the extensive work that would be involved in all sealing approaches.

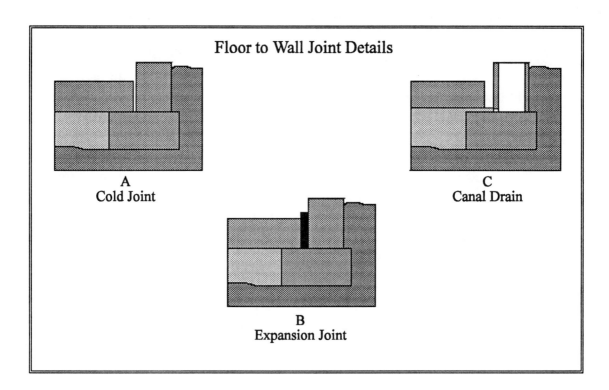

Floor to Wall Joint Details

A
Cold Joint

B
Expansion Joint

C
Canal Drain

Planning Step 2.   Determining what kind of floor to wall joint you have.

There are basically three ways that the builder of your home may have formed the joint between the concrete slab and the foundation wall. You will need to inspect your floor to determine how your home was built. The above illustration shows the three basic methods:

A. Cold Joint.   This is where the concrete slab was poured right up to the wall. As the concrete cured it contracted and pulled slightly away from the wall. Although this may look like a small crack, it is a major entry route and can be a significant air leak for a suction point located nearby. Sometimes this joint may have been grooved with a corner edging tool that will provide a 3/4 inch deep trough at the joint. To seal this area, the joint should be wire brushed and vacuumed and a bead of caulk applied which spans between the floor and the wall. If the joint does not have a groove, plan that a 11 ounce tube of polyurethane caulk will cover 12 linear feet. If there is a groove, plan a tube of caulk to cover 8 feet of perimeter length.

B. Expansion Joint.   This is where a 1/2 inch asphalt impregnated board is placed against the foundation wall and the concrete is poured up to it. This prevents attachment of the concrete to the wall so the slab can "float." This is often found in areas where expansive soils cause a heaving concern. Plan an 11-ounce tube to cover 8 feet of perimeter length.

C. Canal Drains.   This is where a 2 by 4 inch board was laid up against the foundation wall and the concrete was poured up to it. After the concrete has set, the board was removed to form a 2 inch channel along the perimeter of the slab. It is designed to either catch water that drains off the face of the wall so it can either drain to the aggregate beneath the slab, or slope towards a sump. If you have one of these, pay particular attention to how this is sealed so as not to restrict the basement's ability to get rid of drainage water. (see later in this chapter on page 8-7.)

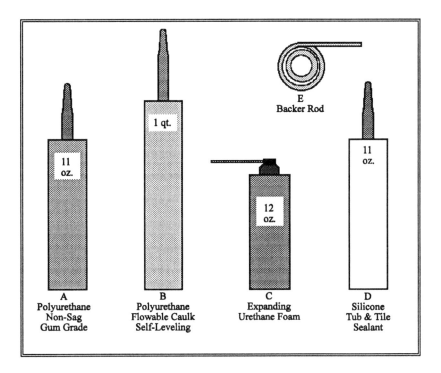

Types of Sealants and Materials to be Used

The types of sealants that you will use will depend upon what you are sealing. Regardless of the type, you must read the material safety data sheets and the manufacturers' instructions.

Polyurethane caulks are most frequently used. They are used for sealing wherever you want to make a permanent seal. Don't get these tubes wet or they will blow out when used. Keep them in a warm interior location prior to use (cold caulk is hard to dispense). It comes in two basic forms: non-sag and flowable. You use many of the sealing materials depicted in the above illustration.

Fig. A.   Non-sag or sometimes referred to as gun-grade polyurethane. This comes in 11 ounce tubes and can be dispensed with a common caulking gun. Examples for use would be concrete floor cracks, floor to wall joints and attaching plastic sheets in sub-membrane systems. This is the most widely used caulk.

Fig. B.   Flowable or self leveling polyurethane caulk is also used for permanent adhesion to concrete. It is used for sealing large areas such as a canal drain or a concrete control joint. This material flows like ketchup, so the void space must be first filled with a backer rod (E) or gun grade caulk to prevent it from being lost down through the concrete. It requires a large caulking gun.

Fig. C.   Canned urethane foams can be purchased and used to fill large void spaces as may be found with a plumbing penetration through a basement wall. Once the material expands, it sets up and can be trimmed with a bread knife. Once used, the can is thrown away.

Fig. D.   Silicon caulk is infrequently used but is the caulk of choice for sump covers, toilet bases, etc., where a permanent bond is not desirable.

Fig. E.   Backer rod is a plastic rope-like material for filling large holes prior to caulking.

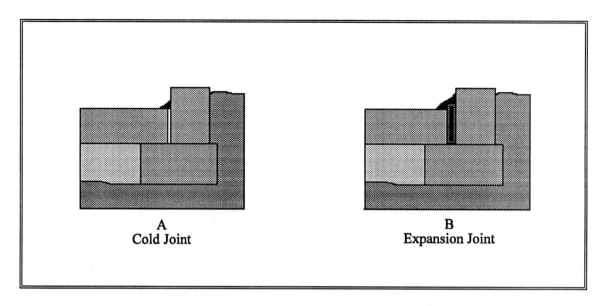

A
Cold Joint

B
Expansion Joint

Caulking Floor to Wall Joints -- Cold Joint and Expansion Joint Types

Cold Joints.   Wire brush the joint to remove loose dirt and concrete spatter. Be sure to brush down into the crack and at least an inch out onto the floor and 1 inch up the wall. *VENTILATE THE WORK AREA* (See later in this chapter and Safety Chapter 10). Use a caulking gun to apply a thick bead of caulk along the joint. *Note:* **You should be applying enough caulk so 1 tube goes no further than 12 feet.** Take a spent tube of caulk and run the butt end of it along the joint so the caulk is smoothed onto the floor and up the wall about 1/2 inch. BE CAREFUL - THIS IS STICKY, STRINGY STUFF AND WILL GET EVERYWHERE IF YOU ARE NOT CAREFUL.

Expansion Joints.   If the joint sticks up above the concrete more than 1/8 inch, then cut it off with a utility knife or a hammer and chisel. DO NOT TRY TO POUND IT DOWN (it will pop back up later on and break the seal). Don't use a grinding wheel either unless you enjoy big messes. Use a utility knife. Brush the top of the expansion joint and at least an inch out onto the floor and 1 inch up the wall. *VENTILATE THE WORK AREA* (See later in this chapter and Safety Chapter 10). Use a caulking gun to apply a thick bead of caulk along the top of the joint. *Note:* **You should be applying enough caulk so 1 tube goes no further than 8 feet.** Take a spent tube of caulk and run the butt end of it along the joint so the caulk is smoothed onto the floor and up the wall about 1/2 inch. BE CAREFUL THIS IS STICKY, STRINGY STUFF AND WILL GET EVERYWHERE IF YOU ARE NOT CAREFUL.

After applying this material be careful not to step in it or allow children or pets into the area for at least 24 hours. It will take several days for it to fully cure, but it should be tack free after 24 hours.

The important thing to remember with either type of joint to be sealed is that you should apply the caulk in a smooth consistent bead - and do not skimp. It is no problem if you put too much on because the excess will be removed when you "tool it" with the back of the caulk tube.

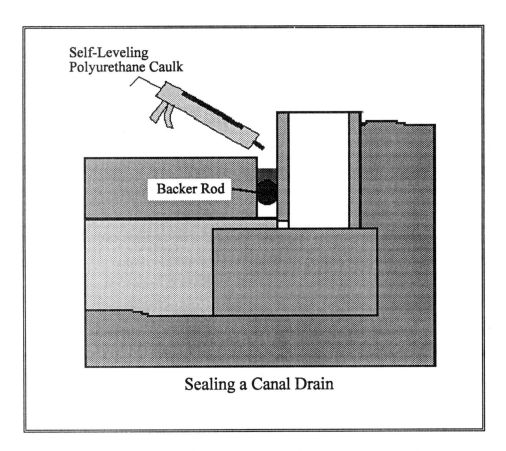

Sealing a Canal Drain

Caulking Floor to Wall Joints -- Canal Drains

The sealing of a perimeter canal drain is not a trivial affair. The key thing to remember is that this channel was placed there to collect water, and that you should not impact this feature. To do this it is important that there is a channel between the top of the slab and the caulking and there is a relief area beneath the caulking to allow for the water in the hollow block wall to drain to the sub-slab aggregate. Therefore, the caulk will be suspended between the top of the slab and the footing. This is accomplished by the use of a backer rod. A backer rod is a flexible close cell styrene material that can be purchased from most building supply stores. It comes in several widths and is coiled.

The canal drain should be cleaned out with a vacuum cleaner. The backer rod should be squeezed down into the canal. Buy the backer rod in a diameter that is slightly larger than the width of the canal. This causes the rod to fit tightly into the canal. Do not push it all of the way down. Use gun grade polyurethane caulk to seal where ends of backer rod meet at corners.

VENTILATE THE AREA. Apply flowable polyurethane caulk to the area above the backer rod. The flowable caulk is a liquid. It will flow to the edges of the canal on top of the backer rod. Make sure that you do not fill up the entire channel between the backer rod and the top of the concrete. Leave at least a 1/2 inch channel for water to collect. Make sure that this channel is directed towards a floor drain or sump in the basement.

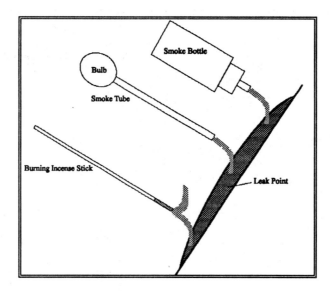

Planning Step 3.   Finding leaks.

After the system has been turned on, a suction will be created in the soil under and around the home. This vacuum catches the radon and other soil gas that would have entered the home. The better the vacuum is, the better the radon reduction will be. A better vacuum can be produced by finding and sealing leaks through a slab. You should check slab cracks, plumbing penetrations, etc., to see if air is being drawn down beneath the slab. The use of smoke saves a lot of time and expense in determining what should be caulked. Simply, if the system does not pull air down -- don't caulk it. Of course you have to do this after the system is installed. Plan on purchasing a few extra tubes of caulk beyond what you need for the floor to wall joints, so you will have enough for this touch up sealing.

Sometimes you can hear air being drawn down through a leak. However, it is best to use some type of smoke generator to detect air being drawn down through the leak. The picture above shows three different types of smoke generators that can be used for this purpose. A flashlight should be used to help see the direction that the smoke moves. If it goes down through an opening, use some caulk to reseal the opening until smoke is no longer seen to flow down. Typically polyurethane caulk is used to seal openings such as concrete cracks and floor to wall joint areas. However, where a seal may need to be broken in the future, the sump lid for example, silicone is to be used. Silicone will allow for future access to a plumbing system like a sump lid, whereas polyurethane will not.

Burning Incense Stick: An incense stick or a "punk" can be purchased and when lit it burns slowly and produces a light smoke. This can be held close to a suspected leak area to see if the smoke is drawn down. If so, seal it with caulk. Because the smoke is warm, it will want to rise on its own; therefore, it is as not as sensitive for finding leaks as the other devices. To compensate for this, put the burning end as close to the opening as possible and shine a flashlight on the smoke and look for small wisps of smoke being drawn down.

Smoke Tube and Smoke Bottle: These are devices that can be ordered from a radon catalog supply house or sometimes from a heating and ventilating equipment supplier. They are filled with titanium tetrachloride (*do not get in eyes or on skin*). When the bulb or bottle is gently squeezed a small amount of the chemical is released into the air. The chemical forms a hydrochloric acid mist in the air (*do not breathe*). This makes this device more sensitive and more likely to find to leaks. Use a flashlight with these devices as well.

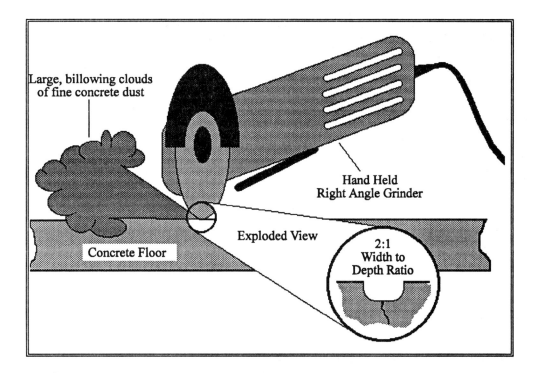

Large, billowing clouds of fine concrete dust

Hand Held Right Angle Grinder

Exploded View

Concrete Floor

2:1 Width to Depth Ratio

Floor Cracks, Slab Cold Joints and Control Joints

Floor cracks generally do not cause a significant concern unless they are close to the suction point or are very wide (greater than 1/16 of an inch). Even cracks that are greater than 1/16 of an inch may be acceptable if the crack forms a "V" in the concrete. A "V" crack is wide on the top of the concrete and narrow on the bottom so there really is not a large pathway for air leakage. An exception to this would be in some areas of the country where little or no reinforcing wire is used in the concrete (Southwest U.S. and other areas where there are no provision for frost and seismic tremors in the local building codes). In these areas when the concrete cracks it makes a wide crack, all the way through the concrete, which will present a large air leakage area. You may not be able to tell how bad a crack is until the system is turned on and a smoke stick is used to check it (see previous page 8-8).

If you do decide to seal the crack merely forcing caulk into the crack is a waste of time. You need to grind out the crack with a hand grinder. BE AWARE THIS WILL CREATE A LOT OF DUST. You should have a shop vacuum wand near the grinding wheel to catch as much as you can. You should cover furniture with drop clothes to protect it. You will have to wear gloves, goggles, a respirator and hearing protection. Grind out the crack to provide a clean surface for the caulk to adhere to and to give it the proper adhesion profile as shown in the figure above.

After the crack has been ground out ventilate the area and apply a non flowable polyurethane caulk into the crack and smooth it out flush with the top of the concrete using a scrap of cardboard or putty knife. Wipe the excess up off the floor with rags. Don't allow children or pets into the area for at least 24 hours to prevent this from being tracked around the house.

This same approached would be applied to cold joints where separate slabs are poured together. Also, if you have control joints in the concrete (straight 1/2 inch grooves in the slab) the method for sealing them is identical except that you **do not need to grind** the joint. Just vacuum out the control joint and apply the caulk.

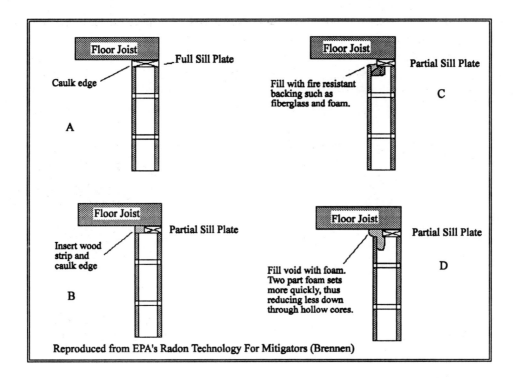

Reproduced from EPA's Radon Technology For Mitigators (Brennen)

Hollow Block Walls

Hollow block walls, if open on top, can present significant air leakage points. After turning the soil depressurization system on, you should use a smoke stick at the top of the wall to see if air is being drawn down them. If this occurs, you may have to seal the void space on the top row of block. This is especially true if so much inside air is drawn out that the combustion appliances backdraft or that the suction pressure beneath the slab is too weak to adequately reduce the radon. Sealing these areas can be difficult. The illustration above shows four different methods depending upon whether the sill plate (the board that sets on top of the block that the floor joists rest upon) covers the entire block or not, and whether you can access the block tops.

A. If the sill plate spans the width of the block, wire brush the point where the sill plate and the block meet. Then run a thin bead of polyurethane caulk along the edge. Use your smoke stick to find leaks, seal, and re-check when done.

B. If the sill plate only spans a part of the width of the block, cut a board of appropriate width and height and place over the gap not covered by the sill plate. Caulk the edge as in A above.

C. As an alternative to B, you can stuff the top of the block with fiberglass insulation to act as a backing and use expanding urethane foam to seal off the open area.

D. As an alternative to B and C, where the walls have been finished and you cannot easily get to block tops, purchase a fast setting two part urethane foam and shoot it into the block tops either from inside the home or through the exterior side of the block after 3/8 inch holes are drilled into each hollow course from the outside. If you drill holes into the block from the outside make sure you drill them above grade and seal them with polyurethane caulk when you are done.

USE VENTILATION WHEN USING THESE SEALANTS, SEE CHAPTER 10.

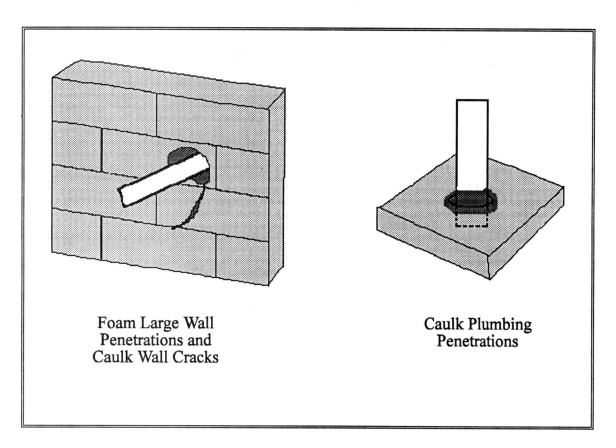

Foam Large Wall
Penetrations and
Caulk Wall Cracks

Caulk Plumbing
Penetrations

Large Wall Openings, Plumbing Penetrations and Wall Cracks

Other places that you should check with your smoke stick to find air leakage are wall and floor penetrations for utility piping.

If the gap is small around the pipe, wire brush it and caulk around the penetration with polyurethane caulk. Make sure you ventilate the area and follow the safety precautions discussed in Chapter 10.

If the gap is large, greater than 1/2 inch, you will have to stuff it first with backer rod and caulk it with polyurethane. Alternatively you can apply expanding urethane foam into the opening. Remember that this material expands to three times the volume applied. It will grow into the void that you want to seal off. Much of it will expand into the room. After it sets up you can cut the excess off with a bread knife.

You may want to check wall cracks to see if they are drawing air into them as well. If so, caulk them as you would a floor crack (grind it first).

Floor and wall coatings offer little value for reducing air leakage. The most economical approach is to find the holes and caulk them, rather than covering an entire wall or floor with a material that will crack as the wall moves.

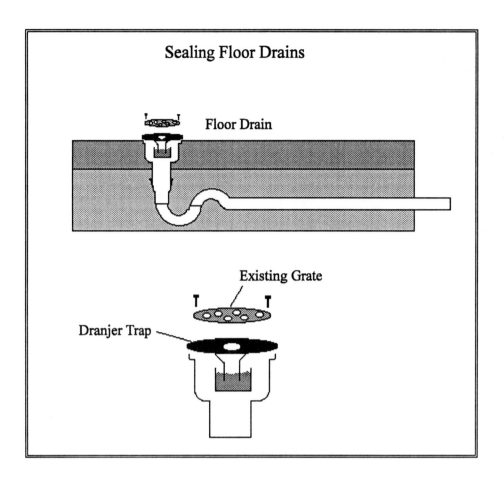

Sealing Floor Drains

Floor Drain

Existing Grate

Dranjer Trap

Floor Drains

At times air leakage can occur around and down floor drains. Use a smoke stick to determine this. Some floor drains have slip joints beneath the drain in the soil. Once a vacuum is applied to the soil, air from inside of the house could be lost. This would especially be true if a suction point was located near a sub-slab plumbing pipe.

Floor drains can be sealed with a proprietary device called a Dranjer. It is consists of a rubber sheet with a pipe in the center of it. Connected to the pipe is a small cup trap. Water can still drain from the floor through the cup trap, but the trap forms a water seal to prevent air passage. It is installed by removing the grate over the floor drain and setting the trap into it. The excess rubber is trimmed off and the grate screwed back down onto the rubber seal.

Note: DO NOT SIMPLY BLOCK OFF THE FLOOR DRAIN WITHOUT A MEANS SUCH AS THIS TO ALLOW WATER TO FLOW INTO IT.

Another use for these water traps, and others like them, are for sump lids. If your interior water drainage system was designed to allow water to weep down walls and across the floor to a sump, and you have sealed the sump with a lid, a trapped floor drain should be installed to allow for water to get into the sump. This would be the case if you have had to seal off a canal drain as was described earlier in this chapter.

Caulking and Sealing

The following is a list that you can use for determining the materials that you may need for sealing air leakage points. Note that this material would be in addition to the materials that you may need for the actual active soil depressurization system itself.

Area	Item	Feet	Ft/tube	√
Safety	Goggles/safety glasses			
	Dust mask			
	Leather gloves			
	First aid kit			
	Ventilation fan			
	Flashlight			
	Coveralls or old clothing			
Material	**Gun grade polyurethane caulk**			
	Perimeter expansion joint		8	
	Cold joints (perimeter or where slabs adjoin)		12	
	Control joints		10	
	Floor cracks		12	
	Wall cracks		12	
	Flowable caulk			
	Perimeter canal drain 2 inch by 1/2 inch volume		10	
	Backer rod			
	Perimeter canal drain			
	Other large openings (oversize so it squishes in)			
	Silicone caulk			
	For sealing around bath tubs, etc.		12	
	Expanding foam			
	Holes in walls, etc. (one can will expand to 350 cubic inches)			
	Drain trap			
Tools	Smoke stick			
	Hand grinder with composite wheel suitable for concrete			
	Caulking gun			
	Wire brush			
	Shop vacuum			
	Drop clothes			
	Broom & dust pan			
	Trash container			
	Utility knife			
	Rags			

Summary

Relative to the installation of the caulking and sealant material, the only advice that can be provided is:

♦   Not all openings need to be sealed. Seal the ones that show smoke being drawn down.

♦   Ventilate the area very well when applying the caulking.

♦   Use polyurethane caulking unless you are sealing something that you may have to remove in the future such as a toilet base. In that case use silicone caulk.

♦   Carefully follow the manufacturer's instructions carefully, and obtain **and read** the Material Safety Data Sheets before proceeding (see Chapter 10).

♦   Keep kids and animals away from caulking so they do not track it around the house.

Chapter 9

Combining Radon Mitigation Systems Together

Where More Than One Foundation Type Exists

and

Discussion of Other Mitigation Techniques

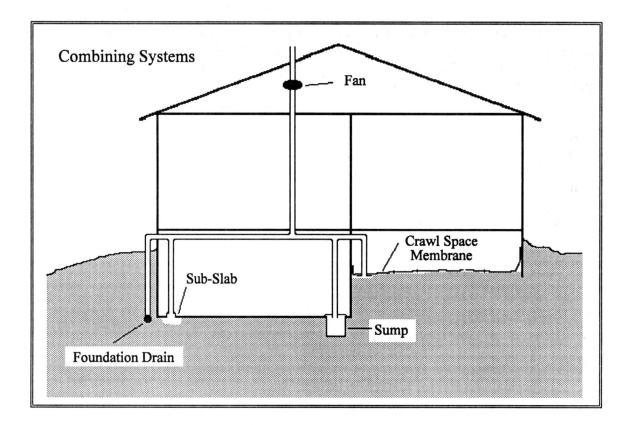

Combining Systems

Fan

Crawl Space
Membrane

Sub-Slab

Sump

Foundation Drain

Combining Mitigation Approaches

If your home is built completely over a crawl space, or completely over a basement, or completely as a slab-on-grade home, the techniques that have been described in Chapters 4 through 8 can be applied as described. However, there are often times that a house has both a crawl space and a basement, or both a crawl space and a slab-on-grade slab. The question is how do you approach these more complex foundation designs?

The good news is that the specific systems previously described can be installed and connected to a common depressurization system and fan. This will save considerable cost compared to a separate piping and fan system for each foundation type. However, in order to tie these different mitigation systems together, you will need to plan your piping accordingly.

The illustration above shows how several systems can be connected together. The number of systems and the exact location of the connections will depend on your specific house but the following are a list of commonly connected systems:

1. Sump depressurization and crawl space. Often the sump is found near the wall separating the crawl space from the basement. Both systems are to be installed with their own separate risers from the plastic sheeting and from the sump lid. The two risers should be connected by way of the simplest and most direct pathway. Any horizontal run should be sloped to either or both risers (i.e., towards the sump or towards the crawl space).

2. Foundation drain and crawl space. If the drain is exterior, it will generally run along the inside of the footing of the wall separating the crawl from the basement, or sometimes on the exterior of the crawl space foundation wall. The crawl and the foundation drain system can be tied together within the crawl or on the outside wall.

3. Foundation drain and sub-slab. If the foundation drain runs completely around the footprint of a basement home, a tie-in to a sub-slab point should not be necessary. However, if the drain is only around two or three sides, a sub-slab suction point may be necessary to cover a portion of the slab that does not have a drainage pipe along side it.

4. Crawl space and sub-slab. If there is both a crawl space and a basement or a crawl space and a slab-on-grade portion, consider locating the sub-slab suction point at the end of the slab that is the furthest from the crawl space. Often the vacuum applied to the plastic sheeting on the crawl space will extend well under the adjacent slab. This extension of the vacuum would eliminate the need for adding a suction point to the slab area. Do the sub-membrane system first then re-test before you install the sub-slab system. This is where a sequential process for installing multiple systems is helpful.

Phasing of Multi-Component Systems

The question that often arises in dealing with homes which may need a multiple approach is: Do I need to install all of these systems in order to reduce my radon level? The answer is often no, but sometimes it is yes. There are no good methods for predicting this. However, there is an approach used by professional mitigators to minimize the amount of unnecessary work done. This is called "phasing".

Phasing is where the individual system that has the greatest potential for reducing radon is installed first. The system is then fine tuned with as much sealing as is reasonable (see Chapter 8). Next, a short-term test device is placed in the home utilizing the methods described in Chapter 2 to determine how well the first system has worked. If the test shows an acceptable level, you are done. If the test is not acceptable, proceed to the next method until you are satisfied with the post mitigation results.

The key to phasing is to plan your depressurization piping in a manner that will allow you to easily extend it to the next system that **may be** installed. The other key to phasing systems is to determine which single technique will provide the biggest reduction. The following relative ranking should provide some guidance. To make two techniques work in concert with each other, run the depressurization piping for your primary system as you would if it were the only system to be installed. The only difference would be that you would install a tee with a cap on it so a second system could be easily connected to it.

Relative Ranking of Effectiveness of Reduction Techniques

1. **Crawl Space Depressurization**

2. **Sump Depressurization**

3. **Exterior Foundation Drain**

4. **Sub-Slab Suction Points**

The relative rankings of the techniques above are guidelines and not hard and fast rules. A crawl space that is attached to a basement generally represents a large entry point for radon and is an area that always has to be treated to adequately reduce the radon. In some cases a vacuum drawn under a plastic sheet in a crawl space that has been sealed well will draw radon from beneath an adjacent slab, even when the slab is at a lower elevation than the crawl space.

An interior sump or a foundation drain approach will provide a better distribution of the applied vacuum under a slab than one or two suction points in a slab. Of course, if there is a crawl space adjacent to the slab, go after it first but make provisions to be able to tie into the sump or drain line.

If there is no crawl space or drainage system the choice is obviously sub-slab depressurization. The fact that it is listed last should not diminish your confidence in this measure. It is very effective but may require several suction points to accomplish the full reduction.

Other Mitigation Techniques

There are mitigation techniques that can be used other than those detailed in this book. They are techniques that are generally used in the rare case when the basic Crawl, Drainage, or Sub-Slab Systems do not fully reduce the radon. They are also used if there are other problems with the house such as other indoor pollutants or water drainage problems. These approaches have been left out of this book, either because their installation is more complex than that which can be handled by the typical home repairman or they could present health risks or high operating costs if not properly installed. This is where a professional mitigator is the most valuable. Those who have been trained at recognized training centers and have passed the EPA Contractor's Proficiency Exam are aware of the peculiar aspects of these other systems.

If the homeowner wishes to obtain information on this, the voluminous reference below may be obtained from your local EPA office.

> *"Radon Reduction Techniques for Detached Houses - Technical Guidance (second edition)" U.S. EPA Publication "EPA/625/5-87-019"*

This document was published in 1988 and does not include all of the most current approaches and may not be universally available. A new edition is scheduled to be issued late 1993 or early 1994.

The following is a list of some of the techniques that require specialized skills:

Method	Advantages	Disadvantages
Heat Recovery Ventilation	Can dilute other indoor air contaminants. Applicable when levels of radon are 8 pCi/L or less.	Expensive and difficult to install. Can add significant costs to heating and cooling bills.
Block Wall Depressurization	Can reduce radon infiltration by creating a vacuum on the blockwalls.	High potential for back drafting combustion appliances if the openings in the block tops and sides are not well sealed.

Baseboard Depressurization	Can reduce radon by creating a vacuum within a channel built over the floor-wall joint. Can be used for basement de-watering as well.	Difficult to install properly. If not done right both back drafting and drainage system problems can occur.
House Pressurization	Can reduce radon by blowing air into home.	Can result in high heating and cooling bills, and introduce allergens into home.
Basement Pressurization	Can reduce radon by blowing air from upstairs into basement.	This can back draft fireplaces and combustion appliances as well as increase building utility costs.
Soil Pressurization	Can reduce radon by blowing air from outside to beneath a slab in order to force the radon away from the house.	Can sometimes increase the radon entry into the building, and its effectiveness can vary with frost or rain content of soil around the house. The soil depressurization techniques described in this manual are generally more reliable.
Crawl Space Depressurization	Reduces radon in home by using a fan to suck air out of the crawl space without the use of a plastic membrane.	This can cause significant house air to be drawn down into crawl space. The potential for back drafting is high with these systems and can increase building utility bills.

Next to the active soil depressurization techniques described in this book (which comprise more than 90% of the mitigation approaches used in the U.S. today), the heat recovery ventilator is the next most used. Its application is best suited for reducing other indoor air quality concerns or when the active soil depressurization systems have reduced to close 4 pCi/L and just a little dilution air is needed to finish the reduction.

In any event, do not attempt the techniques described in the previous table unless you have consulted with a professional radon mitigator, or if you desire give the authors a call. Also in the appendix of this manual is a copy of the U.S. EPA's Consumers Guide that can explain these systems and provide some cost factors as well.

Chapter 10

General Safety Precautions and

Backdrafting Concerns

General Safety Precautions

Performing the repairs described in this manual will expose a person to many risks. Using power drills, hammer drills, digging holes, working in confined spaces and working with solvent containing caulks and glues present many injury opportunities. The risks are greatly minimized if one uses caution and does not attempt anything they are neither comfortable nor experienced in doing. This chapter is designed to point out some of the potential hazards and to offer advice as to how to avoid these. Most accidents occur because of poor planning and haste. Think first, assemble your materials and take your time. Remember that although radon levels are certainly a concern, they present a long-term exposure risk and do not require hasty actions on the part of the homeowner. A few general pieces of advice are:

1.   Plan and design your system at least two weeks prior to performing the work. It will take a couple weeks to obtain the special materials needed.

2.   Assemble everything before starting - especially your safety equipment.

3.   If you need to complete the actual installation sooner than a few weeks, such as in a real estate transaction, then you are probably better off calling a professional. Professional mitigators have all the right equipment inventoried and can generally complete most repairs in one day. To quote one of the contributors of this manual, "The only difference between an amateur and a professional is the price of his tools and the time it takes to do the job." *Allow yourself sufficient time.*

4.   Arrange to have a helper work with you. It is a lot easier to have someone hold the other end of the pipe as you run it, but **more** importantly if one worker gets hurt, the other can call for help.

5.   Don't do anything you are **not** trained to do! Don't run your own 110 volt system unless you are a trained electrician. There are alternatives such as hiring an electrician or using packaged low voltage systems.

6.   Read all the instructions and Material Safety Data Sheets (called MSDS) provided by the suppliers of the equipment caulks and glues. Ask for the specific MSDS's at the information center of the hardware store you are buying materials from.

7.   Remember no one ever planned to have an accident.

The majority of the potential accidents that can occur are minor (if you are careful). The potential for cuts and bruises is high, especially if you find yourself belly crawling through a crawl space filled with nails, busted glass and an occasional rattlesnake. These can be avoided with protective clothing such as gloves, safety goggles and coveralls. If you don't have these **get them** before starting work. They'll come in handy for other home improvement projects as well.

The primary areas that need specific protection are your skin, eyes, hands, ears and lungs. The following illustration depicts the basic and most fashionable attire for the do-it-yourself mitigator.

Task and Recommended Safety Gear

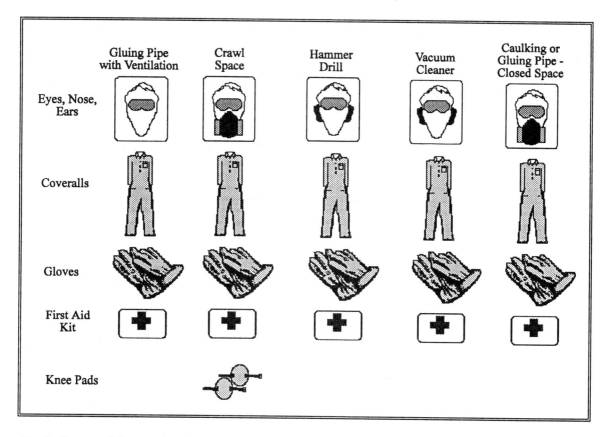

Basic Personal Protective Gear

The illustration above shows the minimum requirement of personal safety gear for different tasks that you may be performing. Notice that in all of the operations cited above each visual list the following items are always used:

1.   Safety Goggles. These protect your eyes from glue that can drip into them when applying it to a fitting overhead. They also protect your eyes from those wires and nails that are always hanging down in dimly lit crawl spaces and not easily seen. Goggles also protect you from the flying bits of concrete when operating hand and concrete hammer drills. They are also useful when caulking in closed spaces and when you wipe the side of your face with a sleeve that has caulk gobbed on it. **Wear safety goggles all of the time while working.**

NEVER wear contacts while doing this type of work. Chemical fumes from the caulks and glues irritate your eyes. However the biggest concern is when chemicals are splashed into an eye. If this happens some of the material can get behind the contact lenses and prevent the eye from being quickly and thoroughly washed out. Safety goggles can be purchased that will fit over your glasses. **Don't wear contact lenses.**

2.   Coveralls. Durable outerwear offers excellent protection from the debris found in crawl spaces, the grunge found in sumps and the insulation in the attic. Although an old pair of pants and work shirt will help, coveralls offer more protection since they are one piece. The problem with a shirt and a pair of pants is that the shirt comes out and then your mid-section is exposed. Pants will scoop up dirt as you belly crawl through the crawl area.

3. Gloves. A well fitting pair of leather gloves are a necessity for protecting your hands from sharp objects. Sharp objects are found everywhere in this work, whether it be in crawl spaces, pulling dirt from a suction pit through a basement slab, or when your drill slips off the screw you're driving in. Of course these won't protect you from cutting a finger if you tangle with a saw, but that goes back to being familiar and careful with your equipment. Of course, gloves offer no protection if you do not have them on. Buy a pair of gloves that are not too big and clumsy. If they are too big, you will not be able to pick up anything and they will soon be off and in a corner. A tight fitting pair of leather gloves works best (ropin' gloves).

Gloves can cause problems while caulking if you get caulk on the glove. With a glove you cannot feel the caulk; therefore, you are not apt to clean it off before you smear it on something you touch. The best advice is to wear good leather gloves. Take your time caulking and do not get it all over yourself. Be prepared to throw the gloves away if you're not careful with the caulk and glue.

4. First Aid Kit. A first aid kit that has disinfectant, small and large butterfly bandages, and knuckle bandages is mandatory. Make sure that there is running water available to flush an eye with if something spills into it. If you are entering a confined area such as crawl space that could have spiders and snakes in them, don't rely on some of the patent medicines that are available. Don't go in if you feel these critters are in there. Call a professional pest exterminator or call your local extension office to find out how you can drive them out. Remember once you are face to face with a rattlesnake or a skunk, there is not a lot of freedom of movement to make a hasty retreat. The best thing to do is to shine a lot of light into the crawl space before entering and to make a lot of noise as you go in to scare them away.

5. Knee Pads. These are handy for crawl space work since you will be supporting half of your weight by your knees. There are few things as painful as a nail through the knee because not only do you hurt your knee, but you also whack your head when you react to the pain.

6. Head Protection. Wear something on your head. A hard hat is best, but when you are bent over into a sump or are in a crawl they are hard to keep on. If you are not accustomed to wearing one they can limit your range of vision. A bike helmet works well, too. It even has a chin-strap to keep it in place. At least, wear a snug fitting heavy baseball hat to soften a blow when you bump into a floor joist.

7. Ear Protection. Hammer drills, electric drills and shop vacuums create more noise than you think, especially if they are going all at once. Get some of the soft insertable, and disposable, foam ear plugs. You can also purchase "ear-muff" style ear protectors. However, the foam ear plugs provide good protection and are more comfortable to wear.

Remember: **Prevention is cheap compared to fixing bodily damage.** As an example, a short visit to the emergency room will cost at least $150.00 for a minor laceration. Compared to this, a $15.00 pair of gloves is a good investment.

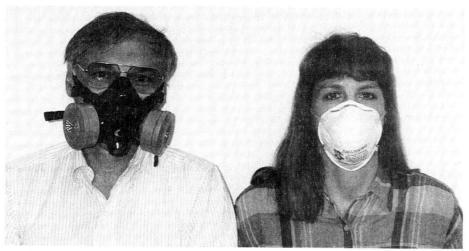

A	B
Half Face Negative	Half Face
Air Respirator	Disposable Respirator

Respirator Protection

The above picture shows two alien looking creatures wearing different types of half face respirators. These are designed to offer different levels of protection from breathing air borne particulate and chemical vapors. The next section, on ventilation, will describe a more practical way of protecting yourself from most respiratory hazards. However, you may find yourself in an area where you do not know the hazards when you enter it. Increased ventilation may deal with one problem but stir up dirt and dust at the same time. Respirators are good devices to have for the investigation side of your project as well as the actual installation.

A. **Half-face negative air respirator.** This is a respirator that can be fitted with many different types of filters against different types of contaminants. They are called negative air because you have to suck air in through the filters as you breathe.

Note: NOT EVERYONE HAS THE LUNG CAPACITY TO WEAR THESE FOR A PROLONGED BASIS WHILE ENGAGED IN PHYSICAL ACTIVITY. You should **NOT** wear one of these unless your doctor has approved it. They should fit snugly. You should not rely on them to work in an area with asbestos.

IF YOU FIND ASBESTOS - LEAVE IT TO A PROFESSIONAL. Once asbestos gets in your lungs, it stays there and continues to do damage.

B. **Half- face negative air disposable respirator.** These often can be found in hardware stores. They operate the same as respirator A above, except that they are not as difficult to breathe through. They do not provide the same level of protection as respirator A. They are suitable if you have not had a physical, or just need something keep the dust out. However, never depend upon these for full protection against hazardous materials such as asbestos.

When purchasing these devices, look for cartridges for respirator A, or the actual mask in the case of respirator B, that will provide protection against dusts and organic chemical fumes.

Protection from:	Respirator A Cartridges NIOSH /MSHA ID #s	Protection From:	Respirator B Masks NIOSH ID #
Radon decay products, asbestos	TC-21C-231 TC - 21C-346	Nuisance level dusts	TC-21C-132
Organic vapors	TC-23C-107 TC-23C-661	Nuisance level organic vapors	TC-21C-234
Radon decay products, asbestos, and organic vapors	TC-23C-458 TC-23C-672		

Ventilate The Work Area

It is best not to let the vapors from the caulking or glues to build up rather than wearing a respirator at all times. The best way to prevent vapor build up is to ventilate the work area. The following illustration shows one method for doing this:

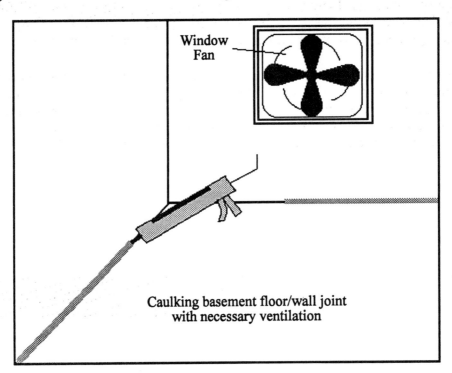

Window Fan

Caulking basement floor/wall joint
with necessary ventilation

Use a window fan, or blowers that can be rented, or temporarily hook up the depressurization fan to either supply or exhaust air into the work area. Caulk will out-gas as it cures so continue ventilating while the caulk dries. If you dilute the vapors and remove them from the house as they are released from the caulk or glue, you may not need to wear a respirator. Remember, don't ventilate an area where asbestos is present. This will stir it up and create a significant health hazard. Again if you find asbestos, **STOP AND CALL** a professional trained in asbestos abatement. Ventilation will also reduce the radon concentrations in the work area as well. This is particularly important when you work in confined areas such as crawl spaces, sumps or when you first cut the suction pit through the concrete floor. The only time you will need to shut fans off will be when you perform air leak smoke tests. The air flow from the fan will disrupt the smoke direction.

Chemical Hazards:

The materials described in this manual are not particularly hazardous unless:

A.   You very sensitive or allergic to some chemical vapors.

B.   You don't follow directions and misuse them.

To avoid problems you should read the instructions for the material's use very carefully (caulks, glues, foams, etc.). You should also obtain what is called the "Material Safety Data Sheet" (MSDS). By Federal Law all manufacturers must supply these sheets. If you are not provided one, demand it. If you are still not provided one, shop elsewhere. An example of the type of information that can be obtained from these follows this page. It describes the chemical content as well as the health risks known about the specific material. Use precautions, flammability and other good information provided on the sheet. There is first aid information if an accident does occur from your use or due to accidental ingestion by children or pets. Read the MSDS thoroughly before you use the material and always ventilate the work area.

Note: The example that follows this page may look a little different from what you receive from your supplier. MSDS sheets can vary in format. Regardless of the format, the same type of information can be found on first aid, flammability and toxicity. This information is required to be made available to you by federal law. Don't just shop for price. Look at the hazards that may be associated with a specific product to determine if paying a little more will reduce your health risk.

Material Safety Data Sheet

May be used to comply with
OSHA's Hazard Communication Standard,
29 CFR 1910.1200. Standard must be
consulted for specific requirements.

U.S. Department of Labor

Occupational Safety and Health Administration
(Non-Mandatory Form)
Form Approved
OMB No. 1218-0072

IDENTITY (As Used on Label and List)

Note: Blank spaces are not permitted. If any item is not applicable, or no information is available, the space must be marked to indicate that.

Section I

Manufacturer's Name	Emergency Telephone Number
Address (Number, Street, City, State, and ZIP Code)	Telephone Number for Information
	Date Prepared
	Signature of Preparer (optional)

Section II — Hazardous Ingredients/Identity Information

Hazardous Components (Specific Chemical Identity; Common Name(s))	OSHA PEL	ACGIH TLV	Other Limits Recommended	% (optic.

Section III — Physical/Chemical Characteristics

Boiling Point		Specific Gravity (H_2O = 1)	
Vapor Pressure (mm Hg.)		Melting Point	
Vapor Density (AIR = 1)		Evaporation Rate (Butyl Acetate = 1)	

Solubility in Water

Appearance and Odor

Section IV — Fire and Explosion Hazard Data

Flash Point (Method Used)	Flammable Limits	LEL	UEL

Extinguishing Media

Special Fire Fighting Procedures

10 - 8

Unusual Fire and Explosion Hazards

Section V — Reactivity Data

Stability	Unstable		Conditions to Avoid
	Stable		

Incompatibility (*Materials to Avoid*)

Hazardous Decomposition or Byproducts

Hazardous Polymerization	May Occur		Conditions to Avoid
	Will Not Occur		

Section VI — Health Hazard Data

Route(s) of Entry: Inhalation?   Skin?   Ingestion?

Health Hazards (*Acute and Chronic*)

Carcinogenicity: NTP?   IARC Monographs?   OSHA Regulated?

Signs and Symptoms of Exposure

Medical Conditions
Generally Aggravated by Exposure

Emergency and First Aid Procedures

Section VII — Precautions for Safe Handling and Use

Steps to Be Taken in Case Material Is Released or Spilled

Waste Disposal Method

Precautions to Be Taken in Handling and Storing

Other Precautions

Section VIII — Control Measures

Respiratory Protection (*Specify Type*)

Ventilation	Local Exhaust		Special
	Mechanical (*General*)		Other

Protective Gloves	Eye Protection

10 - 9

Other Protective Clothing or Equipment

Work/Hygienic Practices

Other Hazards:

Electrical hazards, power tool use, and falling from heights are the other installation hazards associated with this work.

When using power tools make sure that you are using a grounded, three prong extension cord connected to a GFI (ground fault interrupter) circuit. Buy and use a GFI receptacle box that can be put in the circuit with your extension cord. Don't use a three prong to two prong plug adapter. Use at least a 15 amp rated extension cord. Don't stand in water when using power equipment around sumps and drains.

When using power tools keep the safety guards in place - for example, like these on circular saws. When using hammer drills, hold the drill in front of you so when it twists it does not turn and kick you in the legs or elsewhere. Never use the "constant on" switch of a power tool that may have one. You will either use a 1/2 inch electric drill or a right angle drill with hole saws for cutting holes through floors. Position the drill against a wall or something solid so when, not if, the saw binds, the drill handle will not slam into you or twist your wrist.

You will be climbing step ladders and going into attic spaces. Use a strong step ladder, not a chair, and stay off the top step. When going into attics make sure that you can climb back out without having to jump onto a ladder. Be careful that you walk on the ceiling joists, or lay a board out on top of the joists to support and spread out your weight while in the attic. This is safer and more comfortable. It will also prevent the drywall ceiling nails from popping out.

When climbing up on the roof use a good solid extension ladder. To keep it from sliding side to side, tie it to the roof. Place a stake in the ground at the base of each of the two feet of the ladder and tie it off to keep it from kicking out. Wear tennis shoes or some other rubber soled shoe to provide good traction on the roof. Wait for a good weather day to get up on the roof. Don't climb the roof in the snow or in the rain.

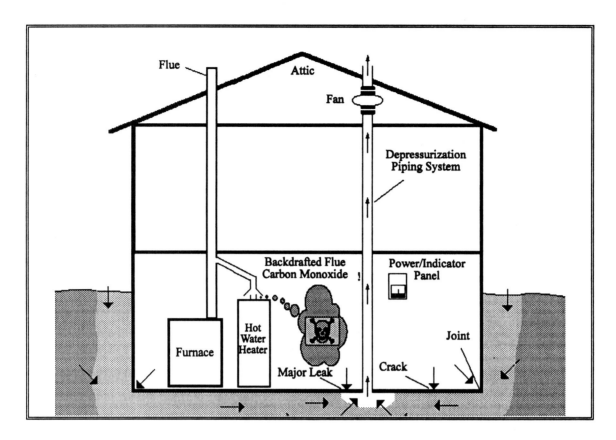

Backdrafting:
Possible effect on ability of combustion flues to operate properly.

Chimneys and flues are designed to vent the exhaust gases from combustion appliances safely out of the home. In most homes these gases exhaust out because the combustion gases of hot water heaters and furnaces are warm and naturally rise up the flue. This is similar to the stack effect that was discussed in Chapter 3. However, in this case, it has the beneficial effect of causing unwanted gases to leave the home. If there is a competing force in the building, like an exhaust fan running or an air leak into a defective radon system, the gases can be prevented from rising up the flue. If the flues cannot "draft" properly, these gases can accumulate in the home and can lead to carbon monoxide poisoning. Carbon monoxide can cause severe nerve damage and death. Like radon, carbon monoxide is colorless, odorless, and invisible. You cannot detect this deadly gas with your human senses.

It is possible that even a properly installed system could add to the forces that compete with the proper venting of the flue. This is especially true if you have not sealed large openings in a slab, you have not sealed your sump well, there is an un-trapped floor drain emptying into it, or you did not seal the plastic in the crawl space well. The EPA states in its radon mitigation standards that all mitigation systems must be tested for backdrafting immediately after installation.

Testing for backdrafting and the presence of carbon monoxide is not a trivial matter. It should be done by a professional home inspector or qualified heating and cooling technician. *A simple kitchen match test is not adequate.*

If a backdrafting problem is detected it very well may be due to a faulty flue rather than the radon system itself. Therefore, it is felt by the authors that the backdraft test should be done whether you fix your house or not. You should also consider having this repeated every couple of years to insure that your flues have not changed or become clogged. Also, if you decide to hire a contractor to install your radon system, rather than installing it yourself, make sure that this test is done before they leave. Your safety depends upon it.

Another consideration is that the radon system was installed properly and the combustion flue worked properly as it should. The ability of a flue to draft properly would certainly change if: a child broke the depressurization piping, a repair person working in the crawl space cut the plastic and did not repair it, or a sump lid was removed without shutting off the fan. When major breaches in the piping like this occur, the potential for backdrafting significantly increases. Labels recommended in this book should be placed in a easily visible location for maintenance people and future homeowners to see. Make sure that the label instructs the reader that they should shut off the depressurization system fan before making major breaks in the system. This is also why the system indicators described in Chapter 7 should be reliable and placed in a location that you will see frequently. Don't cut corners on the quality of the indicator.

It is recommended that you:

1.   Install your system as best you can.

2.   Temporarily turn it on long enough to perform the smoke tests to finish the sealing.

3.   Turn it off. Arrange for an inspector to come to the home to test the flue.

4.   After the flue has passed the backdraft test, turn the system on. Now start your post-mitigation test. If the flue backdrafts **turn the system off** until it can be fixed by a competent heating contractor.

Don't ignore this important step. The authors are not saying this to satisfy their attorney's concerns, but rather, that many "marginal flues" exist whose problems have not been caused by radon systems. However, the extra suction could be just enough to amplify an existing problem. We have seen three homes with backdraft problems out of a few thousand. This may seem like too small of a percentage to be concerned about, *unless it is your home that is bad!*

Last Bit Of Advice

Our goal in this chapter wasn't scare you to death. If you take your time and use your head you will probably do a better job than many contractors. We have seen some strange and dangerous designs and installations over the years installed by contractors who have **not** been specifically trained in radon mitigation. If you decide to use a contractor, because you are concerned about some of these issues, use the guidances in this book to make sure that they observe the same precautions as you would - if you were to do it. Remember that training and certification is only a requirement in a **minority** of states in the U.S. So lets be careful of what we do and whom we trust with our health and safety.

Appendix

*Safety Equipment, Tools, and Material Checklist
Listing of Materials and Suppliers*

U.S. EPA's Citizen's Guide to Radon

U.S. EPA's Consumer's Guide to Radon

*U.S. EPA's Radon Contractor Proficiency Program -
Interim Radon Mitigation Standards*

SAFETY EQUIPMENT
TOOLS
and MISCELLANEOUS MATERIALS

AREA	ITEM	√
SAFETY	Protective eye wear (safety glasses or goggles)	
	Head protection (hard hat or bump cap)	
	Hearing protection (earplugs or industrial earmuffs)	
	Respiratory protection (half face mask or dust/mist respirator mask)	
	Hand protection (industrial light duty leather gloves)	
	First aid kit	
	Ventilation-large window type fan	
	Coveralls or old clothing	
	Knee pads	
TOOLS	Shop vacuum-2 horsepower *	
	2" Vacuum cleaner suction hose-2 lengths of hose (at least 6' in length) *	
	Electric rotary hammer drill *	
	1/4 inch by 12 inch bit for hammer drill *	
	3/8 inch by 12 inch bit for hammer drill *	
	Portable 3/8" hand drill with assorted bits *	
	Electric hand grinder *	
	Heavy duty extension cords (2)	
	Caulking gun	
	Flashlight	
	Work lights (2)	
	25' measuring tape	
	Utility knife	
	Utility hammer	
	Assorted screw drivers	
	Assorted wrenches	
	24" Level	
	PVC pipe saw	
	Hole saw	
	Broom and dust pan	
	Shovels	
	Rake	
	Trash can	
	Wire brush	
MISC.	Duct tape	
	Plumber's putty	
	PVC or ABS pipe cleaner	
	PVC or ABS glue	
	Assorted self tapping sheet metal screws	
	Clean rags	
	Paper towels	
	Drop cloth	

* These items should be available at most home rental centers.

MAIL ORDER RADON PRODUCT PROVIDERS
that wish to deal directly with the public.

PROFESSIONAL DISCOUNT SUPPLY, INC.
525 EAST FOUNTAIN BLVD. SUITE 201
COLORADO SPRINGS, COLORADO 80907
Orders and Technical Assistance: 800-688-5776
FAX: 719-632-9607

RADON CONTROL, INC.
511 INDUSTRIAL DRIVE
CARMEL, INDIANA 46032
OFFICE: 317-846-7486
FAX: 317-846-5882

PINEDA PRODUCTS, INC.
425A PINEDA COURT
MELBOURNE, FLORIDA 32940
OFFICE: 407-254-7785
FAX: 407-259-7979

Note that plumbing and hardware stores carry many of the materials to perform the work described in this manual. If you purchased this manual from one of these stores they probably carry a full line of radon reduction products in addition to pipe, glue and caulking.

MATERIAL LISTING
PRODUCT PROVIDER LISTING

ITEM	HW	PDS	RCI	PP	
IN-LINE CENTRIFUGAL RADON FANS					
LOW VOLTAGE FAN SYSTEM FOR SELF INSTALLATION					
KTA-150		X	X	X	
120 VOLT FANS FOR INSTALLATION BY ELECTRICIAN					
FANTECH FR-150		X	X	X	
GAUGES AND ALARMS FOR SYSTEM MONITORING					
KTA TOTAL SYSTEM		X	X	X	
DWYER MARK II MANOMETER		X	X	X	
FLEX-TUBE U-TUBE MANOMETER			X	X	
MAGNEHELIC DIFFERENTIAL PRESSURE GAUGE			X	X	
CAULK-GUN GRADE:					
GEOCEL 2100	X	X	X	X	
VULKEM 116				X	
SILICONE CAULK	X				
BACKER ROD	X	X	X	X	
SELF LEVELING SEALANT:					
SONOLASTIC SL-1		X			
VULKEM VS-30			X		
VULKEM 45				X	
CROSS LAMINATED POLYETHYLENE FOR CRAWL SPACES					
(Use 4 mil, high density, cross laminated white polyethylene)					
TU-TUF (20' X 100')		X			
RADON RETARDER (22' X 100')			X		
RUFCO (22' X 100')				X	

PDS-PROFESSIONAL DISCOUNT SUPPLY, INC.
RCI-RADON CONTROL, INC.
PP-PINEDA PRODUCTS, INC.
HW-HARDWARE AND BUILDING MATERIAL STORES

MATERIAL LISTING
PRODUCT PROVIDER LISTING

ITEM	HW	PDS	RCI	PP	
DOWNSPOUT VENTING SYSTEMS					
4" X 3" METAL DOWNSPOUT		X			
SQUARE TUBING PVC SYSTEM			X		
4" X 4 " ROUND TO SQUARE PIPE ADAPTER	X	X	X		
OTHER MITIGATION PRODUCTS					
6" X 4" RUBBER REDUCERS FOR FAN INSTALLATION	X	X	X	X	
RADON MITIGATION SYSTEM LABELS		X	X	X	
6" X 4" PVC DWV REDUCER USED FOR SUB SLAB SUCTION HOLE		X			
SUMP COVER LIDS		X	X		
ROOF FLASHINGS/ROOF JACKS	X	X	X		
DRANJER RETRO-FIT FLOOR DRAIN SEALS		X	X	X	
COSMETIC FLANGES FOR 4" PVC PIPE		X	X		
J HOOK FOR PVC PIPE INSTALLATION		X	X		
DRAIN CHECK FOR PERIMETER DRAIN INSTALLATIONS		X	X		
FIRE BARRIER PRODUCTS FOR FIRE WALL PENETRATIONS	X	X	X	X	
HYDRO-SEP FOR PROTECTING FAN FROM WATER		X			
CLASS I URETHANE FOAM SEALANT	X	X	X		
PVC OR ABS PIPING	X				
PIPE STRAPPING	X				
FAN HOUSINGS		X	X	X	
RADON TESTING KITS					
CHARCOAL CANISTERS	X	X	X	X	
ALPHA TRACK DEVICES	X	X	X	X	
RADON IN WATER TEST KITS		X	X	X	

PDS-PROFESSIONAL DISCOUNT SUPPLY, INC.
RCI-RADON CONTROL, INC.
PP-PINEDA PRODUCTS, INC.
HW-HARDWARE AND BUILDING MATERIAL STORES

United States Environmental Protection Agency	U.S. Department Of Health and Human Services	U.S. Public Health Service
Air And Radiation (ANR-464)	402-K92-001	May 1992

&EPA A Citizen's Guide To Radon (Second Edition)

The Guide To Protecting Yourself And Your Family From Radon

EPA Recommends:

▼ *Test your home for radon–it's easy and inexpensive.*

▼ *Fix your home if your radon level is 4 picocuries per liter (pCi/L) or higher.*

▼ *Radon levels less than 4 pCi/L still pose a risk, and in many cases may be reduced.*

Radon is estimated to cause thousands of cancer deaths in the U.S. each year.

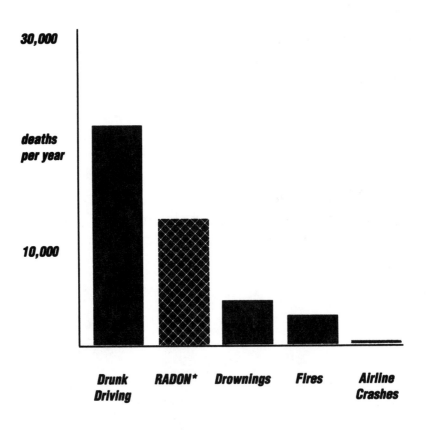

* Radon is estimated to cause about 14,000 deaths per year–however, this number could range from 7,000 to 30,000 deaths per year. The numbers of deaths from other causes are taken from 1990 National Safety Council reports.

Radon is a cancer-causing, radioactive gas.

You can't see radon. And you can't smell it or taste it. But it may be a problem in your home.

Radon is estimated to cause many thousands of deaths each year. That's because when you breathe air containing radon, you can get lung cancer. In fact, the Surgeon General has warned that radon is the second leading cause of lung cancer in the United States today. Only smoking causes more lung cancer deaths. **If you smoke and your home has high radon levels, your risk of lung cancer is especially high.**

Radon can be found all over the U.S.

Radon comes from the natural (radioactive) breakdown of uranium in soil, rock and water and gets into the air you breathe. Radon can be found all over the U.S. It can get into any type of building – homes, offices, and schools – and build up to high levels. But you and your family are most likely to get your greatest exposure at home. That's where you spend most of your time.

You should test for radon.

Testing is the only way to know if you and your family are at risk from radon. EPA and the Surgeon General recommend testing all homes below the third floor for radon. EPA also recommends testing in schools.

Testing is inexpensive and easy – it should only take a few minutes of your time. Millions of Americans have already tested their homes for radon.

You can fix a radon problem.

There are simple ways to fix a radon problem that aren't too costly. Even very high levels can be reduced to acceptable levels.

HOW DOES RADON GET INTO YOUR HOME?

Any home may have a radon problem.

Radon is a radioactive gas. It comes from the natural decay of uranium th[at is] found in nearly all soils. It typically moves up through the ground to the a[ir] above and into your home through cracks and other holes in the foundati[on]. Your home traps radon inside, where it can build up. Any home may have [a] radon problem. This means new and old homes, well-sealed and drafty homes, and homes with or without basements.

Radon from soil gas is the main cause of radon problems. Sometimes radon enters the home through well water (see page 8). In a small number of homes, the building materials can give off radon, too. However, building materials rarely cause radon problems by themselves.

RADON GETS IN THROUGH:

1. Cracks in solid floors.

2. Construction joints.

3. Cracks in walls.

4. Gaps in suspended floors.

5. Gaps around service pipes.

6. Cavities inside walls.

7. The water supply.

Nearly 1 out of every 15 homes in the U.S. is estimated to have elevated radon levels. Elevated levels of radon gas have been found in homes in your state. Contact your state radon office (see page 15) for general information about radon in your area. While radon problems may be more common in some areas, any home may have a problem. The only way to know about your home is to test.

Radon can be a problem in schools and workplaces, too. Ask your state radon office (see page 15) about radon problems in schools and workplaces in your area.

HOW TO TEST YOUR HOME

You can't see radon, but it's not hard to find out if you have a radon problem in your home. All you need to do is test for radon. Testing is easy and should only take a few minutes of your time.

The amount of radon in the air is measured in "picocuries per liter of air," or "pCi/L." Sometimes test results are expressed in Working Levels (WL) rather than picocuries per liter (pCi/L). There are many kinds of low-cost "do it yourself" radon test kits you can get through the mail and in hardware stores and other retail outlets. Make sure you buy a test kit that has passed EPA's testing program or is state-certified. These kits will usually display the phrase "Meets EPA Requirements." If you prefer, or if you are buying or selling a home, you can hire a trained contractor to do the testing for you. Make certain you hire an EPA-qualified or state-certified radon tester. Call your state radon office (see page 15) for a list of these testers.

There are Two General Ways to Test for Radon:

SHORT-TERM TESTING:
The quickest way to test is with short-term tests. Short-term tests remain in your home for two days to 90 days, depending on the device. "Charcoal canisters," "alpha track," "electret ion chamber," "continuous monitors," and "charcoal liquid scintillation" detectors are most commonly used for short-term testing. Because radon levels tend to vary from day to day and season to season, a short-term test is less likely than a long-term test to tell you your year-round average radon level. If you need results quickly, however, a short-term test followed by a second short-term test may be used to decide whether to fix your home.

LONG-TERM TESTING:
Long-term tests remain in your home for more than 90 days. "Alpha track" and "electret" detectors are commonly used for this type of testing. A long-term test will give you a reading that is more likely to tell you your home's year-round average radon level than a short-term test.

How To Use a Test Kit:

Follow the instructions that come with your test kit. If you are doing a short-term test, close your windows and outside doors and keep them closed as much as possible during the test. (If you are doing a short-term test lasting just 2 or 3 days, be sure to close your windows and outside doors at least 12 hours **before** beginning the test, too. You should not conduct short-term tests lasting just 2 or 3 days during unusually severe storms or periods of unusually high winds.) The test kit should be placed in the lowest lived-in level of the home (for example, the basement if it is frequently used, otherwise the first floor). It should be put in a room that is used regularly (like a living room, playroom, den or bedroom) but **not**

Testing is easy and should only take a few minutes of your time.

your kitchen or bathroom. Place the kit at least 20 inches above the floor in a location where it won't be disturbed—away from drafts, high heat, high humidity, and exterior walls. Leave the kit in place for as long as the package says. Once you've finished the test, reseal the package and send it to the lab specified on the package right away for study. You should receive your test results within a few weeks.

EPA Recommends the Following Testing Steps:

Step 1. *Take a short-term test. If your result is 4 pCi/L or higher*, take a follow-up test (Step 2) to be sure.*

Step 2. *Follow up with either a long-term test or a second short-term test:*

- *For a better understanding of your year-round average radon level, take a long-term test.*
- *If you need results quickly, take a second short-term test.*

The higher your initial short-term test result, the more certain you can be that you should take a short-term rather than a long-term follow up test. If your first short-term test result is several times the action level—for example, about 10 pCi/L or higher—you should take a second short-term test immediately.

Step 3.
- *If you followed up with a long-term test: Fix your home if your long-term test result is 4 pCi/L or more*.*
- *If you followed up with a second short-term test: The higher your short-term results, the more certain you can be that you should fix your home. Consider fixing your home if the average of your first and second test is 4 pCi/L or higher*.*

* 0.02 Working Levels (WL) or higher.

WHAT YOUR TEST RESULTS MEAN

The average indoor radon level is estimated to be about 1.3 pCi/L, and about 0.4 pCi/L of radon is normally found in the outside air. The U.S. Congress has set a long-term goal that indoor radon levels be no more than outdoor levels. While this goal is not yet technologically achievable in all cases, most homes today *can* be reduced to 2 pCi/L or below.

Sometimes short-term tests are less definitive about whether or not your home is above 4 pCi/L. This can happen when your results are close to 4 pCi/L. For example, if the average of your two short-term test results is 4.1 pCi/L, there is about a 50% chance that your year-round average is somewhat below 4 pCi/L. However, EPA believes that any radon exposure carries some risk—no level of radon is safe. Even radon levels below 4 pCi/L pose some risk, and you can reduce your risk of lung cancer by lowering your radon level.

If your living patterns change and you begin occupying a lower level of your home (such as a basement) you should retest your home on that level.

Even if your test result is below 4 pCi/L, you may want to test again sometime in the future.

RADON AND HOME SALES

More and more, home buyers and renters are asking about radon levels before they buy or rent a home. Because real estate sales happen quickly, there is often little time to deal with radon and other issues. The best thing to do is to test for radon NOW and save the results in case the buyer is interested in them. Fix a problem if it exists so it won't complicate your home sale. If you are planning to move, call your state radon office (see page 15) for EPA's pamphlet "Home Buyer's and Seller's Guide to Radon," which addresses some common questions. During home sales:

- *Buyers often ask if a home has been tested, and if elevated levels were reduced.*

- *Buyers frequently want tests made by someone who is not involved in the home sale. Your state office (see page 15) has a list of qualified testers.*

- *Buyers might want to know the radon levels in areas of the home (like a basement they plan to finish) that the seller might not otherwise test.*

Today many homes are built to prevent radon from coming in. Your state or local area may require these radon-resistant construction features. Radon-resistant construction features usually keep radon levels in new homes below 2 pCi/L. If you are buying or renting a new home, ask the owner or builder if it has radon-resistant features.

Test your home now and save your results. If you find high radon levels, fix your home before you decide to sell it.

RADON IN WATER

Compared to radon entering the home through soil, radon entering the home through water will in most cases be a small source of risk. Radon gas can enter the home through well water. It can be released into the air you breathe when water is used for showering and other household uses. Research suggests that swallowing water with high radon levels may pose risks, too, although risks from swallowing water containing radon are believed to be much lower than those from breathing air containing radon.

While radon in water is not a problem in homes served by most public water supplies, it has been found in well water. If you've tested the air in your home and found a radon problem, and your water comes from a well, contact a lab certified to measure radiation in water to have your water tested. If you're on a public water supply and are concerned that radon may be entering your home through the water, call your public water supplier.

Radon problems in water can be readily fixed. The most effective treatm is to remove radon from the water before it enters the home. This is called point-of-entry treatment. Treatment at your water tap is called point-of-use treatment. Unfortunately, point-of-use treatment will not reduce most of th inhalation risk from radon.

Call your state office (see page 15) or the EPA Drinking Water Hotline (800-426-4791) for more information on radon in water.

If you've tested the air in your home and found a radon problem, and your water comes from a well, have your water tested.

HOW TO LOWER THE RADON LEVEL IN YOUR HOME

Since there is no known safe level of radon, there can always be some risk. But the risk can be reduced by lowering the radon level in your home.

A variety of methods are used to reduce radon in your home. In some cases, sealing cracks in floors and walls may help to reduce radon. In other cases, simple systems using pipes and fans may be used to reduce radon. Such systems are called "sub-slab depressurization," and do not require major changes to your home. These systems remove radon gas from below the concrete floor and the foundation before it can enter the home. Similar systems can also be installed in houses with crawl spaces. Radon contractors use other methods that may also work in your home. The right system depends on the design of your home and other factors.

Ways to reduce radon in your home are discussed in EPA's "Consumer's Guide to Radon Reduction." You can get a copy from your state radon office.

The cost of making repairs to reduce radon depends on how your home was built and the extent of the radon problem. Most homes can be fixed for about the same cost as other common home repairs like painting or having a new hot water heater installed. The average house costs about $1,200 for a contractor to fix, although this can range from about $500 to about $2,500.

RADON AND HOME RENOVATIONS

If you are planning any major structural renovation, such as converting an unfinished basement area into living space, it is especially important to test the area for radon before you begin the renovation. If your test results indicate a radon problem, radon-resistant techniques can be inexpensively included as part of the renovation. Because major renovations can change the level of radon in any home, always test again after work is completed.

Most homes can be fixed for about the same cost as other common home repairs.

Lowering high radon levels requires technical knowledge and special skills. You should use a contractor who is trained to fix radon problems. The EPA Radon Contractor Proficiency (RCP) Program tests these contractors. EPA provides a list of RCP contractors to state radon offices (see page 15). A contractor who has passed the EPA test will carry a special RCP identification card. A trained RCP contractor can study the radon problem in your home and help you pick the right treatment method.

Check with your state radon office for names of qualified or state certified radon contractors in your area. Picking someone to fix your radon problem is much like choosing a contractor for other home repairs – you may want to get references and more than one estimate.

If you plan to fix the problem in your home yourself, you should first contact your state radon office (see page 15) for EPA's technical guide, "Radon Reduction Techniques for Detached Houses."

You should also test your home again after it is fixed to be sure that radon levels have been reduced. Most radon reduction systems include a monitor that will alert you if the system needs servicing. In addition, it's a good idea to retest your home sometime in the future to be sure radon levels remain low.

FAN

SUBSLAB SUCTION

SEALANT

SEAL FLOOR & WALL CRACKS

SUMP SUCTION

PIPES PENETRATE BENEATH SLAB

THE RISK OF LIVING WITH RADON

Radon gas decays into radioactive particles that can get trapped in your lungs when you breathe. As they break down further, these particles release small bursts of energy. This can damage lung tissue and lead to lung cancer over the course of your lifetime. Not everyone exposed to elevated levels of radon will develop lung cancer. And the amount of time between exposure and the onset of the disease may be many years.

Like other environmental pollutants, there is some uncertainty about the magnitude of radon health risks. However, we know more about radon risks than risks from most other cancer-causing substances. This is because estimates of radon risks are based on studies of cancer in humans (underground miners). Additional studies on more typical populations are under way.

Smoking combined with radon is an especially serious health risk. Stop smoking and lower your radon level to reduce your lung cancer risk.

Children have been reported to have greater risk than adults of certain types of cancer from radiation, but there are currently no conclusive data on whether children are at greater risk than adults from radon.

Your chances of getting lung cancer from radon depend mostly on:

- *How much radon is in your home*

- *The amount of time you spend in your home*

- *Whether you are a smoker or have ever smoked*

Scientists are more certain about radon risks than risks from most other cancer-causing substances.

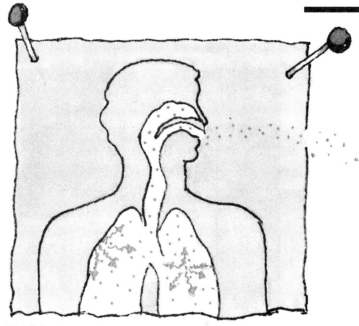

RADON RISK IF YOU SMOKE

Radon Level	If 1,000 people who smoked were exposed to this level over a lifetime. . .	The risk of cancer from radon exposure compares to. . .	WHAT TO DO: Stop Smoking and. . .
20 pCi/L	About 135 people could get lung cancer	← 100 times the risk of drowning	Fix your home
10 pCi/L	About 71 people could get lung cancer	← 100 times the risk of dying in a home fire	Fix your home
8 pCi/L	About 57 people could get lung cancer		Fix your home
4 pCi/L	About 29 people could get lung cancer	← 100 times the risk of dying in an airplane crash	Fix your home
2 pCi/L	About 15 people could get lung cancer	← 2 times the risk of dying in a car crash	Consider fixing between 2 and 4 pCi/L
1.3 pCi/L	About 9 people could get lung cancer	(Average indoor radon level)	(Reducing radon levels below
0.4 pCi/L	About 3 people could get lung cancer	(Average outdoor radon level)	2 pCi/L is difficult)

Note: If you are a former smoker, your risk may be lower.

RADON RISK IF YOU'VE NEVER SMOKED

Radon Level	If 1,000 people who never smoked were exposed to this level over a lifetime. . .	The risk of cancer from radon exposure compares to. . .	WHAT TO DO:
20 pCi/L	About 8 people could get lung cancer	The risk of being killed in a violent crime	Fix your home
10 pCi/L	About 4 people could get lung cancer		Fix your home
8 pCi/L	About 3 people could get lung cancer	← 10 times the risk of dying in an airplane crash	Fix your home
4 pCi/L	About 2 people could get lung cancer	← The risk of drowning	Fix your home
2 pCi/L	About 1 person could get lung cancer	← The risk of dying in a home fire	Consider fixing between 2 and 4 pCi/L
1.3 pCi/L	Less than 1 person could get lung cancer	(Average indoor radon level)	(Reducing radon levels below
0.4 pCi/L	Less than 1 person could get lung cancer	(Average outdoor radon level)	2 pCi/L is difficult)

Note: If you are a former smoker, your risk may be higher.

It's never too late to reduce your risk of lung cancer. Don't wait to test and fix a radon problem. If you are a smoker, stop smoking.

RADON MYTHS

MYTH: *Scientists aren't sure radon really is a problem.*

FACT: **Although some scientists dispute the precise number of deaths due to radon, all major health organizations (like the Centers for Disease Control, the American Lung Association and the American Medical Association) agree with estimates that radon causes thousands of preventable lung cancer deaths every year. This is especially true among smokers, since the risk to smokers is much greater than to non-smokers.**

MYTH: *Radon testing is difficult, time-consuming and expensive.*

FACT: **Radon testing is inexpensive and easy--it should take only a little of your time.**

MYTH: *Radon test kits are not reliable and are difficult to find.*

FACT: **Reliable test kits are available through the mail, in hardware stores and other retail outlets. Call your state radon office (see page 15) for a list of test kit companies that have met EPA requirements for reliability or are state certified.**

MYTH: *Homes with radon problems can't be fixed.*

FACT : **There are simple solutions to radon problems in homes. Thousands of homeowners have already fixed radon problems in their homes. Radon levels can be readily lowered for about $500 to $2,500. Call your state radon office (see page 15) for a list of contractors that have met EPA requirements or are state certified.**

MYTH: *Radon only affects certain kinds of homes.*

FACT: **House construction can affect radon levels. However, radon can be a problem in homes of all types: old homes, new homes, drafty homes, insulated homes, homes with basements, homes without basements.**

MYTH: *Radon is only a problem in certain parts of the country.*

FACT: **High radon levels have been found in every state. Radon problems do vary from area to area, but the only way to know your radon level is to test.**

MYTH: *A neighbor's test result is a good indication of whether your home has a problem.*

FACT: **It's not. Radon levels vary from home to home. The only way to know if your home has a radon problem is to test it.**

MYTH: *Everyone should test their water for radon.*

FACT: **While radon gets into some homes through the water, you should first test the air in your home for radon. If you find high levels and your water comes from a well, contact a lab certified to measure radiation in water to have your water tested.**

MYTH: *It's difficult to sell homes where radon problems have been discovered.*

FACT: **Where radon problems have been fixed, home sales have not been blocked or frustrated. The added protection is some times a good selling point.**

MYTH: *I've lived in my home for so long, it doesn't make sense to take action now.*

FACT: **You will reduce your risk of lung cancer when you reduce radon levels, even if you've lived with a radon problem for a long time.**

MYTH: *Short-term tests can't be used for making a decision about whether to fix your home.*

FACT: **A short-term test followed by a second short-term test may be used to decide whether to fix your home. However, the closer the average of your two short-term tests is to 4 pCi/L, the less certain you can be about whether your year-round average is above or below that level. Keep in mind that radon levels below 4 pCi/L still pose some risk. Radon levels can be reduced in most homes to 2 pCi/L or below.**

STATE RADON CONTACTS

Alabama **800/582-1866**
Alaska **800/478-4845**
Arizona **602/255-4845**
Arkansas **501/661-2301**
California **800/745-7236**
Colorado **800/846-3986**
Connecticut **203/566-3122**
Delaware **800/554-4636**
District of Columbia **202/727-5728**
Florida **800/543-8279**
Georgia **800/745-0037**
Hawaii **808/586-4700**
Idaho **800/445-8647**
Illinois **800/325-1245**
Indiana **800/272-9723**
Iowa **800/383-5992**
Kansas **913/296-1560**
Kentucky **502/564-3700**
Louisiana **800/256-2494**
Maine **800/232-0842**
Maryland **800/872-3666**
Massachusetts **413/586-7525**
Michigan **517/335-8190**
Minnesota **800/798-9050**
Mississippi **800/626-7739**
Missouri **800/669-7236**

Montana **406/444-3671**
Nebraska **800/334-9491**
Nevada **702/687-5394**
New Hampshire **800/852-3345 x4674**
New Jersey **800/648-0394**
New Mexico **505/827-4300**
New York **800/458-1158**
North Carolina **919/571-4141**
North Dakota **701/221-5188**
Ohio **800/523-4439**
Oklahoma **405/271-5221**
Oregon **503/731-4014**
Pennsylvania **800/237-2366**
Puerto Rico **809/767-3563**
Rhode Island **401/277-2438**
South Carolina **800/768-0362**
South Dakota **605/773-3351**
Tennessee **800/232-1139**
Texas **512/834-6688**
Utah **801/538-6734**
Vermont **800/640-0601**
Virginia **800/468-0138**
Washington **800/323-9727**
West Virginia **800/922-1255**
Wisconsin **608/267-4795**
Wyoming **800/458-5847**

FOR FURTHER INFORMATION

For more information on how to reduce your radon health risk, ask your state radon office to send you these guides:

• **Home Buyer's and Seller's Guide to Radon**

• **Radon in Schools**

• **Radon: A Physician's Guide**

• **Consumer's Guide to Radon Reduction**

• **Technical Support Document**

If you plan to make repairs yourself, be sure to contact your state radon office (see above) for a current copy of EPA technical guidance on radon mitigation, "Application of Radon Reduction Techniques for Detached Houses."

SURGEON GENERAL HEALTH ADVISORY:

"Indoor radon gas is a national health problem. Radon causes thousands of deaths each year. Millions of homes have elevated radon levels. Homes should be tested for radon. When elevated levels are confirmed, the problem should be corrected."

ISBN 0-16-036222-9

90000

For sale by the U.S. Government Printing Office
Superintendent of Documents, Mail Stop: SSOP, Washington, DC 20402-9328
ISBN 0-16-036222-9

9 780160 362224

Environmental Protection
Agency

August 1992

Air and Radiation 6604J

Consumer's Guide To Radon Reduction

How to reduce radon levels in your home...

&EPA

Consumer Federation of America strongly urges consumers to have elevated radon levels in their homes reduced. EPA's *Consumer's Guide to Radon Reduction* will assist these individuals and offers very good advice for selecting and working with a qualified radon contractor.

ISBN 0-16-036255-5

9 780160 362552

90000

For sale by the U.S. Government Printing Office
Superintendent of Documents, Mail Stop: SSOP, Washington, DC 20402-9328

ISBN 0-16-036255-5

INTRODUCTION

You have tested your home for radon, but now what? This booklet is for people who have tested their home for radon and confirmed that they have elevated radon levels - 4 picocuries per liter (pCi/L) or higher. This booklet can help you:

- Select a qualified contractor to reduce the radon levels in your home
- Determine an appropriate radon reduction method
- Maintain your radon reduction system

If you want information on how to test your home for radon, call your state radon office (see p. 17) and ask for a copy of *A Citizen's Guide to Radon.*

OVERVIEW

Reduce Radon Levels In Your Home

Radon is the second leading cause of lung cancer. The Surgeon General and the EPA recommend testing for radon and reducing radon in homes that have high levels. Fix your home if your radon level is confirmed to be 4 picocuries per liter (pCi/L) or higher. Radon levels less than 4 pCi/L still pose a risk, and in many cases may be reduced. If you smoke and your home has high radon levels, your risk of lung cancer is especially high.

Select A State Certified And/Or RCP Contractor

Choose a radon contractor to fix your home who is state certified and/or listed in EPA's Radon Contractor Proficiency (RCP) Program. RCP contractors are trained, must pass a comprehensive exam, and must agree to follow standards developed to ensure effective radon reduction. Call your state radon office (see p. 17) for a list of qualified contractors in your area.

Radon Reduction Techniques Work

Radon reduction systems work. Some radon reduction systems can reduce radon levels in your home by up to 99%. The cost of fixing a home generally ranges from $500 to $2500. Your costs may vary depending on the size and design of your home and which radon reduction methods are needed. Thousands of people have reduced radon levels in their homes.

Maintain Your Radon Reduction System

Maintaining your radon reduction system takes little effort and keeps the system working properly and radon levels low.

HOW RADON ENTERS YOUR HOUSE

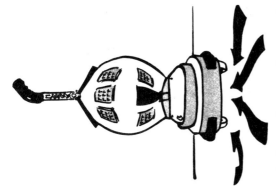

Radon is a naturally occurring gas produced by the breakdown of uranium in soil, rock, and water. Air pressure inside your home is usually lower than pressure in the soil around your home's foundation. Because of this difference in pressure, your house acts like a vacuum, drawing radon in through foundation cracks and other openings. Radon may also be present in well water and can be released into the air in your home when water is used for showering and other household uses. In most cases, radon entering the home through water is a small risk compared to radon entering your home from the soil. In a small number of homes, the building materials can give off radon, although building materials rarely cause radon problems by themselves.

RADON IS A CANCER-CAUSING, RADIOACTIVE GAS

Radon is estimated to cause many thousands of lung cancer deaths each year. **In fact, the Surgeon General has warned that radon is the second leading cause of lung cancer in the United States.** Only smoking causes more lung cancer deaths. If you smoke and your home has high radon levels, your risk of lung cancer is especially high.

WHAT DO YOUR RADON TEST RESULTS MEAN?

The amount of radon in the air is measured in "picocuries of radon per Liter of air," or "pCi/L." Sometimes test results are expressed in Working Levels, "WL," rather than picocuries per Liter of air. A level of 0.02 WL is usually equal to about 4 pCi/L in a typical home.

WHY USE A TESTER OR A TEST KIT THAT MEETS EPA REQUIREMENTS?

Whether you use a short or long-term test, use a device and a testing company that is state certified, and/or is listed in EPA's Radon Measurement Proficiency (RMP) Program. If you want to use a do-it-yourself test kit, use one that displays the phrase "Meets EPA Requirements." EPA's RMP Program is designed to help assure that consumers get reliable radon measurements. If you want to hire a professional to take the measurement, contact your state radon office for a current list of state certified and/or RMP listed companies and individuals (see p. 17). Listed RMP Program participants must follow quality assurance and EPA measurement procedures and have demonstrated the ability to take reliable measurements with specific devices. Your state may also have additional requirements for professional radon testers.

Any radon exposure has some risk of causing lung cancer. The lower the radon level in your home, the lower your family's risk of lung cancer. The U.S. Congress has set a long-term goal that indoor radon levels be no more than outdoor levels; about 0.4 pCi/L of radon is normally found in the outside air. EPA recommends fixing your home if the results of one *long-term test* or the average of two *short-term tests* taken in the lowest lived-in level of the home show radon levels of 4 pCi/L (or 0.02 WL) or higher. A short-term test remains in your home for two days to 90 days, whereas a long-term test remains in your home for more than 90 days. With today's technology, radon levels in most homes **can** be reduced to 2 pCi/L or below.

HAVE YOU CONFIRMED YOUR RADON TEST?

If your first short-term test result is 4 pCi/L or higher, (or 0.02 WL or more), EPA recommends that you take a second test to be sure. For a better understanding of your year-round average radon level, take a long-term test. If you need results quickly, take a second short-term test and average it with the first. The higher your initial short-term test result, the more certain you can be that you should take a short-term rather than a long-term follow up test. If your first short-term test result is several times the action level — for example, about 10 pCi/L or higher — you should take a second short-term test immediately.

WHY HIRE A CONTRACTOR?

EPA recommends that you have a qualified contractor fix your home because lowering high radon levels requires specific technical knowledge and special skills. Without the proper equipment or technical knowledge, you could actually increase your radon level or create other potential hazards. But, if you decide to do the work yourself, get information on appropriate training courses and copies of EPA's technical guidance documents from your state radon office.

WHY USE A STATE CERTIFIED AND/OR RCP CONTRACTOR?

EPA recommends that you use a contractor trained to fix radon problems. EPA's Radon Contractor Proficiency (RCP) Program requires contractors to take training courses and pass an exam before being listed in EPA's National RCP Report. The Report lists radon contractors who meet RCP requirements. RCP contractors carry a current RCP photo identification card and all RCP contractors are required to follow EPA standards to make sure that their work meets minimum quality standards. A number of states have their own contractor certification programs which have additional requirements. Check with your state radon office (see p. 17) to see if the contractor you are considering is state certified and/or RCP listed.

HOW TO SELECT A CONTRACTOR

Get Estimates

Choose a contractor to fix a radon problem just as you would choose someone to do other home repairs. It is wise to get more than one estimate, to ask for references, and to contact some of those references to ask if they are satisfied with the contractors' work. Also, ask your county or state consumer protection office for information about the contractors.

Use this check-list when evaluating and comparing contractors and ask the following questions:

YES   NO

☐   ☐   **Will the contractor provide references or photographs, as well as test results of 'before' and 'after' radon levels of past radon reduction work?**

☐   ☐   **Can the contractor explain what the work will involve, how long it will take to complete, and exactly how the radon reduction system will work?**

☐   ☐   **Does the contractor charge a fee for any diagnostic tests?** - Although many contractors give free estimates, they may charge for diagnostic tests — these tests help determine what radon reduction system should be used, but are not always necessary (see p. 8 for more on diagnostic tests).

☐   ☐   **Did the contractor inspect your home's structure *before* giving you an estimate?**

☐   ☐   **Did the contractor review the quality of your radon measurement results and determine if EPA testing procedures were followed? [An RCP requirement]**

Compare the contractors' proposed costs and *consider what you will get for your money.* Take into account the following: a system that is less expensive to install may have higher operating and maintenance costs than a system that is more expensive to install; the best system for your house may be the more expensive option; and the quality of the building material will effect how long the system lasts.

Do the contractors' proposals and estimates include:

YES   NO

☐   ☐   **Proof of liability insurance and being bonded and licensed?**

☐   ☐   **Proof of state certification and/or RCP listing?**

☐   ☐   **Diagnostic testing prior to design and installation of a radon reduction system?**

☐   ☐   **Installation of a warning device to caution you if the radon reduction system is not working correctly? [An RCP requirement]**

☐   ☐   **Testing after installation to make sure the radon reduction system works well? [An RCP requirement]**

☐   ☐   **A guarantee to reduce radon levels to 4 pCi/L or below, and if so, for how long?**

WHAT TO LOOK FOR IN A RADON REDUCTION SYSTEM

I n selecting a radon reduction method for your home, you and your contractor should consider several things, including: how high your initial radon level is, the costs of installation and system operation, your house size and your foundation type.

Installation and Operating Costs

For most homes, radon reduction measures are no more expensive than having a new hot water heater installed or having the house painted. The cost of a contractor fixing a home generally ranges from $500 to $2500, depending on the characteristics of the house and choice of radon reduction methods.

Most types of radon reduction systems cause some loss of heated or air conditioned air, which could increase your utility bills. How much your utility bills will be affected depends on the climate you live in, what kind of reduction system you select, and how your house is built. Systems that use fans are more effective in reducing radon levels; however, they will increase your electric bill. The table on p. 16 lists the installation and average operating costs for different radon reduction systems and describes the best use of each method.

How a Radon Reduction System May Affect Your Home

In order to minimize the effect of installing a radon reduction system in your house, ask your contractor before any work starts, how the system can be made to blend with its surroundings. For instance: radon vent pipes may be encased with materials that match the exterior of your house, or the pipes may be routed up through closets.

The Contract

Ask the contractor to prepare a contract before any work starts. Carefully read the contract before you sign it. Make sure everything in the contract matches the original proposal. The contract should describe exactly what work will be done prior to and during the installation of the system, what the system consists of, and how the system will operate. Carefully consider optional additions to your contract which may add to the initial cost of the system, but may be worth the extra expense. Typical options might include a guarantee that the contractor will adjust or modify the system to reach the promised radon level, or, an extended warranty and/or a service plan.

Important information that should appear in the contract includes:

- [ ] **The total cost of the job, including all taxes and permit fees; how much, if any, is required for a deposit; and when payment is due in full.**

- [ ] **The time needed to complete the work.**

- [ ] **An agreement by the contractor to obtain necessary licenses and follow required building codes.**

- [ ] **A statement that the contractor carries liability insurance and is bonded and insured to protect you in case of injury to persons, or damage to property, while the work is being done.**

- [ ] **A guarantee that the contractor will be responsible for damage and clean-up after the job.**

- [ ] **Details of warranties, guarantees, or other *optional* features, including the acceptable resulting radon level.**

- [ ] **A declaration stating whether any warranties or guarantees are transferable if you sell your home.**

- [ ] **A description of what the contractor expects the homeowner to do (e.g., make the work area accessible) before work begins.**

RADON REDUCTION TECHNIQUES

There are several methods that a contractor can use to lower radon levels in your home. Some techniques prevent radon from entering your home while others reduce radon levels after it has entered. EPA generally recommends methods which **prevent the entry of radon. Soil suction**, for example, prevents radon from entering your home by drawing the radon from below the house and venting it through a pipe, or pipes, to the air above the house where it is quickly diluted.

Any information that you may have about the construction of your house could help your contractor choose the best system. Your contractor will perform a visual inspection of your house and design a system that considers specific features of your house. If this inspection fails to provide enough information, the contractor will need to perform **diagnostic tests** to help develop the best radon reduction system for your home. For instance, your contractor can use a "smoke gun" to find the source and direction of air movement. A contractor can learn air flow sources and directions by watching a small amount of smoke that he or she shot into holes, drains, sumps, or along cracks. The sources of air flow show possible radon routes.

Another type of diagnostic test is a "soil communication test." This test uses a vacuum cleaner and a smoke gun to determine how easily air can move from one point to another under the foundation. By inserting a vacuum cleaner hose in one small hole and using a smoke gun in a second small hole, a contractor can see if the smoke is pulled down into the second hole by the force of the vacuum cleaner's suction. Watching the smoke during a soil communication test helps a contractor decide if certain radon reduction systems would work well in your house.

Whether diagnostic tests are needed is decided by details specific to your house, such as the foundation design, what kind of material is under your house, and by the contractor's experience with similar houses and similar radon test results.

House Foundation Types

Your house type will affect the kind of radon reduction system that will work best. Houses are generally categorized according to their foundation design. For example: **basement, slab-on-grade** (concrete poured at ground level), or **crawlspace** (a shallow unfinished space under the first floor). Some houses have more than one foundation design feature. For instance, it is common to have a basement under part of the house and to have a slab-on-grade or crawlspace under the rest of the house. In these situations a combination of radon reduction techniques may be needed to reduce radon levels to below 4 pCi/L.

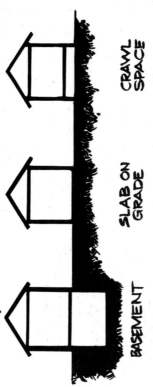

BASEMENT   SLAB ON GRADE   CRAWL SPACE

Radon reduction systems can be grouped by house foundation design. Find your type of foundation design above and read about which radon reduction systems may be best for your house.

Basement and Slab-on-Grade Houses

In houses that have a basement or a slab-on-grade foundation, radon is usually reduced by one of four types of soil suction: **subslab suction, drain tile suction, sump hole suction**, or **block wall suction**.

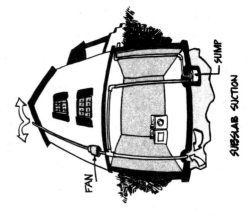

FAN   SUBSLAB SUCTION   SUMP

Active Subslab suction (also called **subslab depressurization**) is the most common and usually the most reliable radon reduction method. Suction pipes are inserted through the floor slab into the crushed rock or soil underneath. They also

Other Types of Radon Reduction Methods

Other radon reduction techniques that can be used in any type of house include: sealing, house pressurization, natural ventilation, and heat recovery ventilation. Most of these methods are considered to be either temporary measures, or only partial solutions to be used in combination with other measures.

Sealing cracks and other openings in the foundation is a basic part of most approaches to radon reduction. Sealing does two things, it limits the flow of radon into your home and it reduces the loss of conditioned air, thereby making other radon reduction techniques more effective and cost-efficient. *EPA does not recommend the use of sealing alone to reduce radon because, by itself, sealing has not been shown to lower radon levels significantly or consistently.* It is difficult to identify and permanently seal the places where radon is entering. Normal settling of your house opens new entry routes and reopens old ones.

House pressurization uses a fan to blow air into the basement or living area from either upstairs or outdoors. It attempts to create enough pressure at the lowest level indoors (in a basement for example) to prevent radon from entering into the house. The effectiveness of this technique is limited by house construction, climate, other appliances in the house, and occupant lifestyle. In order to maintain enough pressure to keep radon out, the doors and windows at the lowest level must not be left opened, except for normal entry and exit.

Some **natural ventilation** occurs in all houses. By opening windows, doors, and vents on the lower floors you increase the ventilation in your house. This increase in ventilation mixes radon with outside air and can result in reduced radon levels. In addition, ventilating your house can help to lower indoor radon levels by reducing the vacuum effect. Natural ventilation in any type of house, (aside from ventilation of a crawlspace), should normally be regarded as a *temporary* radon reduction approach because of the following disadvantages: loss of conditioned air and related discomfort, *greatly* increased costs of conditioning additional outside air, and security concerns.

NATURAL VENTILATION

---

may be inserted below the concrete slab from outside the house. The number and location of suction pipes that are needed depends on how easily air can move in the crushed rock or soil under the slab, and on the strength of the radon source. A contractor usually gets this information from visual inspection, from diagnostic tests, and/or from experience. Acting like a vacuum cleaner, a fan connected to the pipes draws the radon gas from below the house and then releases it into the outdoor air. **Passive subslab suction** is the same as active subslab suction except it relies on air currents instead of a fan to draw radon up from below the house. Passive subslab suction is generally not as effective in reducing high radon levels as active subslab suction.

Some houses have **drain tiles** to direct water away from the foundation of the house. Suction on these drain tiles is often effective in reducing radon levels if the drain tiles form a complete loop around the foundation.

One variation of subslab and drain tile suction is **sump hole suction**. Often, when a house with a basement has a sump pump to remove unwanted water, the sump can be capped so that it can continue to drain water and serve as the location for a radon suction pipe.

Block wall suction can be used in basement houses with hollow block foundation walls. This method removes radon from the hollow spaces within the basement's concrete block wall. It is often used together with subslab suction.

Crawlspace Houses

In houses with crawlspaces, radon levels can sometimes be lowered by **ventilating** the crawlspace passively (without the use of a fan) or actively (with the use of a fan). Crawlspace ventilation lowers indoor radon levels both by reducing the home's suction on the soil and by diluting the radon beneath the house. Natural ventilation in a crawlspace is achieved by opening vents, or installing additional vents. Active ventilation uses a fan to blow air through the crawlspace instead of relying on natural air circulation. In colder climates, for either natural or active crawlspace ventilation, water pipes in the crawlspace need to be insulated against the cold.

Another effective method to reduce radon levels in crawl-space houses involves covering the earth floor with a heavy plastic sheet. A vent pipe and fan are used to draw the radon from under the sheet and vent it to the outdoors. This form of soil suction is called **submembrane depressurization**.

A **heat recovery ventilator (HRV)**, also called an **air-to-air heat exchanger**, can be installed to increase ventilation. An HRV will increase house ventilation while using the heated or cooled air being exhausted to warm or cool the incoming air. HRVs can be designed to ventilate all or part of your home, although they are more effective in reducing radon levels when used to ventilate only the basement. If properly balanced and maintained, they ensure a constant degree of ventilation throughout the year. HRVs also can improve air quality in houses that have other indoor pollutants. There could be *significant* increase in the heating and cooling costs with an HRV, but not as great as ventilation without heat recovery (see p. 16).

DOES YOUR CONTRACTOR'S WORK MEET RCP REQUIREMENTS?

There are certain basic requirements that all radon reduction systems should meet. RCP contractors **must** meet the following performance standards (for a complete list of RCP standards call your state office, see p. 17). Some states have similar requirements:

☐ Radon reduction systems *must* be clearly labelled.
- This will avoid accidental changes to the system which could disrupt its function.

☐ The exhaust pipes of soil suction systems *must* vent 10 feet or more above the ground, and away from windows, doors, or other openings that could allow the radon to reenter the house.

☐ The exhaust fan *must* be located in an unlivable area.
- For instance, it should be in a un-occupied attic of the house or outside — *not* in a basement!

☐ If installing an exhaust fan outside, the contractor *must* install a fan that meets local building codes for exterior use.

☐ All active radon reduction systems require electrical connections that *must* be installed according to local electrical codes.

☐ A warning device *must* be installed to alert you if the system stops working properly.
- Examples of system failure warning devices are: a liquid gauge, a sound alarm, a light indicator, and a dial (needle display) gauge.

☐ A warning device *must* be placed where it can be seen or heard easily.
- If your monitor shows that the system is not working properly, call a contractor to have it checked.

☐ RCP contractors *must* make sure a follow up radon test is done within 30 days of system installation, but no sooner than 24 hours after your system is in operation with the fan on, if it has one.
- To test the system's initial effectiveness, a 2 - 7 day measurement is recommended.
- Test conditions: windows and doors must be closed 12 hours before and during the test, except for normal entry/exit.

☐ RCP contractors *must* recommend that you get an independent follow up radon measurement.
- Having an independent tester perform the test, or conducting the measurement yourself, will eliminate any potential conflict of interest.

Your RCP contractor should also check that your radon reduction system's warning device works. Make sure your contractor completely explains your radon reduction system, demonstrates how it operates, and explains how to maintain it. Ask for written operating and maintenance instructions and copies of any warranties.

LIVING IN A HOUSE WITH A RADON REDUCTION SYSTEM

Maintaining Your Radon Reduction System

Similar to a furnace or chimney, radon reduction systems need some occasional maintenance. You should look at your warning device on a regular basis to make sure the system is working correctly. Fans may last for five years or more (although manufacturer warranties tend not to exceed three years) and may then need to be repaired or replaced. Replacing a fan will cost around $250 including parts and labor. By testing at least every two years, you will confirm that your radon level is staying low and that your fan is still performing well.

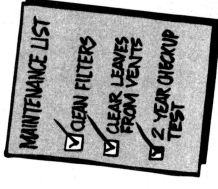

MAINTENANCE LIST
☑ CLEAN FILTERS
☑ CLEAR LEAVES FROM VENTS
☑ 2 YEAR CHECKUP TEST

Remember, the fan should NEVER be turned off; it must run continuously for the system to work correctly.

The filter in an HRV requires periodic cleaning and should be changed twice a year. Replacement filters for an HRV are easily changed and are priced between $5 and $15. Ask your contractor where filters can be purchased. Also, the vent that brings fresh air in from the outside needs to be inspected for leaves and debris. The ventilator should be checked annually by a heating, ventilating, and air-conditioning professional to make sure the air flow remains properly balanced. HRVs used for radon control should run all the time.

Remodeling Your Home After Radon Levels Have Been Lowered

If you decide to make major structural changes to your home after you have had a radon reduction system installed (such as converting an unfinished basement area into living space), ask your radon contractor whether these changes could void any warranties. After you remodel, retest in the lowest lived-in area to make sure the construction did not reduce the effectiveness of the radon reduction system. If you are adding a new foundation for an addition to your house, address the radon problem during construction.

BUYING OR SELLING A HOME?

If you are buying or selling a home and need to make decisions about radon, consult EPA's "Home Buyer's and Seller's Guide to Radon." If you are selling a home that has a radon reduction system, inform potential buyers and supply them with information about your system's operation and maintenance.

If you are buying a new house, consider that it is almost always less expensive to build radon resistant features into new construction than it is to fix an existing house that has high radon levels. Ask your builder if he or she uses radon-resistant construction features. Your builder can refer to EPA

---

guidance about radon and new construction, or your builder can work with a state certified and/or RCP contractor to design and install the proper radon reduction system. To obtain EPA's technical documents contact your state radon office (see p. 17).

All homes should be tested for radon and high radon levels should be reduced.

DO YOU HAVE A WELL?: RADON IN WATER

Well owners with elevated indoor radon levels should test their well water for radon. Radon in your water supply can increase your indoor radon level, although, in most cases, radon entering the home through water will be a small source of risk compared to radon entering from the soil. EPA estimates that indoor radon levels will increase by about 1 pCi/L for every 10,000 pCi/L of radon in water. Call the Safe Drinking Water Hotline at 1-800-426-4791, or your state office (see p. 17) for more information.

What do the results of your water test mean?

Estimate how much the radon in your water is elevating your indoor radon level by subtracting 1 pCi/L from your indoor air radon level for every 10,000 pCi/L of radon that was found in your water (For example: if you have 30,000 pCi/L of radon in your water then 3 pCi/L of your indoor measurement may have come from radon in water). If most of the radon is **not** coming from your water, fix your house first and then retest your indoor air to make sure that the source of elevated radon was not your private well. If a large contribution of the radon in your house **is** from your water, you may want to consider installing a special water treatment system to remove radon. EPA recommends installing a water treatment system only when there is a proven radon problem in your water supply.

How is radon removed from water?

Radon can be removed from water by using one of two methods: aeration treatment or granular activated carbon (GAC) treatment. Aeration treatment involves spraying water or mixing it with air, and then venting the air from the water before use. GAC treatment filters water through carbon. Radon attaches to the carbon and leaves the water free of radon. The carbon may need special handling in its disposal if it is used at a high radon level or if it has been used for a long time. In either treatment, it is important to treat the water where it enters your home (point-of-entry device) so that all the water will be treated. Point-of-use devices, such as those installed on a tap or under the sink, will only treat a small portion of your water and are **not** effective in reducing radon in your water. It is important to maintain home water treatment units properly because failure to do so can lead to other water contamination problems. Some homeowners opt for a service contract from the installer to provide for carbon replacement and general system maintenance. Refer to the table on p. 16 for more information on water treatment systems.

STATE RADON CONTACTS

State	Phone
Alabama	800/582-1866 205/242-5315
Alaska	800/478-4845 907/465-3019
Arizona	602/255-4845
Arkansas	501/661-2301
California	916/324-2208
Colorado	800/846-3986 303/692-3057
Connecticut	203/566-3122
Delaware	800/554-4636 302/739-3787
District of Columbia	202/727-7221
Florida	800/543-8279 904/488-1525
Georgia	404/894-6644
Hawaii	808/543-4383
Idaho	800/445-8647 208/334-6584
Illinois	800/325-1245 217/786-6384
Indiana	800/272-9723 317/633-0150
Iowa	800/383-5992 515/281-7781
Kansas	913/296-1560
Kentucky	502/564-3700
Louisiana	800/256-2494 504/925-7042
Maine	800/232-0842 207/789-5689
Maryland	800/872-3666 301/631-3300
Massachusetts	413/586-7525
Michigan	517/335-8190
Minnesota	800/798-9050 612/627-5012
Mississippi	800/626-7739 601/354-6657
Missouri	800/669-7236 314/751-6083
Montana	406/444-3671
Nebraska	800/334-9491 402/471-2168
Nevada	702/687-5394
New Hampshire	603/271-4674
New Jersey	800/648-0394 609/987-6396
New Mexico	505/827-4300
New York	518/458-6451
North Carolina	919/571-4141
North Dakota	701/221-5188
Ohio	800/523-4439 614/644-2727
Oklahoma	405/271-5221
Oregon	503/731-4014
Pennsylvania	800/237-2366 717/787-2480
Puerto Rico	809/767-3563
Rhode Island	401/277-2438
South Carolina	800/768-0362 803/734-4700
South Dakota	605/773-3351
Tennessee	800/232-1139 615/741-3651
Texas	512/834-6688
Utah	801/538-6734
Vermont	800/640-0601 802/828-2886
Virginia	800/468-0138 804/786-5932
Washington	800/323-9727 206/753-4518
West Virginia	800/922-1255 304/558-3526
Wisconsin	608/267-4795
Wyoming	800/458-5847 307/777-6015

INSTALLATION AND OPERATING COST TABLE

Technique	Typical Radon Reduction	Typical Range of Installation Costs (Contractor)	Typical Operating Cost Range for Fan Electricity & Heated/Cooled Air Loss (Annual)	Comments
Subslab Suction (Subslab Depressurization)	80 - 99%	$800 - 2500	$75 - 175	Works best if air can move easily in material under slab
Passive Subslab Suction	30 - 70%	$550 - 2250	There may be some energy penalties	May be more effective in cold climates; not as effective as active subslab suction
Draintile Suction	90 - 99%	$800 - 1700	$75 - 175	Works best if draintiles form complete loop around house
Blockwall Suction	50 - 99%	$1500 - 3000	$150 - 300	Only in houses with hollow blockwalls; requires sealing of major openings
Sump Hole Suction	90 - 99%	$800 - 2500	$100 - 225	Works best if air moves easily to sump under slab; or if draintiles form complete loop
Submembrane Depressurization in a crawl space	80 - 99%	$1000 - 2500	$70 - $175	Less heat loss than natural ventilation in cold winter climates
Natural Ventilation in a crawl space	0 - 50%	none $200 - 500 if additional vents installed	There may be some energy penalties	Costs variable
Sealing of Radon Entry Routes	0 - 50%	$100 - 2000	None	Normally used with other techniques; proper materials & installation required
House (Basement) Pressurization	50 - 99%	$500 - 1500	$150 - 500	Works best with tight basement isolated from outdoors & upper floors
Natural Ventilation	Variable	none $200 - 500 if additional vents installed	$100 - 700	Significant heated / cooled air loss; operating costs depend on utility rates & amount of ventilation
Heat Recovery Ventilation	25 - 50% if used for full house 25 - 75% if used for basement	$1200 - 2500	$ 75 - 500 For continuous operation.	Limited use: best in tight house; for full house, use with levels no higher than 8 pCi/L; no higher than 16 pCi/L for use in basement; less conditioned air loss than natural ventilation
Water Systems: Aeration	95 - 99%	$3000 - 4500	$40 - 90	More efficient than GAC; requires annual cleaning to maintain effectiveness & to prevent contamination; carefully vent system
Granular Activated Carbon (GAC)	85 - 99%	$1000 - 2000	None	Less efficient for higher levels than aeration; use for moderate levels (around 5000 pCi/L or less); radon by-products can build on carbon may need radiation shield around tank & care in disposal

*NOTE: The fan electricity and house heating/cooling loss cost range is based on certain assumptions regarding climate, your house size, and the cost of electricity and fuel. Your costs may vary. Numbers based upon 1991 data.

Radon Contractor Proficiency Program
Interim Radon Mitigation Standards

December 15, 1991

This document outlines basic minimum performance standards for participants in the Radon Contractor Proficiency (RCP) Program involved in the reduction of radon in buildings. The purpose of these standards is to help ensure the protection of the general public from the risk of elevated indoor radon. State and local regulatory agencies may choose to expand and use these standards in assessing performance of professionals involved in radon mitigation. While this document outlines minimum requirements for participation in the voluntary Federal program, there may be other practices necessary to achieve quality radon mitigation installations. Radon mitigation contractors agree to follow these standards as a condition for inclusion in the U.S. Environmental Protection Agency (EPA) National Radon Contractor Proficiency Report, and as a condition for EPA approval. Failure to comply with these standards may result in loss of EPA approval and the contractor's name being removed from the RCP Program Proficiency Report.

This document replaces the RCP Program Radon Mitigation Guidelines issued in October 1989. The Standards incorporate revisions intended to clarify required practices of RCP Program listed contractors. RCP contractors are not required to retrofit work performed prior to December 15, 1991 as relates to these mandatory practices. The word **"shall"** is highlighted and used to indicate practices that are mandatory for program participants. At a later date the Agency may supersede these Interim Standards by issuing final Radon Mitigation Standards which will establish more definitive specifications for the installation of radon mitigation systems.

For Further questions concerning these Interim Mitigation Standards please call your EPA Regional Office. For extra copies of these Standards please call your nearest Regional Radon Training Center (see page 4.)

Definition: "mitigator", "contractor" - the individual approved and listed in the RCP Program.

1.0 Initial Client Interview - Radon Measurements

The mitigator **shall** review and assess the quality of any previous radon measurements made by the client and ascertain whether or not these measurements were made in accordance with EPA "Indoor Radon and Radon Decay Product Measurement Protocols" (EPA 520-1/89-009), "Interim Protocols for Screening and Follow-up Radon and Radon Decay Product Measurements" (EPA 520/1-86-014-1), or subsequent revisions or additions to these documents. If the contractor determines that the procedures outlined in these documents were not followed, the contractor **shall** advise the client of this and retesting **shall** be recommended.

2.0 Building Investigation

The contractor **shall** conduct a visual inspection prior to the initiation of any installation activities to assist in designing the most effective mitigation system.

3.0 Temporary Risk Reduction Measures

3.1 In dwellings with elevated radon levels, the mitigator **shall** advise the client whether or not temporary measures should be used to reduce occupant exposure until a permanent mitigation system can be installed. This could include temporary measures such as natural ventilation, or mechanical ventilation with unconditioned outside air, or limiting the occupants' exposure by minimizing the time spent in areas of the home with elevated radon levels, or any measures which effectively minimize occupant exposure.

3.2 The contractor **shall not** install a temporary radon reduction system in lieu of a permanent mitigation system.

3.3 Temporary radon reduction systems **shall** be labeled as such. The notice **shall** be legible at a distance of two feet, and contain wording stating that the system should: 1) not be removed until a permanent mitigation system can be installed, and 2) the permanent mitigation system should be installed within 30 days after the installation date of the temporary system. The label **shall** also contain the contractor's name, phone number, and the installation date. If the equipment is not easily labeled, the notice **shall** be posted on the electric service panel, or other prominent location.

4.0 Client Information

The contractor **shall** provide the following information to the client prior to initiating any work:

1. the contractor's RCP Program identification number,
2. the scope of the work to be completed,
3. a statement indicating any known hazards associated with chemicals used in or as part of the installation,
4. a statement indicating compliance with and implementation of all EPA standards and those of other agencies having jurisdiction (e.g., code requirements),
5. a statement indicating any required maintenance by the homeowner,
6. an estimate of the installation cost and annual operating cost of the system.

5.0 Mitigation System Installation

5.1 The mitigation system **shall** be installed as a permanent, integral part of a building.

5.2 The mitigator **shall** comply with all laws, ordinances, local building codes, applicable Occupational Safety and Health Administration (OSHA) standards or regulations of all Authorities having jurisdiction. The mitigator **shall** obtain all licenses and permits required for the work. Examples of these include proper contractor licenses and building permits. In cases where discrepancies occur between these Mitigation Standards and applicable laws, ordinances, local building codes or regulations, the appropriate laws take precedence. Where such deviations from the Mitigation Standards are required by law, they **shall** be reported to the EPA Regional office within 30 days after completion of work.

5.3 Material Safety Data Sheets (MSDS) for sealers, compounds, adhesives, paints, and other materials **shall** be provided to workers and also made available to clients upon request. The contractor **shall** review with the occupants or their representative all materials to be used in the installation of the mitigation system and notify them if the MSDS indicates the possibility for adverse reactions in sensitive people.

5.4 Each active radon mitigation system **shall** have a mechanism to monitor system performance. The mechanism **shall** be plainly visible and simple to read or interpret.

5.5 All visible portions of mitigation systems **shall** be labeled (including the system power or disconnect switch) to identify their function. One central label **shall** be placed on the mitigation system, electric panel or other prominent location, be legible from a distance of at least two feet, and include a system description, a contact name and phone number.

5.6 Depressurization system fans (i.e., sub-slab, sub-membrane, block wall and drain tile depressurization systems) **shall not** be installed in the conditioned (heated/cooled) space of a building, or in any basement, crawlspace, or other interior location directly beneath conditioned space of a building. Appropriate places for depressurization system fans include attics not suitable for habitation, garages, or the exterior of the building.

5.7 To ensure against re-entrainment of radon back into the building and direct exposure to people, exhaust vents from depressurization system fans and radon-in-water aeration systems **shall** be discharged according to all of the following requirements: 1) the discharge point **shall** be ten feet or more above ground level, 2) the discharge point **shall** be ten feet or more, measured directly (line-of-sight) from any window, door, or other openings in the structure (e.g., vents, operable skylights or air intakes) that are less than two feet below the exhaust point, 3) the discharge point **shall** be ten feet or more away from any private or public access, and 4) the discharge point **shall** be ten feet or more from any opening into an adjacent building.

6.0 POST-MITIGATION TESTING

The contractor **shall** ensure that a confirmatory short-term screening measurement is made no sooner than 24 hours, nor longer than 30 days after completion and start-up of the mitigation system. The contractor **shall** recommend that the client obtain an independent radon measurement. The contractor is not required to make a confirmatory radon measurement if he/she can obtain a copy of the test report from a client's or independent third party's test. The contractor **shall** recommend retesting at least every two years. All measurements **shall** be conducted in accordance with EPA protocols as cited in, " Interim Protocols For Screening and Follow-up Radon and Radon Decay Product Measurements" (EPA 520/1-86-014-1) and "Indoor Radon and Radon Decay Product Measurement Protocols" (EPA 520-1-89-010), or subsequent revisions or additions to these documents.

7.0 WORKER SAFETY

Contractors **shall** comply with all applicable OSHA standards relating to worker safety and occupational radon exposure. Please reference the following standards in the Code of Federal Regulations: OSHA "Safety and Health Regulations for Construction", 29 CFR 1926, and OSHA "Occupational Safety and Health Regulations", 29 CFR 1910.

EPA Regional Radon Programs

EPA Region	States Served	Telephone #
1.	CT,ME,MA,NH,RI,VT	(617) 565-4502
2.	NJ,NY,(PR,VI)	(212) 264-4110
3.	DE,DC,MD,PA,VA,WV	(215) 597-8320
4.	AL,FL,GA,KY,MS,NC,SC,TN	(404) 347-3907
5.	IL,IN,MI,MN,OH,WI	(312) 353-9538
6.	AR,LA,NM,OK,TX	(214) 655-7223
7.	IA,KS,MO,NE	(913) 551-7020
8.	CO,MT,ND,SD,UT,WY	(303) 293-1709
9.	AZ,CA,HI,NV,(GU)	(415) 744-1045
10.	AK,ID,OR,WA	(206) 553-7299

Regional Radon Training Centers

Eastern Regional Radon Training Center
Rutgers University
Radiation Science Department
Kilmer Campus, Bldg. 4087
New Brunswick, NJ 08903
tel# (201) 932-2582

Western Regional Radon Training Center
Colorado State University
Department of Industrial Sciences
Fort Collins, CO 80523
tel# (303) 491-7742

Midwest Universities Radon Consortium
University of Minnesota
1985 Buford Avenue (240)
St. Paul, MN 55108-1011
tel# (612) 624-8747

Southern Regional Radon Training Center
Auburn University Housing Research Center
Harbert Engineering Center
Auburn University, AL 36849
tel# (205) 844-6261

ADDENDUM TO THE EPA INTERIM RADON MITIGATION STANDARDS
(Effective October 1, 1992)

This is an addendum to the EPA Interim Radon Mitigation Standards. The standards are required practices for all participants in the Radon Contractor Proficiency Program. Failure to abide by the standards may result in delisting from the program.

The added section requires testing for backdrafting of combustion appliances. Backdrafting can occur when an active depressurizing radon mitigation system creates enough negative pressure in the building that gases from combustion devices (such as furnaces and hot water heaters) spill into the structure. Other causes of backdrafting are: 1) blocked chimneys, 2) air handling equipment that is unbalanced, or 3) other exhaust fans, especially if the dwelling has tight construction. Combustion gases often contain carbon monoxide, as well as carbon dioxide, nitrogen dioxide, sulfur dioxide and water vapor. While backdrafting may not be common, even short exposures to carbon monoxide can be lethal. All EPA approved radon mitigators are required to test for backdrafting whenever an active depressurization system is installed.

EPA Interim Radon Mitigation Standard
5.8   All buildings containing combustion devices where active depressurization systems have been installed **shall** be tested for backdrafting of combustion appliances immediately upon completion of the mitigation system installation. Any backdrafting condition caused by the installed mitigation system **shall** be corrected immediately. The mitigation system **shall** not be operated until backdrafting conditions are corrected. Pretesting the building for potential backdrafting problems may determine the possibility of backdrafting after the system is installed. References mitigators should follow are listed below:

* Chimney Safety Tests User's Manual, Second Ed., January 12, 1988, Scanada Shelter Consortium Inc., for Canada Mortgage and Housing Corp.
* ASHRAE Standard 62-1989, Appendix B, Positive Combustion Air Supply.
* National Fuel Gas Code, Appendix H (p.2223.1-98), 1988, Recommended Procedure for Safety Inspection of an Existing Appliance Installation.

Availability of References

All of the referenced documents are available from your local library. Personal copies can be obtained as specified below:

<u>Chimney Safety Tests User's Manual</u> -- Call you regional Radon Training Center for information on this publication.

<u>ASHRAE Standard 62-1989</u> -- ASHRAE
Attn: Publication Sales
1791 Tullie Circle, NE
Atlanta, GA 30329
(404) 636-8400
$42.00

<u>National Fuel Gas Code</u> -- National Fire Protection Association
1 Batterymarch Park
P.O. Box 9101
Quinsy, MA 02269-9101
(800) 344-3555
$32.65

About the Authors

Douglas L. Kladder, Primary Author

As a consultant and contractor, Mr. Kladder, and his firm Colorado Vintage Companies, Inc., has been involved with the development of radon reduction methods in homes, schools and commercial buildings since 1985. The experience that formed the basis for this book has been gained in all parts of the U.S., including Alaska and Guam. He has assisted in many EPA funded research projects and is a Lead Instructor at the U.S. EPA's Radon Training Center at Colorado State University.

Mr. Steven R. Jelinek, Co-Author

Mr. Jelinek has personally been involved with the design and installation of over 2,000 radon mitigations. His in-depth knowledge of radon mitigation and building construction provided an excellent basis for him to create many of illustrations within this book. He has been involved with EPA demonstration projects and radon mitigation contractor training since 1989.

Dr. James F. Burkhart, Co-Author

Dr. Burkhart is a professor of physics and the Chair of the Physics Department at the University of Colorado at Colorado Springs. He has been involved in the development and practice of radon measurement methods since 1984. He has made significant research contributions in the fields of radon measurements and the evaluation of radon remediation efforts. Dr. Burkhart is a Lead Instructor at the Western Regional Radon Training Center at Colorado State University.

Ms. Julie Hodges, Illustrator and Editor

Ms. Hodges, as owner of Impact Images, has extensive experience in the field of creating illustrations and graphic presentation programs for educational purposes. In this capacity, Ms. Hodges coordinated the mechanical aspects of this project in addition to adapting it into a training program that the manual supplements.

Mr. James F. Gustafson, C.P.A.

Mr. Gustafson is a certified public accountant who has been involved with the administrative and financial aspects of the radon mitigation industry since 1988. In this function, he has gained considerable experience in the identification of radon material sources around the U.S. The identification of material sources along with his non-technical review of this manual was extremely beneficial.

The authors encourage the reader who may have any question or comments on the content of this book to contact them by calling 719-632-1215 or writing them care of Colorado Vintage Companies, Inc. 525 E. Fountain Blvd., Suite 201, Colorado Springs Colorado 80903. Your questions will help us improve future printings of this book.